BUILDING A HEALTHY ECONOMY FROM THE BOTTOM UP

Harnessing Real-World Experience for Transformative Change

ANTHONY FLACCAVENTO

FOREWORD BY BILL MCKIBBEN

UNIVERSITY PRESS OF KENTUCKY

Scholarly publisher for the Commonwealth,
serving Bellarmine University, Berea College, Centre College of Kentucky, Eastern
Kentucky University, The Filson Historical Society, Georgetown College, Kentucky
Historical Society, Kentucky State University, Morehead State University, Murray
State University, Northern Kentucky University, Transylvania University, University
of Kentucky, University of Louisville, and Western Kentucky University.

Editorial and Sales Offices: The University Press of Kentucky
663 South Limestone Street, Lexington, Kentucky 40508-4008
www.kentuckypress.com

Library of Congress Cataloging-in-Publication Data

Names: Flaccavento, Anthony, author.
Title: Building a healthy economy from the bottom up : harnessing real-world
  experience for transformative change / Anthony Flaccavento ; foreword by
  Bill McKibben, University Press of Kentucky.
Description: Lexington, Kentucky : University Press of Kentucky, [2016] |
  Series: Culture of the land | Includes bibliographical references and
  index.
Identifiers: LCCN 2016000230| ISBN 9780813167343 (hardcover : alk. paper) |
  ISBN 9780813167596 (pbk. : alk. paper) | ISBN 9780813167367 (pdf) |
  ISBN 9780813167350 (epub)
Subjects: LCSH: Community development—United States. | Sustainable
  living—United States. | Sustainable development—United States. | United
  States—Economic conditions--2009-
Classification: LCC HN90.C6 F574 2016 | DDC 307.1/40973—dc23
LC record available at http://lccn.loc.gov/2016000230

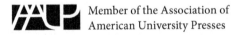

To Laurie, Josh, Maria, and Alex. Thanks for hanging in there with me through all of our experiences of trying to live a somewhat better, healthier life together; for tolerating my periodic rants and despair about the world; and for the illuminating discussions and exchanges we've had over many years. This book is dedicated to each of you, and to the memory of Kayla Jean Mueller.

Contents

Foreword

There is more than enough to be depressed about on our planet—if you gave me an hour, I'd still be listing bullet points when the clock ran out. Melting glaciers, acidifying ocean, rising inequality, increasing flow of refugees, declining soils, on and on and on. It's easy to make the case that we're doomed. And even easier to make that case if you look at the responses coming from our governments. The problems they don't ignore they try to paper over. On climate change, they're trying to spin physics and sweet-talk chemistry; instead of acting on inequality, they're turning our elections over to billionaires.

But say you looked a little deeper—say that, instead of taking the standard-issue journalist's view from 30,000 feet, you got down on the ground and examined the much-talked-about "grass roots." That's what Anthony Flaccavento has done, and he's emerged with a real story to tell, one that offers realistic hope even in a difficult moment.

Fifteen years or so ago—in no small part because of Flaccavento's work along the Appalachian spine—the local food movement began surging in our country. All across America, all of a sudden, local farmers markets were the fastest-growing part of the food economy. This had good environmental consequences (the 10-mile tomato beats the continent-crosser any day), and it definitely made for tastier meals. But maybe the most important part of the equation was how it changed communities. The average shopper at a farmers market had ten times more conversations than the average shopper at a supermarket. That's how communities start to rebuild—how they start to emerge from the withering emphasis on a kind of hyperindividuality that had managed to become America's curse.

Because once people start talking to each other, the ideas begin to flow. It's clear now that we need a farmers market for more than carrots. We need—and are beginning to get—a farmers market in electrons (that's what it means when people by the millions put solar panels on their roof and turn a one-way power connection into a two-way true grid). We need a farmers market in capital—that's what happens when local banking begins to reemerge from the monopoly of the money-center banks that crashed our economy. The farmers market in ideas that we call the Internet is already thriving.

It's a moment for connections, and it strikes me that that's what these wonderful stories that Flaccavento is telling have in common. There's every reason to despair (and every reason to keep engaged in the global fight against the plutocrats), but there's also reason enough to hope that some alternative exists. Once you've read these stories, you won't be able to say our future is inevitable—and once you understand that change is possible, you have no choice but to go to work!

Bill McKibben

Introduction

Economic Transitions in Surprising Places

When we tune out politics, when we abandon hope, we aren't being cool or hip or ironic or even realistic—we are being played.
—Robert McChesney, *Blowing the Roof off the Twenty-First Century*

If you stay in one place too long, you know you'll root.
—Janisse Ray, *Ecology of a Cracker Childhood*

History has a way of surprising us, especially in times when serious change seems impossible.
—Gar Alperovitz, *What Then Must We Do?*

When I first met Martin Miles in 1999, he had been raising tobacco for nearly forty years on his small farm in rural Lee County, Virginia. For generations, tobacco had been the reliable cash crop for small mountain farmers, but by then it was in steep decline. Many were thinking of quitting altogether, worn down by the relentless work of farming and discouraged by the steady decline in income. Bumper stickers proclaiming "Tobacco Put My Kids through College" were becoming less common. That sentiment had been replaced by the newly widespread belief that "nothing can replace tobacco."

Martin was among that smaller group of farmers looking for alternatives. When he heard me pitch the idea of raising organic produce for sale to supermarkets, he was interested. So, too, was John Mullins, a younger man who lived just down the road from Martin. By the following summer, several acres of organic peppers, tomatoes, eggplants, and other crops were growing along Wallens Creek as Martin and John became leaders in a transition from raising tobacco to growing healthy fruits, vegetables, and other foods.

That first year, about ten farmers grew organic produce and, with help from a local organization I had started, Appalachian Sustainable Development, sold it to a number of supermarkets in the region. A section of Martin's tobacco barn was converted into a "packing shed," including a secondhand walk-in cooler at the back end. Where the big leaves of the burley tobacco plants once hung to dry, boxes of produce raised nearby now began to fill the space. A small refrigerated truck, which functioned now and then, carried this "Appalachian Harvest" produce from the packing shed to supermarket docks in nearby Abingdon as well as Richmond, Virginia, and Asheville, North Carolina. Though these types of "food hubs" have since spread throughout much of the country, fifteen years ago they were few and far between, especially in the heart of burley tobacco country.

Appalachian Harvest has grown and evolved over time, including moving from the barn to a larger structure with a better design and considerably more capacity. Since its inception, it has helped nearly two hundred local farmers, in different ways, from tobacco farmers shifting to new crops to new farmers learning the ropes of commercial production. Many farmers have grown for the network for a period of years, then focused on other markets they've developed, or shifted to direct sales to consumers. The parallel growth of farmers markets in many small communities during this time has created another set of opportunities for farmers and eaters alike. All told, the system that Martin helped launch has been a leading part of a regionwide shift in the food and farming economy, one that now includes other parts of Virginia, as well as West Virginia, Kentucky, and Tennessee.

When I started to tell the story about Martin and other tobacco farmers shifting to organic produce, it almost always surprised people. Theirs seemed like an unlikely part of the country to help start a movement toward healthy foods. But then, transitions often surprise people.

This book is about transitions, primarily of an economic sort, but also involving shifts in priorities, in ways of thinking and doing, and in politics and public policy. The transitions we'll consider are in relatively early stages, new enough that we're still very much learning from these experiences, knowing that they'll evolve as they take hold in hundreds of different places. At their core, all of the transitions share this central characteristic: *they are emerging from the bottom up*, from small groups of people, local communities, and innovative business and organizations. In the process, these communities are beginning to buck the trend of increasingly concentrated wealth and power. They are building economies that work better for people and the places where they live; in some places they've

Martin Miles, from Lee County, Virginia, was the first tobacco farmer to make the transition to raising organic produce as part of the Appalachian Harvest enterprise. Author's collection.

also begun to revitalize public spaces and civic life. The question is, can these transitions grow and mature to the point that they reshape the broader economy and the politics behind it? Can they help create, in Marjorie Kelly's words, "an economy that *in its normal functioning* tends to create fair and just outcomes, benefits the many rather than the few, and enables an enduring human presence on a flourishing earth?"[1]

In this context, it is important to note just how big a challenge this represents. Tobacco farming and coal mining, two of the pillars of many Appalachian communities for generations, bring into sharp relief what is in fact a widespread problem in our economy: *How can people make a decent living without doing harm to the land or to the health and well-being of others?* Most folks would agree that the shift from tobacco to other crops or enterprises in many Appalachian communities is a good (though certainly insufficiently broad) transition. But should we also be making a shift away from the big-box stores that destroy small businesses and lower overall wages, from fast food that contributes to obesity and diabetes, from oil and gas drilling to renewable energy, from hedge funds that profit from home foreclosures? Every one of those industries employs many thousands of people. The harm they do may be less obvious than that done by tobacco, but it is substantial nevertheless.

For that reason, the transitions we'll consider also embody an integrated approach to economic development and prosperity, where different goals—job creation, good wages, health, ecological stewardship—are viewed not as competing interests but as equally important outcomes; as opportunities for innovative strategies that enable us to do things better. In a very real sense, we'll be examining the potential for a shift from an economic system utterly dependent upon collateral damage to one based upon, in Wendell Berry's words, "solving for pattern." That is, developing strategies that fit into the larger system and broadly promote health, resilience, and capacity. Finding solutions that generate more solutions rather than solutions that create whole new sets of problems. That's solving for pattern.

The other challenge is in creating these opportunities such that they work for people with a range of educational levels and different types of experience, including farmers, miners, construction workers, and other so-called blue-collar occupations. So many of these folks have been hard hit by the profound changes in our economy, and at the same time, are often forgotten by those espousing a "knowledge economy" or talking about the rise of "the creative class." Farmers, mechanics, builders, and other working folks employ a great deal of knowledge and creativity in bringing the rest of us the real stuff that makes our seemingly virtual lives possible. They need to be in the thick of things as we work toward building better economies. Van Jones has called this the "green collar economy."[2]

I've been working in this arena for the past three decades, primarily in the Central Appalachian region of Virginia, Tennessee, and neighboring states. Thirty years ago, we thought of this work in terms of *economic diversification* and *economic justice*. In the early 1990s, we started to call it *sustainable development* as our efforts increasingly focused on long-term, ecologically sustainable strategies. Soon thereafter the concept of *triple-bottom-line* businesses emerged to capture not only the ecological but the social and community dimensions of economics. By the end of that decade, *asset-based development* and *place-based development* joined the lexicon, describing the efforts of leaders in Appalachia, the Delta, and other places to build on what we had, on our strengths, rather than just focusing on what we lacked. Most recently, I've begun to think of all of these elements as pieces of a *bottom-up economy*, the polar opposite of trickle-down economics, both in theory and practice (and believe me, if you read on, we'll talk about that distinction in great detail). I'll probably use the term "bottom-up economy" more than any other in this book, but know that I'm generally including all of those other elements as well.

Throughout these three decades, there have been scores of experiments, pilot projects, and attempts at building new "models" for the economy. They've arisen out of the private sector, the public sector, and the non-profit world, often involving a bit of all three. Some have endured, grown, and even been replicated or adapted well beyond their original places. We'll look at several of these in the chapters that follow. Others have limped along with modest impact. And certainly many have failed or, as they say in non-profit circles, "provided learning opportunities." It's important to note that these efforts at building a better economy are now in every region of the United States and certainly many other parts of the world. They include urban and rural, small towns and big cities, and cover nearly every sector of the economy.

Because we live in a time of such cynicism, such despair about our leaders and our world, I want to hook you and reel you into this book with hope—not hope premised upon what's theoretically possible, *but hope based on what is already happening.* If you, like me, often despair over the state of our nation and world, it might help to know that:

- A rural town in south Georgia has reversed its decline through community theater, public art, and a new marketplace, all built around the stories of their community.
- A fisherman from Massachusetts has created a form of integrated "vertical farming" that simultaneously restores degraded marine ecosystems and provides an abundance of delicious seafood and useful crops.
- One of the poorest communities in Buffalo, New York, has created businesses and good jobs, turned vacant lots into parks and gardens, and weatherized and upgraded scores of homes through a "green development zone."
- A buying club in New Mexico has grown from a room in a house to a worker-owned cooperative with seventeen thousand members and six retail stores, buying from hundreds of local farmers.
- An entrepreneur and community leader in Phoenix persuaded city officials to reform their building codes, enabling the "repurposing"

of fifty abandoned buildings, now home to more than ninety local businesses, all within the last decade.

- Folks in a neighborhood in Washington, D.C., formed a solar cooperative that in fewer than six years had enabled one hundred households to install solar panels, helped form neighborhood solar groups in every district in the city, and launched a national organization to help other communities.
- Nearly 3 dozen localities in the United States are turning over portions of their budget to their community, to their constituents, who decide how the money will be spent.
- Farmers, ranchers, and researchers are discovering that the same practices that increase productivity and drought resilience also pull enormous amounts of excess carbon out of the atmosphere, feeding the soil while helping to mitigate climate change.

These are just some of the stories that comprise the foundation of this book and of the exciting work that is building a better world and what Bill McKibben calls a more "durable future."[3] Some come from my own experiences, many others from colleagues and entrepreneurs in very different parts of the country. Taken together, these initiatives have helped spawn the beginnings of a more just, durable, and sustainable economy in hundreds of communities. It is a very exciting time.

But if we're going to be honest, it really is just the beginning, constituting a very small part of the overall economy, perhaps an even smaller part of economic thinking and policy. Three decades in, we know much more about what works; we have literally thousands of local success stories to help guide the way. But in many respects, the bottom-up economy is still, in the words of my New York friend Vic, little more than "a fucking gnat," a minor irritation to the big economy and the political process upon which it rests. That's the harsh truth. And it's the reason I've written this book.

Methodology—How Do I Tell This Story?

This book begins with a critical assessment of current economic thinking and practice, and the myths that underlie them. Following this introduction, we will explore *six emerging transitions*, each of which is challenging these myths and contributing to better economies and stronger communities. The transitions are distinct from one another but also build upon and reinforce their respective impacts. Most are economic in nature, though some also deal with media and public debate, and politics and public policy. I contend that we must make all six transitions to have broad and lasting impact. The final chapter makes the case for how they fit together, forming a new narrative about our economy and society.

Each transition will be the focus of a chapter, and each of these will follow the same basic format:

- We will begin by examining successful examples of experience on the ground, initiatives that help illustrate and exemplify the transition. Some of these will come from my own experience, while most will be drawn from other communities in different parts of the country. We will focus on the United States, though it is clear that similar transitions are emerging in other parts of the world as well. The stories I relate are but a tiny sampling of the dynamic and highly effective work under way, from big cities to very rural places. I've left out far more than I've included.

- Following the descriptions of these initiatives, I will attempt to analyze what the transition represents in terms of its potential to help build better opportunities for more people, stronger communities, and a more ecologically sustainable overall economy (i.e., we'll use a "triple-bottom-line" framework for evaluation). To do this, we'll consider what seems to be working, what the current limits or challenges are, and to what degree the transition supports or enables other positive transitions.

- Last, we'll examine current and potential public policy, looking at policies that hinder or undermine the transition as well as those that might support and propel it. This is done with the understanding that public policies are, in essence, the "rules of the game," and as such shape what can and cannot be done, what is rewarded, and what is penalized. The focus will be on federal- and state-level policies, though we will consider some local policies as well.

- At the end of each chapter, I include a brief list of resources that should help deepen your understanding of the issue or, in some cases, provide tools and opportunities for getting involved. As with the examples I use, these reading lists are not meant to be comprehensive but to provide a small sampling of what's out there, focusing on the resources that have been most helpful to me.

On this last point: I have written this book in the hope that the mix of experience, analysis, and policy will enable people to both better understand these issues and at the same time feel more able and ready to act. I'll feel really good if this in fact happens (and I don't often feel really good about things!). But please keep in mind that many people have gone much deeper into the subjects I discuss and offer more comprehensive and thorough examinations of the issues. If I manage to whet your appetite and get you to read some of their books as well, I'll be thrilled.

Whom I Hope to Engage with This Book

As with most people writing a book, I hope to reach a broad range of folks who are interested in a more sustainable economy, one that works far better for ordinary people, the communities where they live, and the ecosystems of which they're a part. I suspect that the first audience for this book will be the thousands of "practitioners" around the country: entrepreneurs and farmers, people working in non-profit organizations, public employees working for local, state, or federal government, environmentalists and sustainability advocates, and community organizers and activists. It is this diverse array of folks, sometimes making for strange bedfellows, who have helped to test and build experiments in economic democracy and sustainable development thus far. Thousands of farmers markets, along with hundreds of revitalizing downtowns, "living economy" business networks, grassroots economic democracy groups, and much, much more now dot our nation's landscape, largely because of the tireless and creative efforts of these practitioners of the bottom-up economy. These are my peers and colleagues, and in many cases, my mentors and inspiration. My hope is that this book will be of use to them in part through the sharing of the experiences of other folks who, like them, are trying to make their community better, healthier, stronger.

I'm also hoping to challenge these same practitioners in the pages that follow through a much-needed analysis of what is working, what is not, and a bit of why. When your work is all-consuming, it is difficult to step back and see what might be done differently and to understand the larger economic and political context in which you're working.

But there's another very important group I hope to engage, folks usually known to the practitioners, people whose support for the bottom-up economy has been essential to what success it has achieved thus far. I'm speaking of the millions of people around the country who are supporting the farmers, entrepreneurs, and practitioners in their communities. Some do this as advocates, some as investors, many as consumers. In a time of well-justified cynicism about civics and politics, I believe this group can rightly be called "hopeful citizens." They are of the utmost importance to the places where they live, indeed, to the direction that our nation and world takes over the ensuing years and decades. I intend for this book to better equip these hopeful citizens to take part in building their local economy *and* engage in the broader discourse about how to move forward as a nation.

I also believe that this book will be useful for college and university students. While it may not be as scholarly as some would like, I hope that the combination of real-world examples with analysis and public policy will be both informative and provocative for teachers and students alike.

Chapter Summaries

Chapter 1. What's Wrong with What We've Got? Rising Tides, Trickle Down, and Other Economic Myths

This chapter presents a critique of the still-dominant economic paradigm and its underlying assumptions, framed as "six myths." This concise critique mostly uses language we've all heard before, for example, "A rising tide lifts all boats." As you read this, please keep in mind that this is the only chapter that focuses almost entirely on problems, on what's wrong. If you're not familiar with the material, it will likely be a bit sobering, but it is essential in order to understand why we need to make big changes and how to go about that. This is also the one chapter that relies mostly on analysis rather than specific stories or experiences. It's the big-picture chapter, and it's pretty damn depressing. Stick it out, though, because the balance of the book focuses on positive economic transitions. By examining our current economic policies and priorities and the assumptions that underlie them, we will be better able to consider the proposed transitions.

Chapter 2. Renewing Households and Communities: From Consumptive Dependence to Productive Resilience

While the larger economy and most economic development efforts continue to pin their hopes on increased consumer retail spending, a growing body of individuals, households, and neighborhood groups are embracing notions of frugality, sharing, and increased self-reliance, as both a practical response to economic hardship and as a way to reduce their ecological footprint. This is helping to stimulate a "reskilling," to quote Wendell Berry, across generations and even, to some degree, across class. This *first transition* will explore a range of these strategies and their role in reducing economic dependence and contributing to the well-being of households, communities, and local economies.

Chapter 3. Unleashing Local Living Economies: From Trickle-Down Problems to Bottom-Up Solutions

More than three decades of trickle-down economic strategies have led to extreme levels of inequality, stagnant or declining wages for most workers, and a competition among states and localities to offer ever-larger tax breaks and subsidies to recruit large, nonlocal companies. It has also fostered the "externalizing" of major costs to our health and to our environment, most notably accelerating climate change. Much of this strategy is based on the notion that "there is no alternative."

The *second transition* will begin to focus in on those emerging alternatives: locally or regionally based, rooted in their communities, ecologically sustainable, driven more by real needs than manufactured wants.

Chapter 4. Building Broadly Based and Durable Prosperity: From Concentrated Wealth and Widespread Insecurity to Worker Ownership and Community Capital

Concentration of economic power encompasses most economic sectors, from seeds, farming, and food to banking and finance. That concentration has led not only to extreme inequality but to many other bad outcomes as well, from economic vulnerability to lower educational attainment, poorer health, and increased levels of incarceration.

This *third transition* will explore the growing force of cooperatives, "community capital," and alternative finance and investment initiatives, which are contributing to more widely based and durable wealth while also helping to make local economies more productive and more democratic.

Chapter 5. Taking Sustainability to Scale: From a Thousand Flickers of Light to Networks of Learning, Doing, and Change

The past two decades have seen the emergence of literally thousands of small, local initiatives around food and farming, healthy living, energy conservation and clean energy, green building, and other local economy initiatives. These efforts have made substantial improvements in countless communities. Unfortunately, they have generally been "out on their own," both underresourced and disconnected from other communities that have launched similar initiatives.

This *fourth transition* will look at the early stages of regional and national networks that are facilitating learning and sharing of best practices, promoting innovation, and encouraging broader impact through joint initiatives and collective action.

Chapter 6. Rebuilding a Meaningful Public Debate: From Debilitating Corporate Media to Energizing Civic Conversations

As community gathering places have disappeared, as most media have become extraordinarily concentrated, and as information technology has made us increasingly autonomous, civic debate and engagement have declined dramatically in most places. They've been replaced, to a significant degree, by the often autonomous and generally much harsher tone of virtual debate.

As local economies emerge, local civic spaces also tend to form, and with them comes the possibility of real dialogue among people of different backgrounds, political parties, and ideologies. In some communities, this has led to surprising allies and partners, usually based on common need or purpose. In the *fifth transition*, some of these examples will be explored along with the role of community art and theater groups, and regional media, both in traditional and new forms.

Chapter 7. Transforming Politics from the Bottom Up: Unleashing a Community-Based Politics of Engagement to Overcome the Lobbyists and Moneyed Elites

The local food movement has attracted and energized a broad base of people. While newer, the "local economy" movement is also building adherents across generations and political affiliations. To date, however, the primary focus of these movements has been on shifting the buying habits of consumers, not on changing public policy or building a base of political power.

This *sixth and final transition* will explore the potential to foster "food citizens" as a critical next step for locavore consumers to begin to shape public policy and help write new rules that promote sustainability, fairness, and resilience. More broadly we'll consider how millions of people, already engaged in their communities, might be mobilized as part of a reenergizing of our democracy. A range of participatory democracy tools and processes will be examined for their potential to rebuild the public sphere.

Conclusion: Creating a New Story from the Bottom Up

The book's conclusion has three components, beginning with a brief recap of the lessons learned from the diversity of bottom-up economy initiatives emerging around the nation, and the potential to expand and accelerate them through better public policy. Based on this, we'll then look at a new narrative or story that integrates the six essential transitions, focusing on how they rely upon and propel one another. Finally, I'll offer a number of ideas for moving forward, beginning with practical steps that can be taken individually and expanding out to the broader national arena.

For the "doers" among you, for those who want to act, the conclusion has a wide range of suggested steps you can consider, based, of course, on your community, what's already going on there, and your own inclinations. You can make some of these choices on your own or as a family, while others will require cooperation with neighbors and fellow citizens, both near and far. I encourage you to adapt what you learn in this book to your own places, to experiment with altogether new ideas, and to constantly learn, both by reading and through action.

While the conclusion contains the most comprehensive list of action ideas, each of the six transitions discussed in chapters 2 through 7 also contains numerous ideas for getting involved in meaningful ways, ranging from marketplace options to policy issues. The potential steps you might take are implied from the discussion of specific examples, the analysis of what's working and what isn't, and the assessment of public policies needed to accelerate that transition. In other words, you don't have to wait until the conclusion to begin thinking about what you might do and how you might get involved.

Most of all, I hope you take this away: "The Economy" is really a mix of many economies, beginning with what we do at home and in our communities. It is not an inscrutable (can't be examined or understood), immutable (can't be changed) force that cannot be changed by ordinary people like you and me—unless we let it be so. *At its most basic level, the economy is simply the system we adopt to produce and distribute what peo-*

ple need to have a decent life. How we do that impacts not only our own prosperity but also the options and problems that future generations will face. I hope this book helps you recognize that truth and claim your role in making it much, much better.

We can do a lot where we live, but local action alone will not overcome the biggest and most important problems we face, including growing poverty, extreme concentrations of wealth and power, obscene levels of incarceration that are substantially based on race, and rapidly accelerating climate change, to name a few. Instead, what's clear is that we need millions of people to engage or, for some, to reengage as activists, protesters, informed citizens demanding change. We need a mass movement for an economy that serves people, builds broadly based prosperity, preserves community and place, and restores rather than degrades the ecosystem.

At the same time, a mass movement demanding such change also needs to be grounded in the vision and reality of the bottom-up, living economy. As Naomi Klein puts it: "Many of us are getting a lot better at standing up to those who would cynically exploit crises to ransack the public sphere. And yet these protests have also shown that saying no is not enough. If opposition movements are to do more than burn bright and then burn out, they will need a comprehensive vision for what should emerge in the place of our failing systems, as well as serious political strategies for how to achieve those goals."[4] The communities and initiatives highlighted in this book can contribute to that vision of "what should emerge," along with ideas for elements of a reinvigorated and truly public politics. They can help spawn and support a mass movement that's as excited about what *could be* as it is angry about what is.

In the months during which I've been focused on writing this book, things have generally gotten worse in our nation and our world. Refugees from war in North Africa are pouring into Sicily, where I was living during much of the writing of this book. Baltimore, where I grew up, has become the latest American city to make the news because of the killing of an unarmed black man by police. For folks like me, who've spent most of their lives trying to build a better world, it's pretty disheartening. That's why the words of the Kentucky farmer and writer Wendell Berry ring so true for me, and perhaps for you: "The things that I have tried to defend are less numerous and worse off now than when I started, but in this I am only like all other conservationists. All of us have been fighting a battle that on average we are losing, and I doubt that there is any use in reviewing the statistical proofs. The point—the only interesting point—is that we have not quit. Ours is not a fight you can stay in very long if you look on victory as a sign of triumph or on loss as a sign of defeat. We have not quit because we are not hopeless. . . . I am looking for reasons to keep on."[5]

I, too, am looking for reasons to keep on. I know that this book will not end economic inequality, overcome injustice and violence, or reverse widespread ecological degradation. And believe me, I'm bummed about that. But in truth, I do intend this book to contribute to overcoming these problems, by sharing the stories of the emerging bottom-up economy, discussing how to strengthen and accelerate these efforts, and proposing public policies that will cultivate stronger, more just and sustainable economies across our country and, by extension, the world. It's a long shot, to be sure, but I invite you to join me in building this better world.

What's Wrong with What We've Got?

Rising Tides, Trickle Down, and Other Economic Myths

There are 47% of the people . . . who are dependent upon the government, who believe they are victims . . . who pay no income tax. My job is not to worry about these people. I'll never convince them that they should take personal responsibility and care for their lives.
—Mitt Romney, 2012

Servants, laborers and workmen of different kinds, make up the far greater part of every political society. But what improves the circumstances of the greater part can never be regarded as an inconveniency to the whole. No society can surely be flourishing and happy, of which the far greater part of the members are poor and miserable. It is but equity, besides, that they who feed, clothe and lodge the whole body of the people, have such a share of the produce of their own labor as to be themselves tolerably well fed, clothed and lodged.
—Adam Smith, *The Wealth of Nations*

Every culture, every nation has certain stories that shape the way its people think, both for good and for bad. At the heart of these stories one often finds "myths," usually broad in scope, sometimes expressed as metaphors. These are myths not because they are completely wrong, but because they form the foundation of our understanding of the world, yet are largely unexamined. Most people accept them without questioning their validity or examining the assumptions behind them.

When many folks think of myths, they picture the ancient Greeks and other early civilizations, people who did not have the benefit of modern science, let alone the vast amount of information available on the Internet. We like to think of ourselves as too well-informed, too rational to be influenced by stories and truisms. But in fact, we are impacted by our own stories, often to the degree that we don't even consider alternative views or accumulating evidence to the contrary. This is particularly true in the realm of economics, its reputation for hard-nosed, unsentimental rigor notwithstanding.

The economic transitions that I propose in this book depend on our recognizing, understanding, and directly challenging these myths. This chapter will do exactly that, focusing on six myths that, taken together, profoundly shape and often skew our nation's discussion about how to build a better economy with more widely shared prosperity.

Understanding America's Stories of Economic Prosperity

The recession of 2007–2009 cost millions of Americans their jobs and sparked angry debates about how to fix our economy. But our economic problems go back much further. For the vast majority of people, incomes have been stagnant and savings and wealth have been declining for more than thirty years.[1] It's not because we haven't been working: on average, Americans work 137 more hours every year than the Japanese, 260 more than folks in the United Kingdom.[2] During that same thirty-year period, our "productivity"—the amount we produce for every hour we work—has almost doubled. Yet wages grew barely 10 percent for the middle class, less still for blue-collar workers.[3]

Working more. Being more productive. Just getting by. Something isn't right.

This first chapter offers a look into what might be wrong with our economy by examining six myths about economic prosperity that shape our thinking and, in many ways, limit our public debate. Remember that by "myth" I mean a widely held belief that may contain some truth but that misleads us for two reasons: First, there is more about it that is wrong than right. Second, it is nevertheless ingrained in us so deeply that we don't think to question it.

Here's an example: *In America, if you work hard, you'll get ahead.* This myth contains some truth, as we know from various rags-to-riches stories we've heard. But it just doesn't hold true for *most* hardworking Americans, especially over the past thirty years, during which time our ability to move up the economic ladder has steadily declined.[4] In fact, among so-called "developed economies," the United States now ranks near the bot-

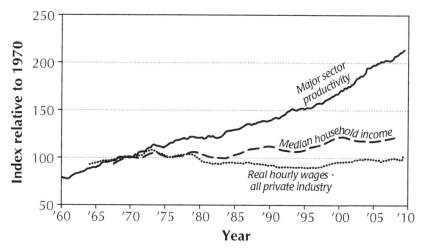

Productivity and real income, 1960–2008. Since 1970, as the productivity of U.S. workers more than doubled, real wages remained virtually unchanged. (Data from Bureau of Labor Statistics, Bureau of Economic Analysis, and census as cited in Maggie Winslow, "Increasing Labor Productivity: A Mixed Blessing?" Triple Pundit, January 24, 2012, www.triplepundit.com.)

tom for economic and social mobility. If you're born into poverty in America, you're more likely to stay there than in most other developed countries.[5]

Certainly, some of these economic myths have been challenged and rebutted by a number of economists, researchers, and scholars. Nevertheless, their influence is still widespread among political elites and pundits, among economic decision makers and everyday people.

Underlying the six myths about economic prosperity is one foundational myth: that the economy is a product of the market, and the market is driven by natural laws, by an "invisible hand" that steers it in ways that are both inevitable and, ultimately, good for us. When politicians try to change that, they just mess things up. And for ordinary people, well, the market's far too powerful and the economy way too big for us to do anything but just try to catch the wave and plug ourselves in. The best policy, then, is to get out of the way and let the market work its magic. This idea of an "invisible hand" that guides the market first came from Adam Smith nearly 250 years ago. He's been quoted innumerable times, often in support of minimal or no market regulation by government. But as we saw in the epigraph to this chapter, Smith's views of the market were actually quite a bit more complex, including concerns about the power of unrestrained corporations and the vulnerability of workers.

Of course, some people question this basic belief about our economy and the role of the market, but most Americans, from the halls of Congress to the sidewalks of Main Street, hold this notion dear. The power and reach of this idea drive not only our economic policies and prescriptions, but much of our political debate as well, far beyond the realm of economic policy.

Flowing from the foundational belief in the wisdom and efficacy of the market, we will examine the following six myths:

Myth 1: Money equals wealth. The more we have, the happier we are.
Myth 2: In business, bigger is better.
Myth 3: Global trade makes everyone—consumers and businesses—better off.
Myth 4: In a free market, "looking out for Number One" is best for everybody.
Myth 5: A rising tide lifts all boats.
Myth 6: Growth is the answer. Always.

This book rests on a wide base of experiences, including extraordinary economic innovations and experiments in nearly every sector of the economy. Many of these offer reason to be optimistic about the prospect for building economies that work better for people and the places where they live. But nearly all of these exemplars of the emerging new economy are hindered or undermined by economic policies and priorities based on one or more of the six myths. We can build a better economy for a few folks, in a few places, but unless we confront these myths, this emerging economy will remain at the margins. So, let's get to it.

Myth 1: Money Equals Wealth. The More We Have, the Happier We Are

This myth opens our discussion because it defines our understanding of prosperity, of what it means to be successful and to live well.[6] Its spirit is captured in the comment a former relative made to me as I started grad school: "When you're driving that big Caddy, it will all be worth it!"

This myth actually encompasses two distinct but related ideas: that money is the same as wealth; and that how much we have largely determines our happiness. As with all myths, there are, of course, axioms or sayings that run counter to its message: "Money can't buy happiness" or "Real riches come from having family and friends." But these ideas have steadily lost ground against what Benjamin Barber refers to as "the emerging world of total commerce,"[7] one in which almost every aspect of life becomes commodified, every want becomes a need that then becomes a market transaction.

Money—in the form of cash, credit card, stocks, or bonds—is intended not to *be* wealth but to represent our ability to secure it, to buy the things we need or want. When we "put money in the bank," we create future buying power, whether saving for a college education or a comfortable retirement. Compared to the old system of bartering goods and services, money is dramatically more flexible, efficient, and convenient.

The problem, then, is not money itself, but *the increasing disconnect between money and real wealth.* Not long ago, people of wealth were thought to be those with large holdings of land, or herds of animals, or the owners of factories, minerals, or mines. But now to be "wealthy" is simply this: to have lots of money. That's a serious problem because, as David Korten has pointed out, this is often "phantom wealth," representing little more than the money itself rather than real goods or productive assets.[8]

Consider *derivatives,* those financial instruments whose worth is *derived* from speculations about what might happen to the value of various assets. Derivatives were conceived as a way of expanding investment opportunities and loosening the flow of money where it might otherwise be tight. Mortgage-backed securities are probably the best-known and most infamous type of derivative, as these were at the center of the Wall Street crisis in 2007. Mortgage-backed securities are pools of mortgages that have been purchased from banks and other lenders and then "packaged" as an investment that is projected to yield a steady return as those mortgages are repaid. It's all quite mind-boggling, but stay with me on this.

You go into a bank and borrow $100,000 to buy a home. In the past, the bank monitored your loan, trying to ensure that you kept up with your payments. If you hit a rough patch, depending upon the bank, they might allow you to restructure your payments, or cut you a bit of slack if you had a sudden change in income. Not that all banks were understanding or flexible, but it was *in their interest for you to keep repaying your loan.*

With mortgage-backed securities, banks quickly sell your loan—and scores of others—to an investment firm and get a lump sum payment for the principal amount. They take it off their books, freeing themselves up to make more loans (and get more money for "closing costs" and other fees) and liberating themselves from the hassle of having to work with the people to whom they originally provided the loans. As this became more commonplace, it did three things: First, it increased the number of mortgage loans being made, well beyond what the banks would have done based on their own collateral and staff resources. Second, it took most of the risk out of "subprime" mortgages, since the people closing the deal quickly sold the mortgage and got their cash. Whether or not the borrower fell behind or defaulted was no longer the lender's concern. Third, it created fantastic amounts of what appeared to be wealth, based on "assets" that weren't real, or at least were greatly inflated in their value. That's what derivatives, unregulated, tend to do.

In 2008 the total market value of all derivatives was estimated to be ten times that of the entire world's gross domestic product (GDP). Let's repeat that: *This single form of financial instrument had a stated value ten times greater than the value of all the products, food, energy, and goods and services produced and sold across the entire planet that year.*[9]

Or not. As the subsequent meltdown of Wall Street and most global stock markets soon made clear, this kind of "wealth" had no lasting value, no real connection to productive human activity in any sense. In many cases, in fact, these new "financial instruments" rose in value in proportion to economic *failure*, whether that was other stocks tanking or homeowners defaulting on their mortgage. The fact that so much money was made *because of* the economic misfortune of millions, specifically their collective loss of their homes and other assets, illustrates just how wide the estrangement between money and real wealth has become.

And derivatives are not the exception, but the rule. Marjorie Kelly's analysis of stock market transactions has shown that less than 1 percent of all money invested in Wall Street in 1999 was actually invested in businesses and their growth. The other 99 percent financed speculation, including such things as credit default swaps.[10] Kelly's careful analysis of money flows on Wall Street in that year substantiates Korten's assertion that much of the economy is based on phantom wealth. In its current form, the stock market is much less a vehicle for investment in companies that create real value than it is, essentially, a gargantuan money-laundering network where money begets more money through a series of mind-boggling, speed-of-light transactions that have almost nothing to do with productive economic activity.

On the other hand, many *real* assets, many of the underpinnings of productivity and wealth, are stressed or in decline, even as both population and rates of consumption continue to grow. A little more than a century ago, we had 14 acres of productive land per person, worldwide. Some of that was farmland and pasture for animals; some was forestland, providing wood, fiber, medicinal herbs, and foods; some was in the form of freshwater lakes and streams. All of this land is "productive" in the sense that it provides or potentially provides things people need, from food to fiber to energy and building materials. Today, that 14 acres has shrunk to just over 3.5 acres for each person, due primarily to population growth but also to the destruction of productive land for so-called development. Compounding the problem, the amount of land required to meet the needs of the average "consumer" increased *fourfold* during that same period.[11]

What's more, a significant proportion of the remaining productive land is stressed or in decline from some combination of overuse, inappropriate use—for example, planting crops on steep slopes or in fragile soils—contamination by air pollution, extremes of heat, drought, or storms, and related problems. A 2011 study by the Environmental Working Group found soil erosion rates on 6 million acres of Iowa cropland that were double the rate at which soil could be replenished.[12] Several studies, including a 2003 analysis by researchers from Cornell and Syracuse Universities, have linked air pollution, especially nitrous oxide, to the declining health of certain tree species and aquatic ecosystems.[13] Thus, while productivity per acre grew dramatically for much of the twentieth century, over the past few decades it has nearly leveled off or, in some cases, begun to decline.

In addition to soils, forests, and other forms of "natural capital," substantial swaths of our human-made capital are also in decline, from degraded roads and failing bridges to aging pipelines and infrastructure for waste and water systems. In its 2013 Annual Report Card, the American Society of Civil Engineers graded U.S. infrastructure overall as a near-failing "D+," with an estimated cost of $36 trillion to bring it up to "a state of good repair."[14]

These examples make clear that we can be awash in money—individually or as a nation—even as real wealth is stagnant or shrinking.

Putting aside questions of what constitutes real versus phantom wealth, most Americans overestimate the importance of income and wealth to their happiness.[15] Several studies that have examined the "money-happiness" link draw similar conclusions: While poverty and its attendant problems clearly erode people's sense of well-being, once we reach a level of relative self-sufficiency, additional income or wealth has very little impact on our happiness.[16] Taken with other research into what makes people happy and unhappy, it's now apparent that a sense of security and fulfillment, along with modest levels of comfort, are the key to happiness for most people, not ever-growing money and wealth. Perhaps that's why the annual surveys of happiness and contentment conducted by the National Opinion Research Council indicate that Americans' happiness peaked in 1956 and has been declining, slowly but surely, ever since.[17] (Which, as it turns out, coincides precisely with my time on earth!) Further evidence of this comes from a 2005 study in *Psychology Today*, which shows that children growing up in affluent suburban households smoke, drank, did more drugs, and had higher rates of anxiety and depression than their urban, lower-income counterparts.[18] Even as our homes doubled in size and as we added many more cars, appliances, computers, and other "amenities," most people's happiness and contentment steadily declined.

Beyond a relatively modest level, for most people money does not, in fact, buy happiness. When money is divorced from real assets, from productive enterprises and endeavors, this disconnect may become even more profound. Phantom wealth, which has come to dominate certain sectors of our economy, has no roots, no connection to specific places and the tangible things in those places. That may be why it is proving to be so terribly unsatisfying, why there is never enough. And why our prosperity myth— that *money equals wealth, and the more we have, the happier we are*—helps sustain a dysfunctional economic focus on consumerism. In the words of Benjamin Barber: "Today's consumerist capitalism profits only when it can address those whose essential needs have already been satisfied but who have the means to assuage 'new' and invented needs. . . . In this new epoch in which the needy are without income and the well-heeled are without needs, radical inequality is simply assumed. If the poor cannot be enriched enough to become consumers, then grown-ups in the First World . . . must be enticed into shopping."[19]

The myth that wealth equals money and money makes us happy is being challenged by people and communities around the nation, as will be described in our first transition to productive resilience (chapter 2).

Myth 2: In Business, Bigger Is Better

Earl Butz said it all. President Nixon's secretary of agriculture admonished farmers to "get big, or get out." This was the only way, they were told, to prosper economically. And it was what the country needed, since bigger farms meant greater productivity and efficiency. Most farmers took the secretary's advice: some got big; many more got out. Three decades later, average farm size had increased to nearly 420 acres, while the number of farms declined by more than 600,000 during those thirty years, continuing a century-long trend.[20]

It seems that most Americans prefer the idea of the family farm to the agribusiness giant, the mom-and-pop store to the big box, the community bank to the transnational financial company. But we are realists who acknowledge that these small to midsize businesses, fun and quirky though they may be, can't compete with the economies of scale that megafarms can attain, or the efficiency and productivity of these multinational corporations. Most of us accept this.

And most of us are wrong. While an expansion in size of almost any enterprise can afford greater efficiencies, there have proven to be limits to the expected "economies of scale." This is true in agriculture as well as many other industries, even in some manufacturing sectors. As Michael Shuman notes: "There is a growing body of evidence that economies of scale in many business sectors, after several generations of modest growth, are beginning to shrink. . . . Firms lower average costs by expanding, *but only up to a point.* Beyond that point, according to the law of diminishing returns to scale, complexities, breakdowns and inefficiencies begin to drive costs back up."[21]

For example, on the basis of production per acre, small to midsize sustainable farms can meet or exceed the output of large farms in terms of both dollar sales and overall output. There are a variety of reasons for this, ranging from the intensity of management possible on a small farm to the potential for more integrated production systems that increase the overall output relative to inputs. A 2012 study looked at diversified organic farms utilizing multicrop rotations with larger, conventional systems and found numerous benefits to this approach: comparable overall yields, reduced needs for fertilizer and pesticides, improved soil quality and fertility, and far less water toxicity.[22] In other cases, farmers managing both livestock and crops (including grains, among others) saw a decrease in input costs and an increase in production from the same piece of land. And this does not include longer-term benefits, like reduced soil erosion and water pollution from excessive use of fertilizers.

Much like the pasture-based livestock systems made famous by Joel Salatin, these and most other integrated farming systems are compatible with small to midsize farms but highly unlikely to be employed by very large farms. These types of operations, often called "management-intensive," require a broader base of knowledge and much closer attention and observation than is feasible on huge acreages. And the return per acre, though likely to be greater, may take some patience as the system is in development.

The same relationship of size to innovation and diversity can be seen in nonfarm enterprises. According to an analysis by the Small Business Administration, small firms produce a staggering sixteen times more patents per employee than large firms.[23] Though very large firms certainly have the capital resources to undertake the research needed for innovation, they often allocate their resources for much shorter-term gain, in large part to increase short-term profits and their stock market share price. In a 2008 study of the pharmaceutical industry, Marc-Andre Gagnon and Joel Lexchin determined that large drug companies actually spent over 80 percent more on advertising and promotion than on research and development.[24]

Small to midsize businesses also generate more jobs and more income for every dollar of sales when compared with large chains and big-box stores. According to studies undertaken by Civic Economics in Anderson, Illinois; Austin, Texas; and other communities, small businesses generate from 25 percent greater to nearly three times the economic impact in their communities per dollar spent, when compared to large chains and big-box stores.[25] There are a variety of reasons for this, but one has to do with how the local firms source the goods and services they need to make their businesses run: In a study of two towns in New Jersey, in-state spending by local firms was nearly four times greater.[26] That's because locally based firms tend to get everything from legal, accounting, and marketing services to office supplies and equipment from other local businesses. Big, nonlocal companies use more national and international suppliers, perhaps saving a few pennies but sending most of their profits out of the community where they do business.

Locally owned banks also generally provide more "bang for the buck." According to a 2012 analysis provided by Stacy Mitchell, locally owned, small to midsize banks provided nearly twice the total lending to home-owners and small businesses even though they had less than half the assets of the largest publicly traded financial institutions.[27] This means that *for every dollar of assets held, they provided four times as much lending to these productive activities.*

In terms of productivity and innovation, it's clear that bigger is not always better; the larger enterprises often lag behind the smaller ones. When we look at the broader impacts of businesses on health, land stewardship, economic stability, and community life—the local banks, businesses, and farms excel even more. Small to midsize banks not only loan more money to local businesses, but they've avoided the need for government bailouts by investing in less risky, more useful community needs. It's the same with credit unions, which have half the loan delinquency rates of traditional banks. Small to midsize farms tend to be more responsive to the interests and needs of their customers, leading the way, for example, in the introduction of more nutrient-dense foods and production practices that increase the healthfulness of produce, grains, and meats. A comparison of farms in the Midwest shows that for every dollar of product sold, diversified vegetable operations paid six times more in wages and created more than three times as many jobs when compared with large commodity farms.[28]

The *bigger is better* myth has certainly propelled a small group of people into the stratosphere of monetary wealth. But for the most part, it isn't creating jobs, building economic opportunity, or strengthening communities. A study by Thomas Lyson of Cornell University looked at two hundred U.S. counties, categorizing them according to how much small-business activity they had versus those with a handful of very large employers. His study showed that those who relied on a few big companies fared much worse—higher rates of disability, substandard housing, low birth weight babies, and poverty—than those with a diverse and larger number of small to midsize businesses.[29] Yet government subsidies to these very large firms exceed $100 billion per year,[30] dwarfing the support that small, locally based firms receive (the annual lending budget of the Small Business Administration is barely over $1 billion).

Much of our agriculture, economic, and tax policy stems in part from the *bigger is better* myth, along with the belief that the wealth created by giant firms and large investors will "trickle down" to the rest of us, the little guys. The emerging local living economies described in chapter 3, presenting the second transition, directly challenge this myth and its underlying assumptions.

Myth 3: Global Trade Makes Everyone—Consumers and Businesses—Better Off

Nearly two centuries ago, the British economist David Ricardo put forward the theory of "comparative advantage," which states that nations should produce or manufacture those products for which they had a "comparative advantage" relative to the nation or nations with whom they were trading. In general, this meant focusing on items they could produce more cheaply, and beyond that, those for which their advantages were greatest. Let's say that New Zealand can produce lamb at half the cost of British farmers, and that it can also produce solar panels for 10 percent less. The comparative advantage in the production of lamb is much greater, so, according to this theory, New Zealand should expand its production and export of lamb while reducing its production of solar panels, instead importing them from Britain. Ricardo believed that through specialization of this kind, every nation could develop a "comparative advantage" in the production of a few things, and that earnings from the export of these items would allow them to buy everything else they needed at lower cost than if they produced it themselves.

Of course, Ricardo lived in an era in which corporations were still based primarily in one nation and in which companies, materials, and people lacked the incredible ease of mobility that we now enjoy. It's not that we've proved his theory altogether wrong so much as that it is now simply outdated; individual megacorporations can simply pack up and move to those places where they find the greatest production advantages, usually defined by lower wages and less health and environmental regulation. Still, the idea that nations—and regions within nations—should specialize in a relatively small number of export items, rather than building a broader, more self-reliant economy, persists. Thus, global commerce has grown inexorably, facilitated by "free trade" agreements pushed by Democrats and Republicans alike. And regions like Appalachia have built economies too narrowly focused on the production and export of a small number of products.

There's no denying it—we depend more than ever on goods produced overseas, on capital from other nations, and on consumers in Europe, Asia, and South America buying the stuff we produce. But is it working? Is it the best strategy to achieve broad prosperity? The simplest measurement to consider is our balance of trade. The United States has had a trade deficit every year but one since 1970. In 2011 and 2012, it hovered near $550 billion.[31] When you buy much more than you sell, you have to borrow money to cover the difference. We've been doing that for a very long time, and that's a major reason for our deficits and debt.

The impact on wages has been mixed, but it is generally negative for American workers. From 1973 to 2006, workers without a college education saw an average decline of 4 percent in their wages attributable to global trade.[32] With nearly three-fourths of Americans employed in so-called blue-collar jobs, it's clear that most have not benefitted from the trade agreements of the past forty years. Those with a college degree, a much smaller portion of the workforce, realized an average gain of only 3 percent during the same period. While education certainly benefits workers in the global economy, those gains are largely offset by the fact that Americans work considerably more hours than they did thirty years ago.

According to a study by Robert Scott, the trade deficit with China led to the loss of 2.7 million American jobs from 2001 to 2011, more than 2 million of which were in manufacturing. For those whose jobs still remain, trade competition with China has led to a decline in wages averaging $1,400 per year during that same period.[33]

The impacts of globalization are mixed at best for the majority of American workers. But according to this myth, there's no alternative, no stopping companies from moving their factories overseas and outsourcing jobs to remain competitive and profitable. Besides, Americans want cheap stuff, and the only way to do this is to "offshore" the production of nearly every product we use, from tennis shoes to tomatoes. Ultimately, the strategy of outsourcing in order to keep product costs low leads to a vicious circle: many low-wage workers, especially in the retail sector, need low-cost items to make ends meet, but the very process that keeps prices low also keeps workers in or near poverty. Not only do many of these workers need cheap goods, but they very often need public subsidies as well, whether food stamps, Medicaid, or housing assistance. *Thus, large companies in effect are subsidized by taxpayers not only to build their facilities but also to help pick up the costs of downsized and low-wage employees.*

The widespread proliferation of cheap goods undeniably creates the opportunity for more people to buy more things. But there can be unintended consequences from this ubiquitous abundance, even for consumers. One of

(in 1,000s)

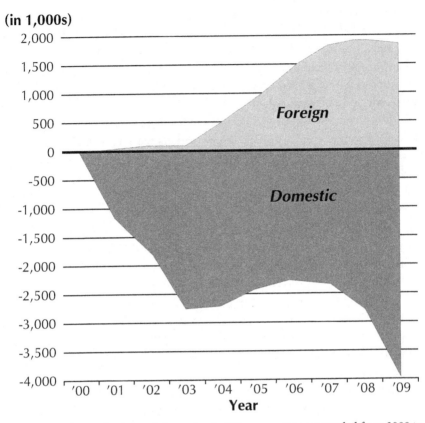

Job gains and losses, foreign and domestic. As U.S. corporations expanded from 2000 to 2009, millions of American jobs were lost, while nearly as many were added overseas. (Excerpted from *Wall Street Journal*.)

these is in terms of diminished product safety and reliability. Between 2005 and 2013, more than one thousand American pets died as a result of eating contaminated "treats" manufactured in China, according to reports in the U.S. press.[34] Further, inspections of human food imported into the United States are minimal, covering barely 2 percent of foods entering the country,[35] including seafood.[36] With such minimal safety testing of imported foods, you might think that labels disclosing where the food was produced, called "Country of Origin Labeling" (COOL) provide a reasonable precaution for consumers. Yet the World Trade Organization ruled in June 2015 that such labels violate "free" trade agreements![37]

Trade among nations, like exchanges among communities, can be a good thing. Iowa has rich soil and tillable land, great for growing crops; Appalachia has abundant hardwood forests; and Louisiana has fertile coastal waters. It makes sense to exchange the things we produce well in these different places. The problem with globalization and so-called "free trade" is not trade, but an increasing *dependence* on that trade for our economic survival. It is also critical to challenge the idea that our various regional and international trade agreements promote free trade. To the contrary, the trade is "free" primarily for the multinational corporations that dominate the rule-making process, as illustrated with painful clarity by the negotiations surrounding the Trans-Pacific Partnership. In this recent example, hundreds of corporate executives have been deeply involved in the secret negotiations under way for more than three years, but virtually no representatives of organized labor, health and environmental groups, or small businesses have been allowed to participate. Workers, citizens, and communities find little in these agreements that enhances their freedom or makes them better off.

What if international trade agreements focused on what people really needed but couldn't readily produce themselves? What if economic policies enabled households, communities, and regions to meet most of their own needs while exporting a few specialized products or services that people in other nations truly need or want? Transitions one and two describe how such productive households and self-reliant economies are being built, such that global trade could be a complement to local businesses rather than an unfair competitor. The third transition (described in chapter 4), focused on building the capital of local workers and communities, illustrates further the alternative to the economic vulnerability and insecurity that global trade agreements have propelled.

Myth 4: In a Free Market, "Looking Out for Number One" Is Best for Everybody

This myth, which has a business side and a worker/consumer side, is sometimes also stated as "greed is good." William Safire succinctly advocated this view in a 1986 *New York Times* column: "Greed is finally being recognized as a virtue. Dressed in euphemism—'the profit motive' or 'the entrepreneurial spirit'—our not-so-deadly sin turns out to be the best engine of betterment known to man."[38] The "greed is good" myth says that the desire to make money in business generates competition among many firms that then spawns countless innovations that improve quality and bring down prices. This in turn makes people rich *and* improves people's lives. Individual consumers contribute to these broader improvements by choosing those products and services that provide the most value for every dollar they spend, while individual workers' desire to make more money makes for hardworking, more productive employees.

Much of the current discourse flowing from this myth also encompasses a highly individualistic view of private property. Without a doubt, private ownership, whether of land, homes, or businesses, can and does generate investment, wealth creation, and longer-term commitment. The challenge is that private ownership has boundaries; the edge of my property is the beginning of someone else's land, and what I do on my property may well create problems for people downwind or downstream.

While running for Congress in 2012, I met with a small group of folks in a rural Virginia community not far from the North Carolina line. One of the people in attendance was a local businesswoman who owned and managed a small retail shop. Echoing what many businesspeople feel, she said to me: "If you get elected, I'm just asking one thing from you. Just leave me alone. Just leave me and my business alone." A few minutes later, I heard her chatting with another person about a local service station that was not properly maintaining its gas tanks, resulting in the leaking of fuel into nearby soil and groundwater. "Something needs to be done about that," they all concurred, including the local businesswoman. "But don't you think," I said, "that the guy running that business just wants the government to leave him alone?"

Clearly, there must be rules within which the market operates, rules that create a level playing field among businesses and that provide reasonable levels of protection for health, consumer and worker safety, and the environment. Unfortunately "government regulation" has become synonymous with "killing jobs" and with bureaucratic meddling. In fact, as the 2010 BP Deep Water Horizon oil-spill disaster demonstrates, a lack of adequate regulations or enforcement in one area can *reduce* the competitiveness of other businesses. This happened when thousands of commercial fishermen, tourism companies, resorts, and other businesses in the Gulf were put out of business or suffered dramatic losses after the spill.

The antiregulatory ethic, combined with unrealistic notions of "perfect competition" in the marketplace, has masked the steady tilt in policies in favor of very large corporations in everything from regulatory frameworks to tax policies and, of course, public dollars spent on so-called incentives. The Dodd-Frank financial regulation that emerged from the 2008 meltdown of the financial sector did very little to prevent the high-risk "investments" that all but evaporated at the start of the recession; likewise, no serious steps were taken to limit the size of the banks that had become "too big to fail." The big boys, in other words, made out just fine. On the other hand, that same legislation has made lending, collateralization, and reporting more expensive for smaller community banks, part of a mix of federal policies that have contributed to the closing of nearly two thousand of these critical institutions since the recession began in 2007.[39] All of this has made both small firms and individual workers far more vulnerable, with fewer protections under the law. As Stacy Mitchell of the Institute for Local Self-Reliance has pointed out, the interests of small businesses are usually more aligned with those of ordinary citizens than they are with huge multinational corporations.[40]

Beyond the problem of externalized costs to the environment and our health, the "looking out for Number One" approach has been disappointing even in the most basic economic terms. A recent survey by Baylor University showed that people working for small firms felt considerably more loyalty than those working for larger companies, and that this in turn led to lower rates of absenteeism. When the business was small and locally owned, employee loyalty increased even further.[41]

This "greed is good" ethic has helped fuel the extraordinary rise in pay for top CEOs, estimated to average nearly three hundred times the pay of the lowest-paid workers in their firms in the United States. Is this exceptional compensation a reward for exceptional performance? Generally not. A study by Michael Cooper of the University of Utah, Huseyin Galen of Purdue, and P. Raghavendra Rau of the University of Cambridge examined CEO pay and company performance from 1994 to 2013. They found that companies whose CEOs were in the top 10 percent pay level had 8 percent *lower* returns than comparable companies; those executives in the top 5 percent best-paid led their companies to 15 percent lower average returns.[42]

At the other end of the spectrum, cooperatives, which hold nearly $3 trillion in assets in the United States, consistently demonstrate higher levels of worker productivity, lower employee turnover, and greater return on investment dollars than comparable enterprises structured around the model of individualism.[43] While cooperatives typically pay senior management more than workers on the floor, the pay differential is miniscule in comparison with the pay disparities in typical U.S. corporations. Cooperative Home Care Associates, the nation's largest worker-owned cooperative, pays its top executive eleven times as much as its workers, compared to a CEO-to-worker pay ratio of 350:1 among large corporations.[44]

And it's not just CEOs who don't necessarily deliver better performance for higher pay. In a 2012 article, Steffie Woolhandler, Dan Ariely, and David Himmelstein summarized an extensive body of research on "pay for performance" incentives in hospitals, schools, and other settings.[45] They found that offering additional pay for better outcomes to both teachers and health care professionals has not usually led to improved performance. What's more, studies show that larger financial incentives tend to yield even worse results, including the tendency of participants—including even doctors—to "cook the books" a bit in order to qualify for the bonuses. Negative financial incentives don't always work as intended, either. An analysis of a preschool that instituted fines for parents who didn't pick their kids up on time found that lateness actually increased when the fines were put in place. Apparently, once the question of timeliness was monetized, other motivations, such as empathy for the day-care staff waiting to go home, diminished. These and other studies quoted by Woolhandler, Ariely, and Himmelstein show that monetary incentives often crowd out so-called "intrinsic motivations," such as empathy for others, doing good, or simply doing the right thing. Greed, or "looking out for Number One," is clearly not the only way, or even the best way, to motivate people toward better performance.

Our obesity epidemic helps illustrate the complexity of self-interest among consumers. Fast-food companies spend more than $4 billion every year to promote their products. They've exploded in number across the United States, exceeding 263,000 in 2012, or more than 600 for every congressional district.[46] As a result of this and changes in work and income patterns, Americans eat more than half their meals away from home, and in the process, eat larger portions and more processed foods. Portion sizes increased by 30 percent or more for most foods from 1977 to 1996,[47] and many have continued to do so for the first decade of the new century, in spite of all the talk about obesity prevention.[48] For the individual consumer, stopping at the drive-through window may make the most sense at that moment, but the sum total is a dramatic decline in health and equally big increases in health care costs. Our "individual self-interest" doesn't always add up to what we really want or need, as individuals or as a society.

Where the "every man for himself" approach to economic prosperity made big "winners" and more and more numerous "losers," a new focus on shared prosperity is taking root in many communities and various sectors of the economy. The emphasis here is not charity, though that is important, but on investments that make networks of small businesses, farmers, or entrepreneurs more viable, in large part by better meeting the needs of people in their communities or nearby. In many cases, businesses are not just searching for "markets" for their products but also are making more long-term investments in an effort to make their own communities better off.

The *Benefit corporation* (or B-Corp) is an example of this new type of business, one where the "bottom line" is not only financial profits but also positive impacts on the community, including the people and environment that make it up. Benefit corporations in the United States are growing rapidly, now totaling more than one thousand, as more companies seek to codify their triple-bottom-line mission, as well as attract the best employees. Some of the best-known are large firms like Patagonia, the outdoor clothing company, and Seventh Generation, which makes recycled paper products, environmentally safe cleaning supplies, and similar items. Many smaller, less well-known companies are also organizing under this model. The future for Benefit corporations looks bright: A 2012 survey by Net Impact found that 70 percent of college students and 50 percent of workers want to work for a company that allows them to have a positive social impact.[49] The experience is similar with cooperatives and employee-owned firms, which have performed better economically while providing better overall compensation to their employees.

The supposed virtue of greed, or looking out for Number One, is in the overall increase in productivity, innovation, and choice that it allegedly generates. Yet the shift to broadly based assets and wealth, the third transition, and the development of regional and national networks, the fourth transition (discussed in chapter 5), both challenge the individualism of this myth with the power of cooperative and community-based strategies that, it turns out, are considerably more productive.

Myth 5: A Rising Tide Lifts All Boats

This idea, sometimes also referred to as "making the pie bigger, rather than cutting smaller slices," has been with us for several generations, The core idea is the same: There's usually plenty to go around. If things get tight, the solution is not to build smaller boats or cut smaller slices, but to *let the market bake a bigger pie*, making everyone better off.

At various periods in our history, a rising economic tide has lifted (most of) our boats. From the end of World War II through the mid-1970s, the incomes of most ordinary Americans grew steadily. During that period, in fact, lower-income people, blue-collar workers, and the middle class saw their incomes grow more, proportionately, than did those of the wealthy. But that all changed beginning about 1979. For the last thirty years, gains in income and wealth have migrated to the wealthiest Americans, while the wages and wealth of the vast majority of people have either stagnated or declined. As Richard Wilkinson and Kate Pickett note: "After slowly increasing from 1950 to 1980, social mobility in the USA declined rapidly as income differences widened dramatically in the latter part of the century. . . . In fact, far from enabling the ideology of the American Dream, the USA has the lowest mobility rate among these eight countries [of comparable wealth]."[50] This trend continued even as the economy began to grow out of the most recent recession. Of the nearly $300 billion in new income gained between 2009 and 2010, 93 percent went to the top 1 percent income bracket, according to calculations by the University of California economist Emmanuel Saez.[51] This shift, now going on for more than thirty years, is not chump change. Had the income distribution patterns of the 1950s and 1960s stayed the same, the average middle-income household would be making $12,000 more per year today.[52]

This shift, better described as a *sucking up* of income, rather than a trickle down, has fueled an accompanying concentration of assets in the United States, where by 2010, 89 percent of all wealth was owned by the top 20 percent, while the bottom 80 percent owned 11 percent of all the assets.[53] To return to the pie analogy, the gains of the past three decades look like this: *One* person in the top 1 percent received one and a half slices of pie; *six hundred* working- and middle-class people shared a single slice.

For the most part, then, hard work and education are not leading people from rags to riches or even from poverty to the middle class. Our economic mobility is stagnant, lower than that of Canada, Germany, France, England, and several other European nations. American men born into poverty remain in poverty as adults 60 percent more often than Danish men born into poverty.[54] Rising tide or not, our boats are stuck in the mud.

Even education, long considered the great equalizer across class, no longer erases the problems of economic inequality. As a 2011 analysis from the Economic Mobility Project shows, poor kids who succeed academically are less likely to graduate from college than richer kids who do poorly in school. Another comparison of children from affluent families with those from low-income families shows that lower-income students with high eighth-grade test scores are still less likely to finish college than richer kids with low test scores.[55]

Of late, some pundits and politicians have labeled efforts to address this inequality a "war on success." The idea behind this is that most everyone at the top got there through their own hard work, intelligence, and education. Anyone else could do the same, if they just put their mind to it. While this has never been entirely true, it is increasingly inaccurate. In fact, even when people from low-income families graduate from college, they are still less likely to achieve wealth than those who never complete college but were born into wealth.[56]

The rising tide of economic output has continued (with a very small pause during the 2007–2009 recession), but instead of lifting more boats, it buoys a small number of ever-grander yachts while most boats are mired in muck. The consequences of this go beyond issues of fairness and income distribution. As Richard Wilkinson and Kate Pickett demonstrate in their insightful book *The Spirit Level: Why Greater Equality Makes Societies Stronger,* the consequences of growing inequality and the lack of social mobility permeate almost every facet of our lives.[57] From our health and life expectancy to drug use and mental health to rates of violence and incarceration, expensive and destructive social problems are virtually all worse in highly unequal societies than in those with greater equality. This is true when comparing richer, more unequal societies like the United States with less affluent, more equal societies, such as Italy. And it is true even within different economic classes in the same society; that is, these health and social problems are more widespread among the middle class of an unequal society than within the middle class of a society with less inequality. Inequality is bad for everyone, except perhaps those at the very top.

John Steinbeck once said that the poor in America see themselves "as temporarily embarrassed millionaires." Yet it's clear that we can't all be rich. While the myth of the "rags-to-riches" self-made man has inspired some people to great economic success, far, far more people struggle to keep their heads above water in a nation of declining opportunity. Confronting this truth is essential if we're going to build real opportunities for the great majority of people. Opportunities not to be rich, but to lead decent, dignified lives doing productive work that benefits their communities and world.

Transitions two and three—building bottom-up, living economies, and building broadly based assets and wealth—demonstrate a fundamentally different, more effective path to prosperity than the rising tide that no longer lifts many boats or trickles down. And transitions five and six (discussed in chapters 6 and 7) describe bottom-up approaches to reinvigorating our citizenship and politics, both utterly essential to challenging the vast concentration of wealth and power that has been obscured by this myth.

Myth 6: Growth Is the Answer. Always

We began this discussion of the six myths by examining one that defines our understanding of success, of prosperity at the individual level. We close with a myth that helps explain how we see ourselves as a people, even as a species. Again, there are two parts: First, that economic growth must always be the end goal because that is what makes prosperity for everyone possible. It's how we make the pie bigger. Second, that such growth can continue forever because human ingenuity and technology will solve whatever problems arise. After all, the "doomsday crowd" has for years been warning of looming shortages, "peak oil," and ecological limits, but we keep finding more resources and making more stuff through technology. One farmer now produces what it used to take fifty farmers to grow; we use less energy for every unit of economic output than we did in the past; we're getting oil and gas from shale and sand. It's all good. Let's go shopping.

As Herman Daly, the noted World Bank economist, has described it, over the two-plus centuries since our nation gained independence, we've moved from "empty world economics" to "full world economics."[58] To illustrate his point, Daly uses a critical measurement known as "net primary productivity" (NPP), that is, the total amount of energy available to all living things, based on the foundation of photosynthesis. Without getting too complicated, photosynthesis, from trees, grass, plants, and algae and other aquatic plants, is the "primary production" upon which everything else depends, regardless of where we are in the food chain. As the graphs show, the world's population in 1776 used only a small fraction of this net primary productivity, less than 10 percent of what was available.

But today, the dramatic increases in both the size of the world's population and the average consumption per person together mean that humanity is consuming four times as much, or nearly 40 percent of terrestrial (land-based) NPP. That figure does not include what the billions of nondomesticated animal species utilize.[59] While we may be able to increase the photosynthetic efficiency of some plants, that is a very difficult thing to do. Unlimited growth will inevitably outstrip primary productivity.

Nearly every economist and politician measures growth using the gross domestic product, or GDP. Simply put, the GDP is the sum of everything we buy, all the goods and services we pay for. Overwhelmingly, it is the main cri-

1776

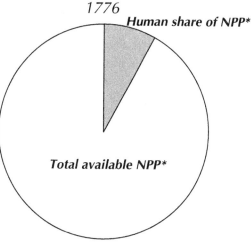

Human share of NPP*

From empty world economics. Around 1776, the total amount of the earth's Net Primary Productivity (NPP) utilized by humanity was less than 10 percent of what was available.

Total available NPP*

NPP - Net Primary Productivity

2009

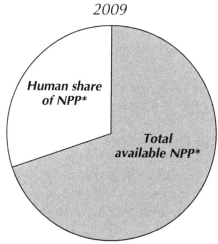

Human share of NPP*

Total available NPP*

To full world economics. By 2009, dramatic increases in both world population and average consumption mean that people are using nearly 40 percent of all available NPP. (Graphs 3 and 4 are based on data contained in Herman E. Daly and John Cobb Jr., *For the Common Good: Redirecting the Economy toward Community, the Environment and a Sustainable Future* [Boston: Beacon, 1994], 143–44.)

NPP - Net Primary Productivity

teria we use to evaluate "how the economy is doing." However, the GDP does not measure what *kind* of economic activity is happening, or who benefits from it. One hundred dollars' worth of cigarettes or cable TV is valued the same as one hundred dollars' worth of organic vegetables or bicycles. A third home in the Hamptons for a stockbroker counts the same as (many) homes built by Habitat for Humanity.

Actually, it's worse than that. Every time we purchase a pack of cigarettes, we contribute to the GDP. If we buy and smoke enough of them, we're likely to get emphysema, heart disease, or cancer. If we do, the hundreds of thousands of dollars we spend in hospitals to treat our disease will also add to the GDP. In a very real sense, the things we do that make us sick or require cleanup after we're gone—think the 2010 BP oil spill—actually contribute more to economic growth than things that preserve our health and environment.

Economists and social scientists would generally agree that economies need to grow to a certain point to create enough total wealth that the potential exists to meet the needs of most people. Unfortunately, in wealthy societies, particularly the United States, further growth alone is doing little, if anything, to benefit most people or the communities where they live. This is true in both pure financial terms as well as in the broader array of measurements we use to determine if people are healthy and happy.

Measuring those indicators of well-being, though challenging, is now being undertaken in several ways. One of these is called the "genuine progress indicator," or GPI. The GPI uses a far broader range of criteria than the GDP's singular focus on economic output, including such things as health, educational attainment, community involvement and volunteerism, family cohesion, levels of crime, drug abuse, and more. Unlike the GDP, bad outcomes, such as drug abuse or water pollution, are *subtracted* from the GPI; positive things that are not purchased, like volunteers building a house for a lower-income neighbor, are added in.

As the graph below illustrates, the GPI in the United States increased only slightly between 1950 and 2002, even as the GDP per capita more than tripled.[60] In other words, as the economy grew much bigger and the total economic output per person increased threefold, the overall well-being of people, their families, and communities was nearly stagnant. By some measurements, the GPI has actually declined since then.

There's no question that scientific understanding and technology have dramatically increased our productivity and in so doing have made it possible for billions of people to eat better, live longer, and have more. However, using our past experience to project a future of unlimited growth is simply bad accounting. It doesn't recognize the depreciation of ecological assets—land, water, air, and nonrenewable resources—that have made this growth possible. This depreciation, this using up of nature's capital, obviously includes fossil fuels, a onetime gift that took millions of years to create but that will be fully exhausted in less than four centuries of modern life.

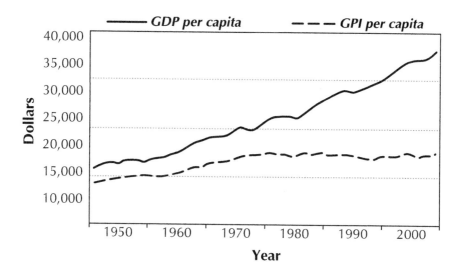

Real GDP and GPI per capita, 1950–2004. While the U.S. Gross Domestic Product (GDP) continued to grow steadily through the second half of the twentieth century, the Genuine Progress Indicator (GPI) stayed flat. (Based on data from Dr. John Talberth, Clifford Cobb, and Noah Slattery, "The Genuine Progress Indicator, 2006: A Tool for Sustainable Development," 19, Redefining Progress, Oakland, CA, 2007, www.rprogress .org.)

Take oil for instance. Recent discoveries of as much as 1 trillion barrels of shale oil in the West have made the notion of "peak oil" seem silly. But these staggering numbers obscure a simple fact: mining, extracting, and processing that oil from shale requires us to *expend* tremendous quantities of energy in order to get the new energy out. This is sometimes called the "energy balance" and is also known as the EROEI, or "energy return on energy invested." The much-heralded new sources of oil from shale and tar sands, as well as natural gas from shale, have a dramatically lower EROEI, ranging from about 5:1 down to some estimates of as little as 2:1. Put another way, it takes a half barrel of oil to get one barrel out. If that doesn't sound bad, consider that oil wells through the mid-twentieth century had an energy balance averaging 100:1, and that even today, traditional oil sources provide, on average, a 17:1 return.[61] So, we may be in the midst of an "oil boom" in the United States, but it won't lead to cheap energy over the long haul.

Coal reserves are greater, on the order of two hundred years, based on current consumption and exports.[62] The total "technically recoverable" reserves of natural gas, including from fracking, exceed 2,000 trillion cubic feet, or an eighty-seven-year supply at current rates of consumption. That figure includes both proven and unproven reserves. The proven reserves of 354 trillion cubic feet are enough for fewer than fourteen years at current consumption rates.[63] It may sound like we have some time to figure out a new way of powering our lives. Unless you consider the climate impacts of burning all these fossil fuels.

It's not just fossil fuels that impose limits to growth. As discussed earlier, the quantity of productive land available per capita globally has shrunk from 14 acres to 3.5 acres over the past century. We have, in other words, 75 percent less land per person to provide food, fiber, building materials, and other necessities, even as we promote the idea of everyone having more. Similarly, there are growing concerns about the warming and acidification of our oceans, both of which are likely to reduce the productivity of the fisheries upon which hundreds of millions of people depend.

Even if we could overcome the ecological limits that continued growth imposes, which we cannot, it's abundantly clear that the bigger pie is not translating to bigger slices for most people. Our economy is nearly 400 percent larger today than it was in Ronald Reagan's first year in office, 1980. During that same period, our population has increased by 40 percent. So, we've grown the economy about ten times faster than the population, yet more people are living in poverty today, and the vast majority of Americans have seen little if any growth in their income. Essentially, we've added ten pies to the table with only one more person in the room, yet most are getting the same size piece, or an even smaller serving. Growth is not making us better off.

Economic growth as we've practiced it has focused almost entirely on quantity over quality, on the physical expansion of our economy, and along with that, our homes, cars, lives, and ultimately ourselves. The myths that *bigger is better,* that *a rising tide lifts all boats,* and that *global trade is good for everyone* are all built on the notion of unlimited growth. We, individual consumers, are encouraged to do our part for growth *by looking out for Number One* and staying focused on the idea that *money can buy happiness.*

Fortunately, a range of new alternatives are emerging that recognize the ecological limits to growth and focus instead on improving our quality of life over simply our quantity of consumption. These emerging alternatives form the foundation of this book.

Summary

The six myths we've examined reinforce each other, are woven together into one big story or belief system about the economy, prosperity, and the role of government, markets, and people. That story goes something like this:

Money is the key to prosperity because it enables us to buy stuff, and the more stuff we have, the happier and more successful we are. To achieve that success, we should all look out for Number One. Businesses and the market will respond by making everyone (who works hard) better off.

When individuals strive to make themselves better off, the market generates a rising tide of prosperity, a bigger pie, so that more and more people can have more stuff. Economic growth is what makes that rising tide possible, so it must continue indefinitely. The only way to sustain that growth is through ever-bigger businesses, farms, and financial institutions, providing the lowest cost goods and services through global free trade.

Left alone, free from all but the bare minimum of government regulation, the market will make this happen.

Because the market rewards hard work and success, there will be some inequality, but overall, everyone who makes an effort will be better off. Problems that arise from economic growth—resource depletion, pollution, health problems, etc.—are short-term. Solutions to these problems will come through market demand and the technological innovation it fosters.

This story is compelling, particularly for us in America, because it focuses on the individual (consumer or business), promises rewards for hard work, and seems to put us all on equal footing in a competition that ultimately makes for a better world. But it hasn't worked out that way, not for millions of Americans, let alone for many more in other countries. The economic and political ideas that this story has generated have brought about record levels of inequality in the United States. This in turn has fostered dramatically higher levels of crime, anxiety, mental illness, substance abuse, and other problems, and poorer overall health, educational attainment, and happiness for us, compared to nations of comparable wealth and income.

The belief in the vast superiority of the market over government, and the widespread cynicism about the public sector, have led many, particularly those in the political middle, to largely withdraw from the public debate, creating space for extreme views and the policies that follow. Many of these views and policies in turn deny or ignore increasingly urgent problems, from the shrinking base of productive land to the growing impacts of climate change.

In a word, it's a mess. And as David Korten has pointed out, we're stuck in the trap of thinking that "the only alternative to the rapacious excess of capitalism is the debilitating oppression of communism."[64] Put another way, there is no alternative to unregulated capitalism, nor to every-man-for-himself consumerism.

In fact, there is. There is an alternative that's emerging all across the nation and in other parts of the world, one that sees the market as a means to better lives and stronger communities rather than as an end in itself. This alternative has not yet been named. Some refer to it as the "local living economy," while others call it "sustainable economies," and others, an economy of "prosperity for all." Regardless of its name, the alternative is based on a different story from the one we've described above, a story that goes something like this:

A strong economy and a healthy society require broadly based, real wealth and widely shared prosperity. This broadly based wealth includes sufficient income and livelihoods for dignified lives but also shared ownership of capital and businesses. This broad base of modest wealth and prosperity is achievable in large part through a diversity of local, independent businesses rooted in and responsive to local communities, and respectful of their places.

To sustain economies and communities, we must sustain the ecosystems upon which they're built, which means learning to live well within limits. Both government and the market have essential and sometimes counterbalancing roles to play to make this happen. Real prosperity includes material progress but also encompasses community, health, and happiness.

This new story is less about different ideas than about different *experiences* emerging in many regions of the country. It is about a laboratory of experimentation unfolding at the local level, led by thousands of businesses, entrepreneurs, and community leaders, more often than not linked together through networks and associations. It is a story, too, about a new generation that seeks not riches but meaning, both in their work and in their communities. The balance of this book is dedicated to this unfolding and very hopeful story.

Further Reading

Berry, Wendell. *The Gift of Good Land.* San Francisco: North Point Press, 1981.

———. *What Matters? Economics for a Renewed Commonwealth.* Berkeley, CA: Counterpoint, 2010.

Daly, Herman, and John Cobb Jr. *For the Common Good: Redirecting the Econ-*

omy toward Community, the Environment and a Sustainable Future. Boston: Beacon, 1994.

Daly, Lew, and Steven Posner. "Beyond GDP: New Measures for a New Economy," Demos Institute, 2011. www.demos.org.

Flannery, Tim. *The Weather Makers: How Man Is Changing the Climate and What It Means for Life on Earth*. New York: Atlantic Monthly Press, 2005.

Kelly, Marjorie. *The Divine Right of Capital: Dethroning the Corporate Aristocracy*. San Francisco: Berrett-Koehler, 2001.

Korten, David C. *Agenda for a New Economy: From Phantom Wealth to Real Wealth*. San Francisco: Berrett-Koehler, 2009.

Shuman, Michael. *The Small-Mart Revolution: How Local Businesses Are Beating the Global Competition*. San Francisco: Berrett-Koehler, 2006.

Stiglitz, Joseph E. *The Price of Inequality: How Today's Divided Society Endangers Our Future*. New York: Norton, 2012.

Stiglitz, Joseph E., Amartya Sen, and Jean-Paul Fitoussi. *Mis-Measuring Our Lives: Why GDP Doesn't Add Up*. New York: New Press, 2010.

Wilkinson, Richard, and Kate Pickett. *The Spirit Level: Why Greater Equality Makes Societies Stronger*. New York: Bloomsbury, 2010.

2

Renewing Households and Communities

From Consumptive Dependence to Productive Resilience

The "Kentucky way" is primarily a system of local knowledge and practice that allows people to exercise control over their livelihood and that provides them with a sense of autonomy. . . . Self-sufficiency is extremely important to people in this region [Appalachia], for it is a strategy of self-reliance, a mark of one's versatility and flexibility and one's ingenuity and cleverness. In this region self-reliance does not serve to isolate people. It is not individualistic or self-serving. Rather, it is a form of outreach to kin and to neighbors in the context of offering multiple goods and services in multiple arenas.
—Rhoda Halperin, *The Livelihood of Kin*

A living economy depends on local control. . . . Wall Street has learned that its ability to generate unearned profits is best served by a system that minimizes local self-reliance and maximizes each locality's dependence on distant resources and markets.
—David Korten, *Agenda for a New Economy*

Early one December morning in 1993, I sat down with my two kids to talk about Christmas. Josh had just turned eleven, and Maria was four. I was a part-time single parent, that is, I was on my own with my kids half of every week. I had a full-time job, but money was very tight. Our 700-square-foot house was in a neighborhood of equally modest homes, walking distance from Kmart, the video store, and Abingdon's little town park.

"Guys, I have an idea about Christmas this year," I started, "and I want to see what you think." I was about to propose something that would impact them, and I wanted to gauge their reactions.

"What if we decide that for every dollar we spend on Christmas gifts this year—for each other, for family and friends—we agree to give the same amount to groups that are helping people? In other words, if we spend $100 on our gifts, we'll also give $100 to these groups."

I'm not sure that Maria was old enough to fully grasp the implications, but both kids knew that we didn't have a lot of money. "It would mean that we'd have to cut back on gifts a bit, since we'd be spending twice that amount altogether," I continued.

Josh answered first, and without hesitation: "Well, sure, Dad, let's do it. I mean, it's better to give money to people who really need it than to buy a bunch of junk for ourselves that we don't need." With his little sister's nod of approval, thus was launched our annual "Christmas tithe." That first year we spent $150 on gifts and gave $150 to two social-change groups; the $300 total was a bit of a stretch for us. Over the ensuing years, the amount spent gradually increased, most years at least, with our contributions going to a wide range of organizations, from the local domestic violence shelter to Oxfam, Doctors Without Borders, Heifer Project, and many others. We'd discuss the possible groups together every year, always including at least one local initiative.

This very simple family tradition had modest but lasting impacts on all of us. For one, it helped keep us out of the malls and big-box stores, where the urge to buy becomes so powerful. Instead, we favored local stores in Abingdon and Bristol for quirky gifts. Mostly, we made things for people, at home, often together, ranging from pasta and biscotti to dark-chocolate candies and granola. (To this day, if I'm lucky enough to have Maria home for the holidays, this is one of the things we do together.) And over time, we contributed a few thousand dollars to groups building a better world, near and far. From a traditional economics point of view, our Christmas tithe was less commendable. After all, cutting back on spending just reduces our contribution to the gross domestic product, the GDP. In a retail-driven consumer economy, what would happen if millions of people bought less stuff at the holidays? Or year-round? It's a complicated but important question, especially if we deliberately set out to build up local resilience and expand what some are calling the "informal economy." We'll return to that question later on in our discussion.

Whatever the implications for the U.S. gross domestic product and jobs in the retail sector, our family's tradition helped us begin to build a *household economy*, as Wendell Berry has aptly described it, a place where family members (or others) work together to produce things they need. This is part of the first of our six transitions, *moving from consumptive dependence to productive resilience.* For us, as for most others I know with similar aspirations, this involved both subtraction and addition: gradually subtracting from our lives some of the things we did not need, things that required a lot of energy to operate, that generated considerable waste, or that propelled further consumption; and adding the skills we needed to meet more of our own needs, along with the tools, rituals, and relationships needed to both sustain and enjoy this life.

Most of this subtraction and addition is incremental, with the occasional "leap." As we increased the size of our garden, we started to can, freeze, and store up for the off-season. This required more time in the kitchen, along with some new skills in basic food preservation. The larger garden required more fertility, so not only did we compost our kitchen scraps and yard waste, but we teamed up with some friends who brought us their leaves, newspapers, grass clippings and trimmings. As we grew more and ate more from our own place, the money saved and the knowledge of what it takes to produce food encouraged us to pay full price for healthy food grown by other folks rather than always seeking out the cheapest items at the big-box stores. And it also propelled us to a small leap: Starting a CSA (Community Supported Agriculture) buying group in 1994, producing a weekly basket of produce for a dozen families out of nothing more than a large backyard garden. Not too long after, we were farming on a small commercial scale.

As a family, we subtracted trips to big-box stores and chains, virtually all fast food, and most processed food outside of cereal. We also worked to eliminate nonrecyclable materials that included most packaged items at that time, and, of course, "a bunch of junk that we don't need," as Josh had described it. For a little while, my new stepson, Alex, referred to this as "the Amish life" because compared to the homes of friends, we had relatively few games, gadgets, and conveniences. But over time he came to appreciate many elements of this somewhat different way of living, ending up with an environmental studies concentration within his geography degree. And when he comes home to visit, he always offers to help with farm chores. Nevertheless, it's good to acknowledge that we all had our adjustments to make in the effort to find our own "new normal."

There were additions too, most fundamentally in the new skills we acquired, and the new habits and rituals my children and I built together.

While we spent much less money on food overall, we still purchased things, including the seeds, tools, and other items we needed for what was then our market garden; canning and freezing supplies (mostly reusable); and plenty of food we could not grow. We may have been contributing less to the GDP than some other folks, but we certainly did not withdraw from the economy in any radical way. Rather, we participated in it more *on our own terms*, as producers as well as "consumers."

Our experience with food—growing, cooking, eating—as a starting point is fairly typical of those households striving to live with less yet enrich their lives. Gardening requires very practical knowledge and regular physical exertion, both of which have been in decline for many folks. It also provides a place to turn household and yard waste into compost, newspapers or cardboard into mulch, scrap building materials into cold frames or hoop houses, and much more. A well-managed garden—and not all of them are, to be sure—provides fresh fruits and vegetables at a fraction of the cost of buying them, even from discount stores. With a few hens added to the mix, as many folks are now doing, you also get eggs, not to mention more nutrients for your soil.

Some studies, including one from Denver[1] and another out of Flint, Michigan,[2] indicate that people who garden are much more likely to eat fruits and vegetables, and to increase their consumption of fresh produce overall. Another study of Latino youth in Los Angeles found that gardening, combined with cooking and nutrition classes, improved young people's diets and reduced obesity.[3] As gardening builds affection for the "fruits of your labors," it also seems to make cooking less of a burden, becoming more of an adventure and over time, part of the family's culture and way of doing things. There have been hundreds of times when we haven't even started preparing supper until 7:00 p.m. or later, after a long day of work. But done together, using some ingredients that you just picked, can be quite enjoyable.

At every step of the gardening-composting-cooking-eating continuum, there are clear opportunities to contribute in meaningful ways for most everyone in the household. Children's chores are less mundane when there's a clear connection to supper or other vital functions, like gathering wood for heating. It's still work, of course, often hard work, and as such is not always undertaken with a smile. But there is just something far more interesting about gathering eggs or turning a compost pile than the demand to "clean your room!"

People pick up plants for use in community gardens in Detroit. Courtesy of Keep Growing Detroit.

Building a household economy that cultivates resilience need not stop with food. Heating our homes, building structures and repairing equipment, reducing waste, improving our health, and finding ways to care for and entertain ourselves and others—each of these presents opportunities for learning, creativity, and production, at home. And in the community. In fact, it's increasingly clear that household economies are strengthened by productive groups of people, in a neighborhood, community, or city.

Before we go any further with this first transition, let's clarify a few terms. "Resilience" is about the ability to rebound from or make it through tough times without coming unglued. Think about the Brits in World War II, relentlessly bombed for months on end but keeping a "stiff upper lip" and salvaging what they could, rebuilding when they could. Or mountain communities in Appalachia finding new ways to make ends meet when whole industries disappeared. Or perhaps your immigrant grandparents, who worked through economic hardship we could barely imagine and bounced back from trying circumstances with few resources available to them. Whether at the household or community level, resilience means the capacity to bounce back from disaster, crisis, or extreme hardship. It is the other end of the spectrum from *vulnerability*.

In some places, it's less about bouncing back from a particular disaster than it is about learning to survive, even thrive, in conditions of chronic crisis and neglect. Citing the author Octavia Butler, Adrienne Maree Brown described this community resilience capacity as "survival-based efficiency."[4]

Being, or becoming, more resilient usually requires that you are also more "productive," that is, able to do more things for yourself or with others nearby. Think about it. If most everything you need requires you to buy it from someone else or have it shipped in from far away, then you're fine . . . so long as you have the cash, so long as "they" can and do produce all those things, and so long as somebody can get those things you need to you when you need them. Like your food, energy, shelter, transportation, medical services, and more.

Self-reliance is different from resilience, though it is typically part of the foundation of resilient places. I use the term "self-reliance" to describe households and communities who have the knowledge, skills, and resources to meet a significant portion of their own needs, and in so doing, reduce their dependence and vulnerability. The idea here is not a totally self-sufficient Grizzly Adams character but rather people who know how to make the most of what they have, connected to others in their communities with different and complementary capabilities. Self-reliance is, for me, not an absolute goal but a way of living that makes your "needs" more modest while increasing your ability to meet some of those needs, close to home.

The effort to foster households that are less dependent upon purchasing everything they need, and communities that are more capable of meeting some of their core needs, is essential to a broader foundation of resilience and sustainability. There are several reasons for this:

- There are now more than 7 billion people in the world and nearly 350 million in the United States. With the world population likely to reach 10 billion people before it stabilizes, the potential for all or even most of those people leading American-style consumer lives is virtually nil. One study demonstrated that should China continue its current rate of growth and match the United States in per capita consumption rates, in twenty years that single nation would be consuming almost 70 percent of the world's entire grain harvest and virtually all of its oil.[5] That does not include India, Indonesia, Brazil, or any part of the industrialized world. *We simply cannot expect the model of unrestricted consumer growth to continue indefinitely.*

- While the efficiency with which we produce things has increased steadily over the past two generations, those efficiency gains have been offset almost entirely by the "supersizing" of our lives in terms of bigger homes filled with more stuff, bigger cars, and, quite frankly, bigger bodies. It's a good thing that it now takes considerably less energy to produce one dollar of economic output (GDP) in the United States than it did when I was a kid. But if the overriding goal of economic policy is to keep increasing the size of the economy, we're simply allowing "more" to negate "more efficient."

- Along with limits to our land base, to the productivity of our fisheries, and to the store of both fossil fuels and critical minerals, like phosphorus, we also face a world with limited capacity to absorb our waste, the so-called "sink" function of our ecosystems. Whether we are talking about the acidification of our oceans, the severe decline in stored groundwater, or levels of carbon in our atmosphere dramatically higher than at any time in human history, *we face increasingly urgent limits to where we put our "stuff" after we've used it up.* A globalized consumer economy makes it hard to keep up with where our stuff comes from, and it also hides—for a while—where it goes when we're done. Nowhere is that more true than with excess carbon in the atmosphere, that is, climate change.

- The need for increasing resilience within our households and our communities is partly driven by the surge in storms and natural disasters. In some cases those disasters are "anthropogenic," or man-made, like the 2010 BP explosion and oil spill in the Gulf of Mexico, or the collapse of coal ash containment ponds in east Tennessee in 2008 and in North Carolina in 2014. Whatever the cause, it's clear that we need not be paranoid to understand that being more resourceful, more frugal, and more capable of "working with what we've got" is a sensible step we should be taking to minimize the impacts of such shock.

- But it's not just disasters that argue for far greater levels of self-reliance and homegrown productivity. The urgency of our social, economic, and ecological problems in many ways demand "big" solutions to our problems. In fact, I will argue for such broad, public steps in this book. Small, strictly local responses to our big problems won't add up quickly enough to address critical economic and ecological problems. Nevertheless, homegrown solutions that make us more resilient and productive must help to influence the direction of larger policy changes and are an essential complement to broader public approaches. Big solutions, in other words, can't work unless we also relearn how to do more with less, on our own and in our communities.

- The global consumer economy upon which almost the entire foundation of our economic policies rests has generated levels of individual household debt that make most people highly insecure, both financially and personally. In 1950, household debt on average was equivalent to just one-third of our net (or "after-tax") income; by 2003, it had reached 115 percent of our net income, meaning that for most of us, what we owe in any given year is more than what we earn.[6] There's no doubt that part of the reason for this has been the long-term stagnation in wages for working-class and middle-income people, a trend that's more than thirty years old. But even if our incomes had risen at reasonable rates during this time, our household debt would still have grown to precarious levels. This helps explain why household bankruptcies still number more than 1 million per year, even though they've declined since 2010.

- Finally, if we were happier, healthier, kinder, and more loving people as an outgrowth of all this debt, trade, and consumption, it might be worth trying to figure out how to sustain this economic model. But we're not, as research cited in chapter 1 points out. The myth that money equals wealth and that monetary wealth makes us happy just doesn't hold up. Anecdotally at least, individuals, families, and communities that are working toward productive resilience do seem to be happier, healthier, more neighborly, and more loving. These families come from both the political Right and the Left, from those who've downsized their consumptive lives voluntarily to those who've learned to live well with less out of necessity. Beyond the folks I know, there's evidence of strong connections between excess reliance on materialism and low self-esteem, the latter being a major impediment to happiness and productivity.[7]

Being able to care for ourselves and those we love, it seems, is more important to us than our buying power.

Overall, then, a strategy to retool our households and build the capacity of our communities—that is, *making the transition from consumptive dependence to productive resilience*—is the necessary starting place in working toward a more just society and sustainable economy. This transition steers us toward more fundamental questions and more holistic solutions. For instance:

We can and we must fight trade agreements and government policies that promote outsourcing of jobs and lower-wage employment. But even if we close those doors, we'll still need to change the question from "Where are the jobs?" to "What is the work we need to do?"

We can and we must work for far greater equality of wealth, income, and opportunity in our nation. But even if we achieve that, we'll still need, collectively, *to learn how to live within our means.*

We can and we must create a government that protects the vulnerable and serves the needs of ordinary people, rather than one increasingly at the service of the few. But even if we win that extraordinary fight, *we'll nevertheless need ordinary people with great skills and intelligence, working with others to make their places worth living in.*

For a wide range of reasons, many individuals and families are working to reduce their consumption and debt, to live with less or "off-grid." As we'll see, some of these folks are forming neighborhood or community networks that make the efforts of households more efficient, contagious, and long-lasting. In the discussion that follows, we'll look at several examples of these networks of local productivity and resilience, from the completely informal to those with more structure and community support.

Emerging Examples of Productive Self-Reliance

A Community Cider Press

Tom and Deni Peterson met more than twenty years ago while working on a small farm in New England. Over time as their relationship grew, so too did their farming, including six years running an organic farm in the Prairie Crossing community outside of Chicago, followed by a move to southwestern Virginia in 2000. Along with day jobs focused on sustainable agriculture and school-based gardening, they also manage a large market garden, selling their organic produce and flowers at the local farmers market and to nearby restaurants. You might say that they work, eat, and sleep plants, but that has not dampened their love of food.

About eight years ago, Tom and Deni started to make apple cider with a very old press that had been given to them by a friend. While they loved the cider they could make from their own apples—and from neighbors' trees—the old press was terribly slow and cumbersome. They started talking to some friends who also loved cider, and by 2009, a group of six families decided to jointly purchase a modern press, along with an electric grinder. The results have been terrific: This small group recently surpassed one thousand gallons of cider between them, or an average of more than thirty gallons per family each year, much of that in the form of so-called hard cider. The cider and grinder together cost about $1,400, requiring each family to put in $235 for the purchase. With hard cider typically valued at more than $10 per gallon, most of the families recouped their investment within the first year.

Here's how they make it work: The equipment is jointly and equally owned by the six families, all of whom live within about half an hour of Abingdon, Virginia. Responsibilities for upkeep and repair, which thus far have been minimal, are also shared equally. When one family dropped out of the group, they were asked to find another to buy in, which they did rather easily. Decisions related to the press, including a recent one to replace and upgrade a small part, are made informally, with discussions primarily by e-mail.

The press moves from house to house, accommodating everyone's different schedules as much as possible, especially given that all of these are working families. While communication happens through e-mail, much of it also takes place face-to-face, as two or three households often come together for a day of grinding and pressing when the apples are in. Everyone is responsible for "sourcing" their own apples, and thus far that has included apples from people's own trees, leftovers from the trees of neighbors, purchasing "seconds" from small orchards in the area, and a bartering arrangement with a person who needed some help reclaiming and maintaining some of their trees. Tom mentions that the downside is that you don't always have the press exactly when you want it, but with just six families, that has been only a minor inconvenience. So long as it doesn't restrict the six core owners, other people are allowed to use the press for a nominal fee of less than two dollars per gallon.

A few folks in the group are talking about buying a larger, faster press in order to produce the cider commercially, still in small batches, but at a considerably faster rate than they can now do. No one has yet decided to take that plunge, but in the meantime, this simple piece of jointly owned capital has paid for itself many times over.

Tool Libraries: Sharing Equipment and Know-How

About thirty minutes from the Petersons in the town of Damascus, Virginia, Cassa Von Kundra and Ron Edins live on a small homestead, replete with solar PV panels, a geothermal heating and cooling system, and a diverse if small garden built around permaculture principles. When they moved into their home, they undertook considerable renovations, which generated a fair bit of scrap materials, leftover appliances, cabinet sets, and more. The father-and-son team who were doing the renovations on their house worked with another neighbor to "find a home" for virtually all of this, ranging from lumber, flooring, and siding to kitchen cabinets and an old stove.

As Ron and Cassa came to know their neighbors more deeply, they became part of other informal sharing networks once so common throughout Appalachia and many other rural communities. One of these includes a log splitter, which Cassa and Ron purchased but which is used by a neighbor with more downed trees and a little more available time. He splits all the wood they need, along with some for himself and a few others close by. One log splitter was bought; several families are getting the benefit.

Sharing equipment with friends and neighbors, though simple enough, has become the exception to the rule over the past fifty years. Most of us were persuaded that each one of us needed everything under one roof, at our fingertips. But as stagnant incomes have made this more difficult, and more people realized that they only needed most such things occasionally, community equipment sharing has emerged in the form of *tool libraries*. The first of these is thought to have emerged in Columbus, Ohio, in 1976. There are now more than forty nationwide, with one of the most recent ones springing up in Greenville, South Carolina. At least twenty-six states now have one or more tool libraries, according to online listings of active sites.[8] Tool-lending libraries vary in size, offerings, and procedures, but most work on the same principle as a public library. Membership is usually free, though some have instituted small, income-scaled fees to help cover costs. Tools and equipment can be checked out for a designated period of

Community members check out tools at the North Portland Tool Library. Internet stock photo.

time, generally one week. Members are responsible to return the tools clean and in working order, and also take the risk associated with using the equipment. Offerings typically include tools for home repair and maintenance, basic plumbing and electrical items, and yard and garden equipment.

The North Portland Tool Library (NPTL) opened in October 2004 in Portland, Oregon, assisted by North Portland Community Works, a community development non-profit. Started by Matt Moritz, Laura Dalton, Jason Hatch, and Jason Henshaw, the library has grown steadily and now boasts more than two thousand tools for everything from carpentry to raised bed gardening. Any adult over eighteen can become a member by registering and demonstrating that they reside in one of the North Portland neighborhoods. By 2014, the NPTL had more than 4,700 registered members. Staffed largely by volunteers, their operating hours are limited to one weeknight and most of Saturday. In spite of these rather limited hours, the library membership has continued to grow.

In addition to the lending of tools, the NPTL provides regular training to members on the proper and safe use of the equipment, along with workshops on building, maintenance, and repair. Additionally, they host a "Repair Café" about four times per year during which skilled volunteers lend their time as scores of folks bring malfunctioning radios, old bikes, and even broken jewelry to be repaired, while also learning to DIY—Do It Yourself.

Tool libraries offer a more formalized version of neighborly sharing networks, combining the tool inventory of major rental companies with "how to" training and the capacity building mission of community associations. While a number charge a small fee either for membership or tool rental, they make access to good-quality tools and equipment feasible for working folks and lower-income families, often the very households most in need of household repairs and improvements, since they are also more likely to live in older, if not substandard dwellings. In a very real sense, tool libraries are becoming an important source of *community capital* in the small towns and cities where they have arisen. We'll talk more about that in chapter 4.

Community Energy Projects

Community energy projects represent another interesting type of sharing network, one that can draw upon private, cooperative, and public ownership to make windmills, solar panels, and other energy sources more affordable and more productive due to their larger scale. The Clean Energy Collective began near El Jebel, Colorado, as a 77-kilowatt solar power installation owned collectively by twenty different households in close proximity to one another. The landscape and latitude of their area made solar a sensible choice, but even so, when they launched in 2010, the cost of solar was still relatively high compared to today, with a payback period of nineteen years. By going in together, they avoided a common pitfall—undersizing their system—instead building enough capacity to largely meet the power needs of all the members. With the efficiency of the larger scale and reduced per-megawatt installation costs, they were able to reduce the payback period by six years, about 30 percent faster than if they had gone out on their own.[9]

From that modest beginning, the Clean Energy Collective (CEC) has grown rapidly and has completed twenty-four projects in eight states, the most recent being a 1-megawatt collaboration with Midwest Energy in Kansas.[10] Thirty more are in development. These projects, which together represent nearly 30 megawatts of power capacity, are designed to be flexible, enabling people to "go solar" incrementally or all at once and, in most cases, to add panels over time.[11] Working with the CEC provides not only the economies of scale in upfront costs but also long-term guarantees—fifty years—over which time reliable power is assured. Ownership of the panels is shared between the CEC and the people in the community. While there is still tremendous room for growth in individual rooftop solar across the country, this model, which integrates individual ownership with community collaboration, may "truly be the path to widely available solar energy," says Nick Safay, vice president of Ecological Energy Systems based in Bristol, Tennessee: "It can open up the field to more solar development in neighborhoods and communities. It might even make it possible for developers to make this part of affordable housing projects for lower-income families."[12]

The drive for greater community control over their utility needs is not limited to the wide open spaces of the American West. The Energy Co-op was started more than thirty years ago in an effort to bring down the costs of home heating oil for people on a tight budget in Philadelphia and neighboring counties. It has grown steadily over the years, now counting more than six thousand members. In recent years it has also widened its scope and put more emphasis on sustainability, making two other important energy sources available to its members: electricity from solar and wind power, and biodiesel fuel, made in part from waste grease. At present, the biodiesel is primarily for commercial trucks and operators in the area, while the electricity is available to both residential and commercial customers. The Energy Co-op uses old-fashioned bulk buying to secure more reliable supplies of energy and to bring down the cost per unit. In 2014, for instance, the Co-op's buying power saved members an average of twenty-one cents per gallon of home heating fuel.[13]

Energy has represented for many families both a substantial part of their budget and a frustrating "dependency" over which most have had little control. Even with the recent increases in domestic oil and gas production, the fact remains that most power consumers have little or no voice when it comes to the gas they put in their tanks or the electricity that lights and powers their homes. When members of communities have come together to create new, local energy sources or to secure better prices through their aggregate buying power, as in the examples above, some of this dependency is substantially reduced.

Scores of communities around the United States are working now to make their own energy sources cleaner, more local, and more responsive to the needs of their citizens. Another example of this is the town of Caroline, near Ithaca, New York. Concerned with the rising cost of utilities and their dependence on distant sources of oil and other fuels, this community of just over three thousand people took the bull by the horns and decided to make things happen themselves. Under the banner of "Energy Independent Caroline," community leaders began promoting both energy conservation and greater use of renewable energy. In 2005, Caroline became only the second community in New York State to switch to 100 percent renewable energy—from nearby wind facilities—for all of its municipal buildings, including its schools. In 2008, ninety volunteers traversed the town for the day, handing out a compact fluorescent bulb to every one of the 1,400 households within Caroline in hopes of jump-starting a community-wide commitment to conservation and efficiency.

It worked. Since then, the people of Caroline have continued their march toward energy independence, completing a new town hall incorporating solar lighting tubes, a geothermal heat pump, solar photovoltaic electricity, and other features that make it a carbon-neutral facility. The 2,000-square-foot facility is so efficient that heating and cooling bills average just seventy-five dollars per month. The natural lighting is so good that, according to Dan Barber, the town manager, "In a typical day, there's no reason to turn on the lights."[14] The "Solarize Caroline" campaign in 2013 led to more than one hundred households signing up for solar panels, three times more than their goal. This helped bring costs of materials and installation down substantially, and helped persuade local contractors to get into the solar business.[15]

In many places, the energy challenge is being addressed with more of a focus on bringing down demand through much greater conservation and efficiency. In the mountains of eastern Kentucky, the Mountain Association for Community Economic Development, or MACED, set about to tackle the widespread problem of high heating bills for thousands of working-class and lower-income families living in older, less well-constructed homes. Because these homes had little insulation, poor-quality windows, and inefficient heating systems, residents were consuming huge amounts of gas, oil, or electricity, even as their homes remained uncomfortably cold in winter. The solution to these problems was clear enough; the problem was that most of these families simply could not afford the insulation, weatherization, and other improvements so desperately needed.

In response, MACED designed and launched an "on-bill financing" system, in partnership with local utilities, designed to help families with limited means. The first step is an energy audit, performed by a certified energy auditor, which identifies the most critical areas where heat is being lost and provides a set of recommendations as to what should be done. Following this, the family is given an estimated cost for different levels of improvements, from simple caulking to installation of double-pane windows. After this, an agreement is made between the utility, the weatherization contractor, MACED, and the family that provides for payment over time, through the monthly power bill. The family puts nothing down but instead pays for the improvements with the monthly savings that result from the weatherization.

The MACED on-bill financing program is one of several that have emerged in the country, with others in Massachusetts, Buffalo, New York, and elsewhere. It is one of the few in rural areas. Begun as a pilot project at the end of 2010, the initiative has now provided energy retrofits to 162 families, 85 percent of whom live in so-called "distressed counties." Since more than half of the participating families to date have low to moderate incomes, the average monthly savings of more than fifty-one dollars is critically important. So, too, are the ten jobs the program has already created or saved, and the 600 megatons of greenhouse gases it has precluded.[16]

Another increasingly common approach to energy savings is popping up in many cities and even midsize towns: sharing of rides, cars, and vehicles. Some such efforts have spawned rapidly growing businesses, such as Zipcar, now owned by Avis, while others have arisen primarily out of informal networks of people who want to save money, gas, carbon, or all three. Offering vehicles in forty-three states and more than two hundred towns and cities, Zipcar is the largest among several companies that use an "on demand" approach to car rental, providing access to vehicles at lower rates and for shorter periods of time (as little as a few hours) than traditional car rental companies.

One of the first bike-sharing programs in a large city was Denver's "B-Cycle" initiative launched in 2010 as a partnership between the City and Denver Bike Sharing, a non-profit organization. Using a simple but reliable electronic system, members are able to check out one of the seven hundred bikes at any of eighty-four different stations around the city. At present, most of the bikes and sharing stations are located downtown, with clusters also in the Cherry Creek and Denver University neighborhoods. One can become a member for a single day, a week, a month, or a year, with declining costs for longer-term commitments. Once in the system, members can check bikes out at any of the eighty-four stations, seven days per week, from 5:00 a.m. to midnight. Short rides are most economical: Any ride of thirty minutes or less is free; after that it costs one dollar for the next thirty minutes and four dollars for every half hour following that.

The program has grown dramatically over the first four years, with memberships more than doubling to 74,000 and the number of bike trips increasing from just over 100,000 the first year to 377,000 in 2014, covering a bit more than 12 square miles of the city. Those trips added up to an estimated

One of the eighty-four bike stations available in Denver through the Denver B-Cycle initiative. Courtesy of Denver B-Cycle.

803,000 miles of bike travel last year. Surveys of riders indicate that roughly 42 percent of the time, the bike replaced what would have been a car trip.[17]

Community-Level Health Care

As depicted by the graph below, expenses for health care have been rising inexorably for nearly fifty years and now represent, on average, nearly twice the amount that we Americans spend on food. Putting aside the likely connections between cheap food and rising health problems, there is no denying that health care costs are one of the biggest challenges we face as a society. A recent analysis of bankruptcy filings in the United States showed that health care and medical costs were the single biggest factor, greater than credit card debt or even home foreclosure. Even people with insurance are not immune, as high deductibles and other out-of-pocket expenses can push people over the financial edge.[18]

While this is a complex issue beyond the scope of this book, two elements of the transition to productive resilience are relevant here: First, we must

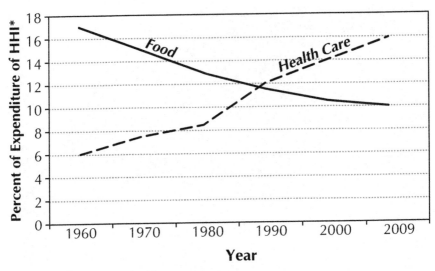

HHI = Household Income

Food and health expenditures as percentage of household income. Since 1960, the proportion of household income on average spent on food has steadily declined, while the amount spent on health care has risen dramatically. (Based on USDA Economic Research Service, "Americans' Budget Shares Devoted to Food Have Flattened in Recent Years," www.ers.usda.gov/data-products/chart-gallery/detail.aspx?chartId=40094; and Henry J. Kaiser Family Foundation, "Health Care Costs: A Primer", May 1, 2012, http://kff.org/health-costs.)

learn, or relearn, how to live healthier lives in order to dramatically reduce our need for expensive medicines and/or hospital care in the first place. Again, this is complicated, involving choices at the individual, household, community, employer, and public levels. There's no doubt that it is easier for middle-class and wealthier people to work on improving their health than it is for working people and the poor, for a wide range of reasons, from access to healthy food to the type of work available. But most all of us need to embark on this effort, and informal networks and communities can play a critical part. We know, for instance, that communities with more sprawl make walking and biking more difficult, and one result, according to a study from the University of Maryland, is that people are on average six pounds heavier in high-sprawl towns.

The second opportunity for decreased dependency and cost in health care is the community-based health clinic and its various spin-offs. Clinics such as these play a critical role in both rural and urban communities, enabling people to get quality primary care close to home at a fraction of the cost of an emergency room, their next most likely option. First launched in the 1960s, there are now more than eight thousand across the country, in high poverty rural and urban communities. Collectively these centers see an average of 20 million people each year, 70 percent of whom earn incomes below the poverty line. The primary and preventive care they offer precludes countless emergency room visits and hospitalizations, saving an estimated $10 billion to $24 billion annually.[19]

Some community health facilities are going a step further toward preventative health care, offering their clients more convenient and low-cost ways to eat healthier foods. One example of this comes from the South Bronx, where the Corbin Hill Food Project has joined forces with the Bronx Lebanon Hospital to bring fresh produce from nearby farms to nearly one hundred families every week for more than twenty weeks. Corbin Hill works with the farmers to coordinate production and provide aggregation and delivery of the produce to more than two dozen community centers throughout Harlem and the South Bronx, including Bronx Lebanon Hospital. Farmers get a good price for the produce that the hospital purchases, and the hospital considers the arrangement to be part of its outreach and wellness efforts.

One novel and highly effective variant of the community clinic can be found in the small mountain town of Floyd, Virginia, where Jack Wall and Kamala Bauers launched Wall Residences in 1995. Inspired by the Community Training Model he had seen working in Michigan in the late 1980s, Jack first piloted his approach when he was director of Mental Health Services in nearby Wythe County. Privately owned by Jack and Kamala, Wall Residences provides high-quality, home-based care and treatment for people who would otherwise be institutionalized with mental disabilities, learning disabilities, and similar challenges. Rather than removing people from the community into institutions, Wall Residences provides an extensive training program to develop paraprofessionals, who then take people into their homes, providing not only a high level of services and support, but the loving, welcoming reality of a family. The paraprofessionals are compensated well for the housing and care they provide, and in turn are expected to provide excellent care and accommodations. Ongoing support and regular, sometimes daily communication help ensure that families are able to meet the medical, technical, and emotional challenges involved.

Due in large part to the excellent outcomes they achieve, Wall Residences has now reached most of the state of Virginia, both urban communities and very rural places, like Floyd. In 2014, 430 people were placed in 280 licensed homes around the state. This family- and community-centered approach costs just one-third of what it does to house people in institutions, averaging $85,000 per person per year versus about $240,000.[20]

Beyond the issue of cost savings, living with a family in a community appears to have very positive benefits for the clients, as they become much better equipped to care for themselves, to hold down a job, to be, in short, members of a community.

Home and Community Gardens

We'll close our survey of community self-reliance and productivity initiatives with what is surely the best-known and most widely employed strategy, home and community gardens. Gardens have ebbed and flowed in the American landscape over the past one hundred years, falling out of favor during periods of intense urbanization and suburbanization, then rebounding, often during times of economic stress. While the Victory Gardens of World War II are deservedly well known, a more gradual but longer period of gardening renaissance has now been under way since the 1970s. Over the past ten to fifteen years, interest in gardening has been spurred not only due to economic need but also as part of the increased concern about healthier eating. Estimates vary, but a study by the National Gardening Research Association estimated that at least 1 million households participate in community gardens each year, and that five times that number are "extremely or very interested" in having a community garden plot available nearby.[21]

In Detroit, a focus on community gardens began a little more than a decade ago, as one of the responses to extreme economic hardship faced by so many families in the city. As a by-product of Detroit's economic decline, thousands of lots became vacant, opening up more than 20 square miles of potentially productive land that, for the most part, was collecting trash and weeds. So great was the amount of open space, with much of it becoming wild, that the longtime Detroit community leader Grace Lee Boggs referred to it, with irony and a bit of hope, as "rural encroachment."[22]

In 2003, there were an estimated eighty community gardens within the city limits. That's when several organizations, including the Greening of Detroit and later, Keep Growing Detroit and the Detroit Black Community Food Security Network, began their push for productive use of this open land to benefit residents. Eleven years later, by 2014, the number of gardens had grown to nearly 1,400, encompassing about 200 acres. Keep Growing Detroit

executive director Ashley Atkinson estimates that 17,000 Detroit residents—
one out of every fifty—are now engaged with a garden somewhere in the city.
The total production of fruits and vegetables from these plots now exceeds
160 tons, or 320,000 pounds of fresh produce annually.[23] While that's still a
small amount for the city as a whole, this past decade of dramatic expansion
has given hope to those who believe that Detroit could produce, within its
own boundaries at least half of all the fresh produce its residents eat.

Gardens, like parks and other well-maintained green areas, help return
vitality and hope to communities while decreasing the likelihood of vandal-
ism and crime. But are gardens reaching the neighborhoods most in need of
a boost? According to surveys done by Keep Growing Detroit, nearly one-
third of all gardeners in the city are low-income people, and a large proportion of the others are either seniors, youth, or working-class folks. Fruits and
vegetables can be hard to afford on the tight budgets most of these folks face,
so gardens make a real difference. A recent analysis of participants' eating
habits showed that those involved in gardens were consuming two and a half
times more servings of fresh fruit and vegetables every day than nongrowers
in the same zip code area.[24]

In Central Appalachia, a concerted effort to train and equip lower-
income people to garden was started five years ago by John-Paul Dejoria,
cofounder of John Paul Mitchell Hair Care Systems. Calling it "Grow Appalachia," Dejoria wanted to invest in people and communities to help bring
back something that had long been a major part of the region's household
economies, the home garden. Focusing more on small, individual plots as
well as community gardens, here the emphasis is on empowering those most
in need to garden, cook, preserve food, and, of course, eat better, for less.
Starting in Kentucky, the initiative now encompasses gardens in thirty-nine
counties in four states, with more than 1,500 families gardening either at
home or at community garden sites.

One of the Grow Appalachia regional initiatives is "Grow Your Own,"
under the auspices of Appalachian Sustainable Development in southwest
Virginia. Now in its third year, the program takes a holistic approach in an
effort to both "grow food and grow community." Each year, the number of
gardeners has expanded, reaching nearly forty low-income families in 2014,
including twenty with home gardens, fourteen who participate in community
gardens, and four with market-gardens who sell some of what they raise.
Nearly 15,000 pounds of produce were raised in these small plots in 2014.
Among the impacts participants cited were improved eating habits, better

exercise, money saved that allowed them to pay other bills, and learning how to can and preserve foods. Grow Your Own found equally enthusiastic responses in their work with high school students with special needs, most of whom have blossomed, so to speak, in the gardening environment. For some of these students, garden planning and work has been added to their individualized educational program (IEP).[25]

Analysis of Transition One

Sharing of tools and equipment might have just been considered neighborliness a couple of generations ago. In much of the country, however, it largely fell out of favor as most of us joined the race toward complete autonomy (of a sort) within our four walls, even within the rooms within those four walls. This relentless drive toward greater personal "choice," achieved by participating in the global consumer economy, is now so widespread, so deeply ingrained—and so utterly convenient—that most of us cannot imagine a serious alternative. In spite of widespread frustration with everything from the pace of life to the rise of superficial materialism, most of us feel stuck in this individualized rat race. In Juliet Schor's words, "We have become a nation that places a lower priority on teaching its children how to thrive socially, intellectually, even spiritually, than it does on training them to consume."[26] We've spent a lot of time and money getting to this place where progress is equated with "growth" and prosperity with "more," two of the core myths discussed in chapter 1. It's going to take some considerable time to change that.

The initiatives described in this chapter represent a tiny sampling of the work under way in the emerging *transition from consumptive dependence to productive resilience*. As part of that transition, people are redefining prosperity and well-being, both on their own and in concert with their neighbors. Among these initiatives and many others like them, certain common characteristics emerge. These efforts in most cases:

1. **Enable people to live more frugally, with less cash required, without compromising their happiness or basic comfort.** In some cases, like the Community Energy Cooperative in Philadelphia, the primary objective was to save money, while in others it is a strong secondary benefit of energy efficiency, such as in MACED's on-bill financing program. Reducing the need for cash is, in fact, an indirect benefit of

sharing of equipment and every other informal network of sharing. And it is often part of a strategy of resistance, of "opting out" of at least some dimensions of the global economy.

2. **Build "community capital,"** whether in the form of jointly owned equipment (apple presses, log splitters, tool libraries), energy-generating infrastructure (e.g., Clean Energy Collective's solar panels), or space and ground for community gardens. This community capital is part of why individuals are able to live more frugally and also part of what builds community bonds or so-called social capital. As we'll see in subsequent chapters, it is also a critical element of building more vibrant, less dependent local economies.

3. **Solve problems closer to home,** both literally, as in the case of Wall Residences' home-based disability care model, or more broadly as in the case of the tool- and skill-sharing networks utilized by both the North Portland Tool Library and ASD's Grow Your Own gardening initiative.

4. **Lessen hidden dependencies,** be they on far-flung energy companies, global retailers, or outside experts. We see this in all of the skill-building and sharing networks, as well as those efforts to build or reclaim local land and other productive capital. It's also one of the by-products of greater local community capacity, as we see in the case of both Caroline, New York, and MACED's energy conservation work in eastern Kentucky.

5. **"Solve for pattern,"** to reuse Wendell Berry's term. When several thousand people utilize hundreds of bikes for tens of thousands of trips—to work, to run errands, to visit friends—a series of positive outcomes begins to multiply, from reducing automobile congestion and emissions to getting a workout without joining a gym. Similarly, when seventeen thousand people become part of nearly 1,400 gardens in Detroit, neighborhoods begin the long process of cleanup, reclamation, and revitalization; more people get regular physical activity, for free, outdoors; people eat better for less money; and some of those gardeners go on to become market gardeners or urban farmers, increasing their own income while helping to expand access to healthy foods.

In each of these five core characteristics, we see seeds of greater productivity, in its most literal sense, and of gradually increasing independence overcoming dependency in many parts of people's lives. These shifts require knowledge, skills, and commitment at the individual level, to be sure. In fact, there is no question that some people pursue self-reliance as rugged individualists, as "preppers" working to prepare themselves for what they believe is impending societal collapse. This is one face of the self-reliance movement. However, as Rhoda Halperin observed about Appalachians in northern Kentucky, there are many more for whom the capacity to meet their own needs is done less for personal survival and more for the good of family, kin, and community. In these settings, individual skills flourish and magnify as parts of more self-reliant networks of people, in neighborhoods, communities, and cities.

It is difficult to know the real number of groups and communities engaged in the wide range of efforts to increase their self-reliance and community resilience, though the number surely seems to be on the rise. One indication of this may come from the growth of the so-called "informal economy"—the cash-based, sometimes barter-based businesses and work happening outside of the tax system and most business legal structures. This informal economy has been central to rural economies in Appalachia and many other places (as described in detail in Halperin's *The Livelihood of Kin*)[27] for generations. Two separate studies in Kentucky[28] and West Virginia[29] estimate that 56 percent and 22 percent of all households, respectively, regularly participate in this "off-the-books" economy. The motivations of entrepreneurs in the informal economy vary, from the desire to "be my own boss" to pure economic survival, the latter far more common in poorer communities.

The informal economy also has a long history among immigrant and minority communities, again both for economic survival and as means for people to pursue their passions and dreams. A study by the Institute for Economic and Social Development focused on the informal economy among African Americans in Chicago and Baltimore, interviewing fifty-five people who made some or all of their livelihood in this way, either as business owners or as wage earners.[30] Like their rural counterparts, the range of enterprises was broad—home repair and construction, yard and lawn work, accounting services, child care, and home health services among them—and most business was generated through family ties and neighborhood networks. About one in five of the informal economy participants also held a job in the formal economy. This study and others from City Heights, San Diego, and from rural Nebraska and Central Appalachia also found that people living in communities with strong informal economies often "shopped first" with their neigh-

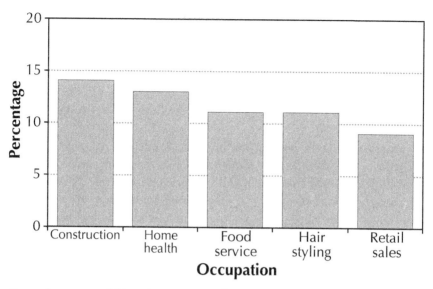

Occupations among African Americans in informal economies of Baltimore and Chicago. In case studies from the two cities, these were the most common occupations among African Americans working in the informal economy. (Compiled from survey data in Jan L. Losby, Marcia E. Kingslow, and John F. Else, "The Informal Economy: Experiences of African Americans," Institute for Social and Economic Development Solutions, September 2003, www.ised.org.)

bors' informal business before entering the formal economy to secure what they needed.[31]

All told, urban and rural, the size of the informal economy is big, with its value estimated at nearly $1 trillion each year in the United States, or about 6 percent of the entire economy.[32] It is safe to say, then, that *a substantial number of people operate businesses, work for wages, and shop in ways that are primarily local and tied to their communities in some way.* This informal economy overlaps those engaged in productive self-reliance, sometimes driven by similar motivations and generating similar outcomes. Overall, however, the size, scope, and impacts of the informal economy should be understood only as an indicator of the number of people able and willing to make some of their livelihood on their own, one component of self-reliance.

This spirit of "making do" and "making the most of what you have" perhaps also suggests a great deal of potential for building more self-reliant people and communities, representing what Colin Williams and Sara Nadin term a "hidden enterprise culture." In their assessment of the informal economy, they found business activity and entrepreneurship to be dramatically undercounted in lower-income communities, precisely because so much of it happens off the books.[33] If we are badly underestimating the entrepreneurial drive and abilities of people in lower-income rural and urban communities, we are almost certainly missing tremendous opportunities to "help people help themselves" while simultaneously building more resilient local communities.

In considering the potential for more localized, productive networks of self-reliance, we should also take stock of the changing nature of work. According to a study from the RAND Corporation in 2004, the shift away from long-term "one job careers" is almost surely here to stay: "We can expect a shift away from more permanent, lifetime jobs towards less permanent, even non-standard employment relationships (e.g., self-employment) and work arrangements (e.g., distance work)."[34] This is another way to say that jobs have become and will remain far less secure and that workers had better get used to it. Even the most conventional economic thinkers and supporters of the current approach recognize that workers are likely in for harder times. No less an authority than Larry Summers, the former U.S. treasury secretary and Wall Street CEO, acknowledges that "there is already a long-term trend towards lower levels of employment in some rich countries" and that technological change increasingly means "capital that effectively substitutes for labor."[35] Which is to say, money will be made, jobs will get done, but with fewer workers.

The reasons for this are surely political as well as technological and economic, owing as much to who's in the driver's seat as to the technology under the hood. From my perspective, we should be fighting like hell against the imbalances in power that are substantially responsible for the growing insecurity of work. But at the same time, we need to be creating the conditions under which people and communities can build good livelihoods, close to home, with or without Wall Street, Big Government, or . . . Big Something.

The other problem we face that points toward more local, frugal, and self-reliant solutions is our massive individual household debt, now at levels that would have been unimaginable two generations ago. The rise in household debt is undoubtedly a result of both stagnant and declining wages combined with the pervasiveness of the "commercializing ethos," as Benjamin Barber describes it.[36] While our incomes have been in decline, the advertising industry has spent upward of $230 billion a year to convince most of us to keep buying stuff, much of it on credit.[37]

Such high levels of personal household debt are unsettling, to say the least, a source of great anxiety for millions of people who are trapped and don't see a way out. It turns out that it is bad for our local communities as well. A 2011 study looked at 238 counties across the United States, sorting them into "high personal debt" and "low personal debt" communities.[38] The investigators found that the high-debt counties have not only lower investment in their homes and residences, and in automobiles and durable goods, but also lower rates of job growth and economic activity overall. Easy credit worked for a spell, but in most parts of the country, the debt that it engendered is now a serious economic obstacle.

The problems just described—rising household debt, reduced investment in homes and communities, and declining job opportunities even as overall wealth increases—are in stark contrast to the movement toward productive resilience. The focus of these efforts, as we've seen, is on building local skills; sharing tools, equipment, and land; creating local sources of energy, expertise, and capital; doing the work that needs to be done and living well, yet living within our means. As I've suggested, the movement toward productive resilience necessitates both subtraction and addition: lessening things like financial debt; dependence on energy and resources over which we have no control; the compulsion and need to buy so many things, wherever and however they may have been made; and dependence on Big Something to provide us with jobs. On the other hand, what's added, to sum it up, is *local capacity*, beginning with people in their households and radiating out to networks of varying size and scope.

The *transition to productive resilience* is thus far small. Its many manifestations are not likely to "replace" the global economy as a source for either goods or employment on a vast scale. But these upwellings clearly represent, at the very least, a substantial and expanding source of livelihood for millions of people, a more satisfying and meaningful way of relating to our kin and neighbors, and, most importantly, a foundation upon which the other transitions we'll explore can build.

Public Policy

The policy landscape, especially at the federal level, has generally not been supportive of many of the elements of community self-reliance and local empowerment (unless one considers the abandonment of neighborhoods and communities as an inducement to be more self-reliant). Nevertheless, at state and local levels, recent years have seen more experimentation that has encouraged productive resilience, either through the relaxation of certain regulatory hurdles or through the creation of incentives for new ideas and ventures. In this brief survey, we'll look at a few policies that still present serious impediments to greater community resilience and self-reliance, and a larger sampling of those that are emerging to more proactively enable this transition.

"Policy," as my colleague Justin Maxson has said, is best understood as "the rules for action" and as "frameworks that influence behavior." Like any set of rules, there are "dos" and "don'ts," things you're allowed to do and things you're prohibited from doing. But because you can't make a rule for everything—though some may try—there is always room for interpretation, gray areas wherein people, groups, and businesses make many decisions based more on a broad understanding of what is expected or acceptable rather than on a step-by-step delineation of exactly what they must do.

As an example, the Organic Food Production Act of 1990 created the National Organic Standards, which include many clear and specific rules. For example, organic farmers like myself can't use Roundup to kill weeds, or 10–10–10 to boost production. That's clear enough, but there are equally important decisions for which there is no specific rule. How, for instance, do I build the health of the soil over the long term so that my plants grow better and provide more nutrients to people eating them? How do I create environments on the farm where insect pests are held in balance, reducing the need for any sort of "pest control," organic or otherwise? The standards themselves don't tell me exactly how to do this, but they do provide a *framework* in which these questions—soil health, nutrients, ecological balance—are always a central concern.

A comprehensive survey of what's wrong or right with public policy is far beyond the scope of this book. Policy, nevertheless, is an essential and largely neglected part of the movement toward more resilient communities and sustainable economies. It's vast, it's complicated, and it's easy to get lost in the weeds.

For this chapter, the most fundamental question is, *Does this policy encourage greater productivity and resilience at the household level, and in local communities?* More specifically, does the policy:

- Enable people to live more frugally, yet live well?
- Build the capacity and "capital" of households and communities?

- Solve problems closer to home, in locally adapted ways?
- Lessen dependencies on far-flung sources of energy, capital, goods, and expertise?
- Solve for pattern, that is, create solutions that solve multiple problems?

Enabling People to Live More Frugally and Independently, with Less Dependence on Consumerism

At the individual level, one of the most important aspects of this challenge relates to household savings, or as we saw in the analysis, the lack thereof. According to a 2013 study, more than half of all U.S. households lack enough liquid savings to cover just three months of normal expenditures.[39] Three months. We know that building savings not only helps insulate people from job loss, medical bills, and other shocks, but it does much more than that. Several studies indicate that the act or habit of savings builds the self-confidence of people, beginning in childhood, and makes for more positive long-term economic outcomes. So, building savings is good, for individuals and the larger society.

At present there are numerous incentives for ordinary people to *spend,* and to spend beyond their means. This comes from many quarters, including massive and relentless advertising by retailers of all types, aided by current tax policy. Virtually all forms of advertising are an allowed business deduction, meaning that when fast-food companies promote their supersized meals or big-box retailers steer consumers away from local businesses to their doors, they are being subsidized by taxpayers in the form of lower taxes.

Easily available consumer credit, beginning at very young ages, is another enabler of sometimes excess spending, again abetted by the lack of penalties companies face for fraudulent inducements, or the ability of some, like "payday lenders," to charge extremely high interest rates; or credit card companies using outlandish penalties for late payments. And, of course, there is the general encouragement of consumerism by our leaders, for example, when President Bush famously encouraged people to "go shopping" shortly after the 9/11 attacks, to show the world that we were getting back to normal.

The impulse to buy, to "go shopping," is encouraged by both culture and policy. Support for *saving* money, by ordinary people, is much harder to come by. As Reid Cramer and Elliot Schreur put it in their 2013 study of savings and tax policy: "As currently designed, our tax system facilitates substantial rewards for high-income earners without advancing the intended social goals of providing inducements to save for the low and middle-income families that need savings incentives the most."[40]

As their examination of current U.S. tax policy revealed, *half* of all the benefits of the major federal tax credits and deductions go to the top one-fifth of wage earners, with 17 percent going just to the top 1 percent. For the mortgage interest deduction, one of the best-known tax inducements to save and build assets, 75 percent of the benefits go to the wealthiest 20 percent, while the "bottom" 60 percent—low-, moderate-, and middle-income folks—see only 8 percent of the benefit. Thus, the people most in need of both inducements and help to build savings in fact get but a very small part of available federal savings benefits.

Cramer and Schreur recommend two policy initiatives to support and encourage savings among low- to middle-income people:

Establish a universal 401(k) system that allows all workers to deposit into these tax-privileged accounts rather than the current system, which relies on employers to provide 401(k) opportunities. For people working temp jobs, or multiple part-time jobs, or low-paying jobs—and that's more and more American workers—the normal 401(k) is not available. They recommend further that the universal 401(k) plans come with a 30 percent tax credit for all retirement savings.

Create a financial security credit that would allow people to directly open a savings account when filing their federal tax forms. Pilot efforts of this sort have shown that, because so many working and moderate-income people are "unbanked," being able to easily open a savings account when filing has proven very effective in getting people on the path to savings. The financial security credit would also provide federal dollar-for-dollar matching of personal savings of up to five hundred dollars per year for low- to moderate-income workers.[41]

The cost of these policies would be well below 10 percent of the federal money currently rebated to (or not collected from) well-to-do people, and would encourage people to spend a bit less and save more, cultivating some of the assets that are critical to household and community resilience.

When people weatherize their homes, the benefits are immediate for them, in terms of comfort, monthly savings, and the overall value of the house. Benefits also accrue to the communities where they live, and the larger world, since reduced energy use also improves air quality and reduces the need to "drill, baby, drill," including in ecologically sensitive areas. The Department of Energy estimates that 20 to 30 million families are eligible for federal weatherization assistance, and that on average, weatherization saves each household more than $350 per year.[42] Yet funding for the federal weatherization is and has been a political football for years, sometimes increasing only to then be slashed or even "zeroed out" in presidential budgets. Weatherizing homes builds people's assets, saves low-income families money, and helps stabilize neighborhoods. We should make a long-term commitment to this at a much higher annual level of at least $1 billion per year.

Building Community Capital

Tool libraries have emerged in more than fifty communities in more than half the states in the nation. They are helping to both build people's skills and to "capitalize" households through the lending of tools that individuals could not afford on their own. This in turn leads to better-maintained homes, lawns, and gardens, longer-lasting appliances, and better-functioning equipment. But tool libraries face a number of challenges, particularly around liability issues and the problem of funding, for the purchase and upkeep of the tools they lend, along with rent, utilities, and other ongoing expenses.

One of the ways to stabilize funding over the long haul, and to potentially increase the efficiency of managing a tool library, is for the local government to take it on as a basic service to the community, just as most do with their public libraries. The City of Oakland, California, does this, housing its tool library in the basement of one of the public library's main branches, sharing space and some administrative duties and costs. The Oakland library touts its tool-lending library, begun in 2000 and now holding more 3,500 tools in its inventory, as one of its most popular public offerings. While the tool library's continuance is not completely assured, the public's heavy use of this program increases the likelihood that it will continue for many years to come, and respond to ideas and needs expressed by citizens.

Another innovative form of capital, community-owned energy facilities, helps reduce energy costs and dependence on unstable sources of energy over which consumers have virtually no say. The adoption of community-scale solar systems, like that pioneered by the Clean Energy Collective in Colorado, typically requires "enabling legislation" related to the State Corporation Commission or other state agencies. At present, only a handful of states encourage the adoption of community-scale energy-generation projects, even though they accomplish several important goals: increase local energy independence; create local jobs related to installation and maintenance; increase the value of homes co-owning or participating in the project; and contribute to cleaner air, water, and reduced carbon pollution. The State of Colorado provides model legislation and institutional policies that have helped spur rapid development of its community-scale solar industry. Other states should examine this and develop comparable policies.

Community gardens are certainly the most common and popular form of "community capital" to emerge in recent decades. The diversity of gardens, by types, size, ownership, and participants, is remarkable, reflecting their rapid adoption throughout the nation, usually led by and adapted to local neighborhoods and communities. Public policy related to community gardens should enable and encourage their growth without encumbering them with unnecessary fees, restrictions, or bureaucratic hurdles. Among the most important policy challenges facing community gardens are security of tenure (i.e., whether they can garden in that spot year in and year out); access to basic infrastructure, such as water sources, fencing, and outbuildings; and questions related to whether people who grow in gardens can also sell what they grow.

The tenure of a garden spot is by no means guaranteed. Because community gardens help beautify and revitalize neighborhoods, often including those in decline, they can over time become vulnerable to real estate development pressures, as happened when Mayor Rudy Giuliani's administration retook possession of scores of active community gardens in 1999, preferring to use the land for the development of high-end housing rather than for the growing of produce by low-income and working-class families in those neighborhoods. Providing community gardens with some security is thus critical to building community involvement for the long haul. With nearly one-quarter of land in U.S. cities estimated to be in vacant lots or abandoned or neglected buildings,[43] the potential expansion of community gardens—and other productive land uses—is enormous.

Several cities have taken steps to increase their long-term support for community gardens, both by amending zoning ordinances to clearly allow them (at least in designated areas for designated purposes), and to enable community gardeners to both eat and sell what they grow. San Francisco created a "Neighborhood Agriculture" category in its land use ordinances, becoming one of several cities that both clarified the role of community gardens and elevated their importance in city planning and management. Philadelphia, Baltimore, Oakland, and others have taken similar steps.[44] Many smaller towns like Roanoke, Virginia; Asheville, North Carolina; and Holyoke, Massachusetts, have also encouraged the growth of community gardens.

In Holyoke, the community gardens grew out of a grassroots organization, Nuestra Raices, which played the lead role in building and managing the network of community gardens, as well as developing the skills and assets of the participants.

One more interesting approach to develop and protect community gardens and green space from undue development pressures is found in Atlanta, with the Land Bank Authority of Atlanta. This local, public bank functions to provide land over the long term, at affordable tax rates, to community gardens, small parks, and other productive green space projects that help bring new life to communities and neighborhoods.[45]

Solving Problems Closer to Home

When we empower people to solve their own problems closer to home, we tend to get solutions that are better suited to that place, that last longer, and that don't cost as much. While this is not always the case, every effort should be made in local, and even more so, state and federal policies to encourage these homegrown solutions.

In the case of Wall Residences' home- and community-focused system for people with mental disabilities, there is no doubt that better results are secured for a fraction of the cost. Yet funding—and most other state resources—still move primarily to costlier, less effective, and less humane institutional approaches. State-level policies related to mental health and mental disabilities should encourage innovative, community-focused approaches through expanded availability of funding and through licensing and fee structures that make this more plausible on a wider scale.

Almost every community in the country is struggling with health problems arising from obesity. There are federal incentives, for example, in the so-called Farm Bill, that encourage greater availability of fresh produce and healthier school lunches. These should be expanded, at least until improved eating is far more widely established in our country. But even more important is the array of policy options that enable health, diet, and wellness challenges close to home.

Lessening Hidden Dependencies

Renewable energy is expanding rapidly in many, but not all, states in the nation. In some places, including much of the Appalachian region and the Southeast, the utilities are not yet going along, in some cases actively fighting greater adoption of renewable energy. Their rationale: It will increase costs for consumers; and it will require the utilities to expand their standby capacity, that is, from coal, gas, or nuclear, because of the intermittent nature of renewables. The first argument is challenged not only by clean energy advocates but by entirely mainstream sources as well. A November 2014 article in the *New York Times* cites several examples of utilities increasing purchase of renewables, as costs continue to decline and in some regions have begun to beat fossil fuels strictly on price.[46] In the April 24, 2014, edition of *Forbes,* in an article expressing pessimism about solar power, Christopher Helman nevertheless acknowledges that the unsubsidized cost of electricity for solar is down to about thirteen cents per kilowatt hour, compared to twelve cents for advanced coal-fired plants.[47]

General Electric International, which no one would mistake for Greenpeace, examined the standby energy capacity issue in the so-called PJM region, including Virginia, Ohio, Maryland, and part or all of seven other states. What they found: Little or no additional standby capacity would be needed from the utilities in this region should renewables expand all the way to 30 percent of total electricity production.[48] With renewables in the low single digits in most of those states today, there is room for dramatic expansion of these clean energy sources with virtually no additional cost to utilities.

In Virginia and other states, efforts have been under way to assess additional fees on customers who install rooftop solar, a so-called "feed-in tariff." These policies undermine the energy independence of households and communities, and serve virtually no public purpose. The utilities' claims that they need these charges to offset the costs of integrating households into their grids is at best dramatically overstated. Instead, investments in household and commercial energy efficiency, along with renewable energy sources, made Vermont the "most energy-efficient state," according to a 2014 WalletHub study.[49]

The on-bill financing initiative in eastern Kentucky has saved low- and moderate-income residents many thousands of dollars, while greatly increasing both the comfort and value of their homes. Two policies have been critical to the success of this and similar efforts in other states. First, states must allow so-called "third-party financing" of energy improvements, in order that groups like MACED be allowed to secure and provide loan capital for lower-income households. Without third-party financing, the funds will likely not materialize. Second, energy-efficiency tax credits, whether at the state or federal level, help write down a portion of the loan amount, meaning that homeowners can retire their debt more quickly and then reap the full benefits of the energy savings.

Solving for Pattern

We Americans are a relatively straight-shooting people, and we tend to like clear, simple answers to sometimes complicated problems. One example: rising crime rates in the 1960s and 1970s led to a wave of "tough on crime" laws beginning in the Nixon years and continuing more or less to the present. Even though violent crime has been falling steadily for a generation, and even though we know that more than half of our prison population is incarcerated for nonviolent offenses, we still struggle to move away from the "lock 'em up and throw away the key" approach to crime. It is extraordinarily expensive, in terms of public dollars and people's lives, and it simply does not work well. But it is clear and easy to understand and, as such, hard to change.

Solving for pattern is altogether different, focusing on the impacts to the whole system of the actions we choose to take, including a consideration of "unintended consequences." The multispecies, management-intensive grazing systems pioneered by Alan Savory and made famous in the United States by Joel Salatin provide an excellent example of "solving for pattern." In most parts of our country, cattle ranchers let their herds roam over large areas (at least before they're sent off to the feedlots). Unfortunately, under these circumstances, the quality of the pasture tends to decline, weeds spread as the cattle avoid less palatable plants, and shallow root systems make the pasture more vulnerable to drought. Farmers respond by using herbicides to control the weeds, fertilizer to keep the grass growing, and lines of credit when dry weather turns things brown.

A visit to Joel's farm near Swoope, Virginia, demonstrates a very different approach. First, the cattle are intensively "corralled" in small paddocks within the larger expanse of pasture, usually just for one to two days before being moved to the adjacent paddock. Sticking together in groups is what their relatives do in the wild, to ward off predators. In those close quarters, the cattle are not so picky, eating almost everything, not just the sweetest and most tender stuff. This stifles the buildup of weeds. The animals' manure is concentrated, providing an infusion of nitrogen and other nutrients. And having the cattle eat the grass down to just a few inches of height actually stimulates the root system, increasing both subsequent growth and resistance to drought. And there's more. Salatin, and many other "grass-based" livestock farmers, use other animals to further harness and improve the pasture: sheep to eat certain weeds the cattle will not; chickens to eat the flies and bugs left behind, while helping to spread the cattle manure; and in some cases, goats to clean the fence lines of briers. Rather than segregating these animals, the animals' natural inclinations are harnessed to create a system that is both far more productive (animals per acre) and yet much, much less dependent on fertilizers, herbicides, and other off-farm inputs. Alan Savory, Joel Salatin, and many others like them have "solved for pattern."

In the context of productive self-reliance and sustainable economies more broadly, solving for pattern is more of a way of thinking than a specific policy prescription. It means that we need to design public policy to encourage healthy communities, with more capacity to solve future problems. It means moving away from fixing one problem only to create two more. It means understanding the "pattern" of communities and the ecosystems in which they develop.

Public policy that promotes community gardening, discussed earlier, certainly encourages solving for pattern. There are specific problems that usually ignite interest in community gardening, including health, obesity, and lifestyle problems, lack of access to quality fresh produce in whole neighborhoods, underused or ill-used vacant lots, and general community decline. While any one of these problems deserves targeted attention, a robust community garden provides at least a partial solution to all of them, while also offering a number of critically important "social capital" benefits, like community pride, kids and elders working together, and renewed neighborhood associations. In addition to the community gardening policies discussed earlier, several localities have taken steps to inventory vacant lots and then promote their cleanup and productive use through tax credits, fee waivers, or other incentives.

Another opportunity to use policy to promote solving for pattern is in the realm of vehicle sharing, whether of bikes or cars. *Policies for Sharable Cities,* produced by the Sustainable Economies Law Center, contains a wealth of ideas and examples of effective policies in this and other areas.[50] Many of the policy ideas they suggest make bike and car sharing easier, safer, and economically feasible for ordinary citizens. Some of these include: reducing parking fees for shared vehicles; allowing dwellings with driveways or street-front parking to lease space to ride sharers; reducing tax rates on shared vehicles, which are generally very high (based on rates charged to auto-rental companies); and designing future transportation corridors as "complete streets," that is, built for cars, bikes, pedestrians, and mass transit rather than only for cars and letting everyone else fend for themselves. All of this will require new thinking and experimentation in our auto-focused nation, but the pattern benefits will be abundant: less congestion, wasted time, smog, and road rage; more walkers and bikers, leading to more exercise and healthier citizens; and even a bit of community building as the sharing of vehicles and space is likely to forge new associations and perhaps make us a bit more neighborly.

This small sampling of policy just scratches the surface of both what we need to change and what is possible if we make those changes. That's all we have space for here, but you can dig in far more deeply, beginning with the list of resources offered below.

Transition One: Recap and Looking Forward

The first transition, *from consumptive dependence to productive resilience,* provides the foundation for the other five transitions, and for a broader economic, social, and political transformation. Among the most important lessons from this transition:

1. When people have greater control over their lives, they are happier, healthier, more productive, and more neighborly. "Greater control" involves many things, including:
    a. the ability and opportunity to support themselves and their families, that is, a secure livelihood;
    b. the knowledge, skills, and connections (relationships with others) needed to make the most of what they have and to weather difficulties;
    c. less dependence on outside resources, decisions, and priorities; and
    d. sufficient ownership of or access to the resources they need to build secure livelihoods.
2. Livelihood is more than employment; it includes other ways that people secure what they need for a decent life, including both cash and noncash economic activities—gardening, food preservation, fixing things that break, sharing with neighbors, etc.
3. In a world of increasing resource scarcity and declining public investment, promoting secure livelihoods rather than simply "job creation" will be essential.
4. The movement toward self-reliance must encompass both households and neighborhoods/communities rather than taking the course of individual survival, which currently is the preoccupation of some.

Public policy at present largely discourages the transition to productive resilience, favoring as it does consumption—and the marketing that propels it—over savings, debt over investment, and economic dependence over local wealth building and self-reliance. This is true for poor and working people particularly, while more affluent people have dramatically greater tax incentives to save and are rewarded for investment.

Policies are emerging that secure access to land for community gardens and other productive uses; enable community-scale solar energy; enable low- and moderate-income families to access cost-saving household energy retrofits; and shift savings incentives to better fit people of modest means. Such policies need further development and dramatic expansion at local, state, and federal levels if we are to build a broad foundation of resilient communities.

Up next: The shift toward productive resilience engenders creativity, innovation, and a focus on meeting real needs. The skills and mind-set this fosters is critical to the next transition to bottom-up, living economies.

Further Reading

Berry, Wendell. *Home Economics: Fourteen Essays.* New York: North Point, 1987.

Bowman, Ann O'M., and Michael A. Pagano. "Urban Vacant Land in the United States." Lincoln Institute of Land Policy, 1998. www.lincolninst.edu.

Halperin, Rhoda H. *The Livelihood of Kin: Making Ends Meet "The Kentucky Way."* Austin: University of Texas Press, 1990.

"Policies for Shareable Cities: A Sharing Economy Policy Primer for Urban Leaders." Sustainable Economies Law Center and Shareable. September 9, 2013. www.shareable.net.

Sandel, Michael J. *What Money Can't Buy: The Moral Limits of Markets.* New York: Farrar, Straus and Giroux, 2012.

3

Unleashing Local Living Economies

From Trickle-Down Problems to Bottom-Up Solutions

We have long been told that the only alternative to the rapacious excess of capitalism is the debilitating repression of communism. This sets up a false and dangerously self-limiting choice between two extremes, both of which failed because they created a concentration of unaccountable power that stifled liberty and creativity for all but the few at the top.
—David Korten, Agenda for a New Economy

The green economy should not be just about reclaiming thrown-away stuff. It should be about reclaiming thrown-away communities. It should not just be about recycling materials to give things a second life. We should also be gathering up people and giving them a second chance. . . . In other words, we should use the transition to a better energy strategy as an opportunity to create a better economy and a better country all around.
—Van Jones, The Green Collar Economy

In September 2002, a group of folks gathered at a local church in Abingdon to discuss the just-confirmed rumors we'd been hearing: Walmart was working with a local developer to build a supercenter on the southwest side of town, right at one of the major corridors connecting to Main Street. There was already a supercenter 7 miles south of Abingdon, and another 20 miles to the west, but the world's largest retailer wanted one in the heart of town. The initial group that gathered for the most part did not previously know one another. There were local business owners, some farmers, and a wide range of other concerned citizens. Their politics covered the spectrum.

Abingdon is a town of just over eight thousand people in Washington County on the eastern edge of Virginia's coalfields. Agriculture remains the largest part of the economy in the county, although the arts, music, theater, and tourism are major drivers of Abingdon's relative prosperity.

With the help of Marty Wegbreit, an extraordinarily smart and dedicated local attorney, the group pushed forward to develop fact sheets on Walmart, to reach out to other local businesses and the community at large, and, ultimately, to persuade the town council to use its powers to stop the development, or at least make it more difficult to move forward. It worked. By the following June, Abingdon had adopted a "Special Use Permit" ordinance, placing additional requirements on all commercial developments in excess of 50,000 square feet (a typical big-box supercenter is close to 200,000 square feet). Walmart walked away. For a town of just eight thousand to prevail in this battle surprised a lot of people.

We'll talk more about the details of that local policy fight later in this chapter. For now, I'm recalling this story because it marks what is in many ways a defining moment in one small town's decision as to whether or not to let wealth "trickle down," such as it might, or to embrace and work for a locally rooted, "bottom-up" strategy for building opportunities and prosperity. To be clear, Abingdon in 2014 is not utopia. The town, the county, and the wider community face plenty of challenges, economic and otherwise. But those of us who fought so hard to keep the big-box giant out of our community promised to skeptics that something better was possible, and in many respects that hope has materialized. Here's a sampling of some of what has come to pass since June 2003:

- Farmers pieced together a farmers market, small at first, squirreled away in a little parking lot. It grew steadily, such that by 2007, the town built a beautiful pavilion as a permanent home. The Abingdon Farmers Market, a "producer-only market," now has more than fifty vendors most Saturday mornings, and about two-thirds of that number on Tuesday afternoons. The number of customers often reaches nearly two thousand people on a given market day. In spite of the town's small population, it is widely considered to be the best market in the region and one of the best in Virginia.
- That same pavilion comes to life on many evenings and weekends, as Abingdon now hosts live music at its "Thursday night jams,"

along with activities during different festivals throughout the year.

- The town's art and cultural scene has been strong for many years, as Abingdon is home to Barter Theatre, which hosts a permanent acting company and a "Festival of Plays and Playwrights" that help lift up local history and culture; and there are two fine arts centers, one more formal than the other, but both strongly emphasizing local and regional art, sculpture, and design. Complementing these long-standing cultural centers has been the emergence of several other galleries, new artists, and a dance studio.

- There is no Starbucks in town (there *is* one near the Walmart 7 miles down the road), but five years ago a local entrepreneur opened Zazzy'z, featuring wonderful coffee, much of it Fair Trade, along with terrific and affordable breakfast and lunch. At Zazzy'z, you're just as likely to find students and twenty-somethings hanging out as you are to find old-timers chewing the fat.

- While Abingdon had become a great place for middle-aged and older folks, until pretty recently, there just wasn't much for younger people to do at night (just ask my kids!). The growth of the live music scene has helped change that, but the real kicker was our first local brewery, Wolf Hills, which has taken off and added a whole new element to the small town. The emerging local brewery scene in Abingdon and surrounding towns has catalyzed an annual craft beer festival and, more recently, "The Howling," an outdoor beer, food, and music festival that's about as close to Woodstock as a small Appalachian town can get.

- One of the folks deeply involved in the Walmart fight, Susan Howard, is now the director of the Main Street program and works closely with the farmers market, the tourism department, and others to cultivate and support downtown businesses, which have been growing in number.

- The community garden at Faith in Action is connected to a network of gardens being cultivated by people with limited incomes, all coordinated by Appalachian Sustainable Development (ASD), the local organization that helped build the farmers market, among other things.

- ASD also coordinates a network of wood-based businesses providing sustainably sourced hardwood products. Abingdon Millworks is one of the key providers in that network. Ecological Energy Systems, the first major solar company in the region, represents another part of the emerging "green building" economy.

- And as a bit of poetic justice, just off of Interstate exit 14 where Walmart had hoped to build sits the Southwest Regional Higher Education Center, which has steadily expanded over the past decade; a thriving, locally owned building supply store, Berry Builders; and, most recently, Heartwood, a regional center for Appalachian art, music, crafts, storytelling, and food. Heartwood serves as a focal point for a much wider network of traditional music, authentic mountain arts and crafts, and outdoor trails spread across southwest Virginia.

Abingdon is somewhat unique within the Appalachian communities of Virginia, but it is far from alone. The focus on building from within, based more on your strengths than your deficiencies, has begun to take hold in many other parts of the region, helping to pave the way for the Appalachian Regional Commission's "Asset-Based Community Development" strategy, which represented a major shift in its approach and priorities. From Whitesburg, Kentucky, to Huntington, West Virginia, citizens, small businesses, and local leaders are beginning to forge more homegrown economies built around food, culture, tourism, and even some new manufacturing. Make no mistake about it, Virginia's Appalachian region, and even more so, neighboring Kentucky and West Virginia, are struggling mightily as coal mining continues to decline, and as farming communities experiment with alternatives to growing tobacco. But for perhaps the first time in memory, there is reason for hope, and a growing body of people working to make the *transition from trickle-down problems to bottom-up economy solutions* a reality.

Bottom-Up versus Trickle-Down Economies

Before going any further, we need to take a quick look at the difference between bottom-up, local living economies and those based on so-called trickle-down economics. The idea of the trickle-down economy has been around for some time, but it was given new life during Ronald Reagan's administration. In essence, it rests on a twofold notion: first, that economic growth and prosperity for the great majority of people depend upon productive investment by people of wealth and the large businesses in which they invest; and second, that lowering tax rates on this small group of people and businesses is necessary to give them incentives to invest (and grow wealthier in the process).

The principal problem with trickle-down is that, in practice, it hasn't worked. Remember that tax rates on the wealthiest Americans—both those directly on their income and those on capital gains—were cut repeatedly from 1980 until 2007, with only a slight increase during the Clinton years.[1] Yet employment growth and investment were both much slower during those periods following tax cuts. More to the point, the benefits of those lower rates have gone almost exclusively to the top income earners, while the vast majority of the populace has seen stagnant or declining wages. Another indicator is the cash on hand among large banks and multinational businesses, which by 2013 exceeded $1.5 trillion, an 80 percent increase in just seven years.[2] The money is there; in fact, it has been accumulating for years. Yet, even as taxes on the wealthy steadily declined, and tax loopholes and tax breaks enabled companies like GE to pay NO taxes

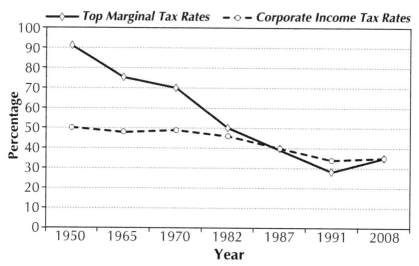

Change in top marginal and corporate income tax rates, 1950–2008. Since the end of World War II, U.S. corporate tax rates have fallen by 30 percent, while the top marginal income tax rates have fallen by 60 percent. (Data on declining top marginal income tax rates drawn from National Taxpayers Union, "Income Tax Rates, Top Bracket, Tax Rate (percent)," www.ntu.org; data on declining corporate tax rates comes from Thomas L. Hungerford, "Corporate Tax Rates and Economic Growth since 1947," June 4, 2013, www.epi.org.)

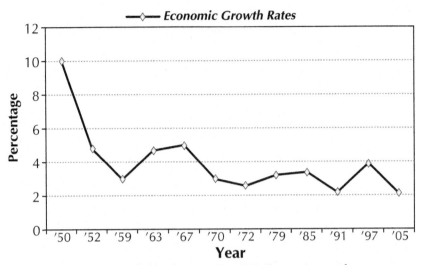

Change in economic growth (GDP) rates, 1950–2005. Economic growth was more than twice as high in the United States during the period of high corporate and top-income tax rates than it is in the recent period of much lower tax rates. (From U.S. Bureau of Economic Analysis, "US GDP Growth Rate by Year," 2015, www.mltpl .com/us-gdp-growth-rate.)

while their cash reserves grew, income and jobs simply have not trickled down from this enormous accumulation of wealth at the top.

So, if trickle-down has not brought about broader prosperity, what is the alternative? Part of that answer lies in *more and more diverse businesses,* which studies repeatedly show are better for workers and the communities of which they're a part. Thomas Lyson's Cornell University study, cited in chapter 1, showed how counties with more small and local business were better off in almost every meaningful way—health, education, crime rates, children's health—than those with economies dependent on a small number of big businesses.[3] Other studies have come to similar conclusions.[4]

But building bottom-up, local living economies is about more than a shift from big to small. As the story of Abingdon, Virginia, begins to hint, it is also about an economic approach that starts with the question, "What do we have here and how can we utilize it for the broadest benefit?" It is economic development made up of more businesses and more diverse types of businesses (and owners), economic development whose foundation, at least, is *the place* where the businesses reside.

And that's another part: It is about "living" businesses and economies. Now, what the heck does that mean? It means enterprises and community economies that evolve and adapt over time, just as living beings do. And in that evolution, they become better suited to their places, or, put another way, they learn to more fully use the strengths of that place while also living within its limits. And last, these economies are "bottom-up" in that most of the ideas, innovations, energy, and, increasingly, the capital don't trickle down but instead come first and foremost from the local people, organizations, businesses, structures, and environment that make up a place, that are from the base, or "bottom." The examples that follow make this quite clear.

Rather than adapting to places or invigorating communities, the prevailing economic model is focused on endless growth achieved through ever-larger global businesses. The myths that "bigger is better" and "growth is the answer," rather than creating broad prosperity, have led to the widespread "externalizing" of costs. This means that some costs of doing business are not included in the price of the product, creating problems that someone else must pay for. The enormous dead zone in the Gulf of Mexico resulting from fertilizer runoff from farms in the Midwest is one example. Coal miners getting black lung is another. Externalities almost always involve problems with people's health or the environment. How big a problem is this? In his book *Agenda for a New Economy: From Phantom Wealth to Real Wealth,* David Korten cites a 1996 study by the accounting professor Ralph Estes that detailed $2.6 trillion in such externalized costs that corporations passed on to the public every year.[5] Two and a half trillion is a lot of dollars, five times greater, in fact, than reported corporate profits in the year of the study.

This chapter briefly reviews the experiences of six other communities in other parts of the country, all of which are working toward this *transition from trickle-down problems to bottom-up solutions.* As you'll see, no community has built an entirely bottom-up economy or, for that matter, even one where that comprises the majority of jobs and economic activity. And several, particularly in bigger cities, are deliberately pursuing a "both/and" strategy. But even in these cases, the idea that we can and should build local economies with less dependence on faraway forces, and more ability to meet their own needs based on their own resources, is proving transformative.

Emerging Examples of Local Living Economies

Appalachian Ohio

Casa Nueva is a fixture in Athens, Ohio, a small college town in the southeastern part of the state. What sets this restaurant apart, even more than its innovative Mexican food, is its commitment to the local community. Casa Nueva is a cooperative, owned by its workers. It's also the single biggest buyer of local farm products, as this was fundamental to the vision of its founder, Leslie Schaller. At the time that it opened in 1977, Casa Nueva's commitment to local farmers and to providing good jobs in the community made it unique. Three decades later, such commitment has become part of the mainstream in Athens and neighboring communities.

Casa Nueva is deeply woven into the fabric of the local economy. Along with its support of the nearby farmers, it is also involved in efforts to incubate new businesses, to cultivate and support local entrepreneurs, and to build connections to local markets. The success of this worker-owned restaurant helped spawn other innovations, often in partnership with ACEnet, the Appalachian Community Economic Network, started in 1988. ACEnet's founder, June Holley, believed that small towns, like small-scale entrepreneurs, needed to be deeply and thoughtfully linked together—"networked"—to have a chance of success vis-à-vis larger urban areas and bigger businesses. June and Leslie launched ACEnet to build these networks in order to magnify and accelerate the impact of local businesses rather than focusing mostly on individual success. One of the centerpieces of their strategy was the development of the Appalachian region's first shared-use commercial kitchen, or "kitchen incubator," now called the Food Ventures Center. With more than 30,000 square feet under roof, the incubator includes state-of-the-art food-processing equipment, along with cooler, freezer, dry storage, and retail space, all part of what they consider to be a "campus" of innovation and entrepreneurial support.

As Casa Nueva, ACEnet, and another key local group, Rural Action, began working to build a more vibrant local economy, they focused their efforts on certain specific needs that were often "missing pieces" for local, independent businesses: The first of these was *incubation,* that is, comprehensive support during the start-up and early development phase, ranging from business training and market analysis to product testing and development. Since its founding, the ACEnet Food Ventures incubator has helped 327 businesses launch, with nearly three-fourths of them still in business after five years, dramatically better than the normal success rate of 20 percent for business start-ups. And several of them have gone on to become substantial companies, including Village Bakery, which now employs twenty people and does $1 million a year in sales, and Casa Nueva,

Tenants of the Food Ventures Center in Athens, Ohio, prepare pumpkins for cooking and processing. Courtesy of Appalachian Community Economic Networks.

with almost $3 million in sales in 2014 and seventy-eight employees (the equivalent of fifty-five full-time workers).

The second missing piece they identified was access to the needed space, facilities, and equipment—that is, *infrastructure*—that small start-up businesses usually can't afford. The Food Ventures Center offers these critical pieces, complementing the marketing, business, and product-development expertise many will need. This enables them to assist about 150 food businesses each year.[6]

The third element is *access to markets,* which they bring about in part by helping businesses develop their own markets and in part through joint promotional, marketing, and branding campaigns, including their Foods You Love brand, which I'll describe later.

Finally, their strategy focuses heavily on the development of *networks of businesses* that create opportunities for buying and sourcing from one another, help secure bulk prices on supplies, and promote more innovation, especially in relation to meeting local needs and developing more sustainable products and practices. Founder June Holley's work on networks is known worldwide, but it all started in the practical laboratory of Athens.

Rural Action, whose origins were more in fighting poverty and environmental injustice through community organizing, has helped ensure a strong grassroots foundation for the collective economic development work, including both rural and small-town communities. Among the initiatives they've launched over the past decade were several aimed at limited-resource farmers. One of these includes Chester Hill Produce Auction in nearby Morgan County, which links more than one hundred local farmers to customers at its weekly auction. Begun in 2009, the auction has grown, with chefs, grocers, schools, and individuals buying nearly a quarter-million dollars of produce through the auction in 2014.[7]

Many other elements have helped ignite the local economy in this southeastern region of Ohio, some spawned by ACEnet or Rural Action, others led by partners in the community, such as the Habitat for Humanity ReStore, which takes old building materials and furnishings and recirculates them in the community; the Athens Farmers Market, launched by ACEnet but now independent, which hosts more than one hundred local farmers and vendors every week; and the Appalachian Partnership for Economic Growth, which strengthens and supports regionally based manufacturers.

From Appalachia to the Great Lakes

When many folks from outside the state think of Michigan, they likely think of Detroit and all its challenges, or Ann Arbor, home to the University of Michigan and one of the most progressive towns in the country. A few may know about the UP, Michigan's verdant Upper Peninsula. But Grand Rapids? Well, sure, we've heard of it, somewhere out there on the western edge of the state, but what is there to tell? An old manufacturing town, built around furniture and, like so many others, beaten down by overseas competition and cheap imports. And not exactly the most experimental place in the world, with the strong conservative underpinnings that many of the city's longtime leaders brought from their traditions and faith.

When Elissa Hillary launched Local First, Grand Rapids, there's no question that there was some truth in at least part of this simplistic description. At that time in 2006, much of the town was indeed in decline: very high vacancy rates downtown, steady urban flight to "the ring" (the suburbs and exurban areas), and disinvestment in much-needed mass transit and other infrastructure. Though Michigan has the second-most diverse agricultural base in the nation, behind only California, and much of that agricultural land is close by, Grand Rapids' farming and food scene was old school: produce as much as you can and sell it across the country and world, with very small profit margins. The 250,000 people in Grand Rapids—well, they can buy stuff from California, like everyone else does.

A Grand Rapids girl, born and bred, Elissa took on a mighty challenge when, at only twenty-four years of age, she set out to revitalize the economy and community of her hometown. One of the principles that guided her was the commitment to building on local strengths as much as possible while also introducing new ideas into the mix. One of those strengths, it turned out, was a goodly number of local, family-owned businesses, many several generations on. For most of these folks, you didn't have to "sell" the idea of local, which to them just seemed like common sense. The challenge, rather, was to find a way to help it come alive once again. The owners of this group of established businesses, who in some way might be said to represent the town's "old guard," were also very committed to their community, as evidenced by their willingness to invest, both philanthropically and in hard dollars. On top of that, they believed in frugality, in minimizing waste and making the most of what you've got. They might not want to be called "environmentalists," but they knew that resources are precious and should be used as such.

In eight short years, an extraordinary renewal has taken hold, built around food, art, breweries, and a small group of critically important manufacturers. The number of farmers markets in Grand Rapids has grown from one to fourteen, and other food-related businesses are opening as well. Local restaurants, content to order from US Foods not long ago, are increasingly embracing—and, more importantly, using—produce, fruit, and meats from nearby farms. One indicator of this growth has been the experience of Western Michigan Farm Link, a food hub that launched in 2011 to connect local farmers to restaurants and other buyers. In its first four years of operation, it has seen more than a fivefold increase in sales of produce, meats, and other local farm items, now exceeding $1 million in annual sales.

The brewery scene is especially notable. While microbreweries have arisen in hundreds of places in the past few years, Grand Rapids now has sixty. On a per-capita basis, that would be equivalent to New York City having almost two thousand independently owned breweries. (They don't even have that many pizzerias!) Those brewers work together very well, promoting the local flavors they provide, helping new breweries get started, even working to source locally grown hops. For most, the spent grains, which are the main waste product, are being returned to the land through local farmers. This is one example of a small but emerging economic sector turning "waste" into a valuable resource. Additionally, two composting businesses have emerged in recent years, and the city's recycled plastic is being used by a private company to manufacture plastic bins.[8]

The Art Prize is an annual event that has helped galvanize efforts to make art a substantial part of the local culture and economy. The three-week-long festival now draws over a quarter-million visitors annually, making it Grand Rapids' single-largest tourism event and propelling the work of local and regional artists to a far wider audience. According to an analysis from the Anderson Economic Group, Art Prize 2013 resulted in more than $22 million of new economic output, leading to at least 250 new jobs.[9] Along with the robust farmers market, food, and beer scene, Art Prize has spawned a growing and very substantial tourism sector in the city. This in turn is helping to propel efforts to revitalize the infrastructure for mass transit and alternative ways of getting around.

Among the most important indicators of the success of the local-first strategy in Grand Rapids has been the revitalization of much of the downtown area, including neighborhoods formerly considered unsafe. As one example of this, when Local First opened its doors in 2006, the section in which it located was in decline, with numerous vacant properties and only five surviving businesses. Today there are twenty.[10] More broadly, vacancies in Grand Rapids have declined by more than half, according to Tim Kelly of Downtown Grand Rapids, Inc., with at least ninety vacant buildings being "repurposed" for housing, offices, and commercial space.[11] Focusing on the reuse of existing, sometimes historic buildings in the city center helps maintain the particular character of Grand Rapids, rather than contributing to the suburban sprawl that is so common in most U.S. cities. The strong base of local realtors and developers has also helped galvanize the interest and the investment to make this possible, helping downtown to become a very walkable community.

The revitalization of urban centers often has a downside: the displacement of longtime residents as rental rates and property taxes rise. This "gentrification" is a fundamental problem in many urban redevelopment efforts and is too often ignored until the process is already well under way. While Grand Rapids also faces this challenge, the city's work to build and protect affordable housing began years ago, long before the more recent resurgence in businesses and real estate. As a result, fully one-third of their

As the economy declined in Grand Rapids, so too did the building stock, with increasing vacancies like this one. Courtesy of Guy L. Bazzani.

As the bottom-up economy took hold, structures like the Bazzani Building were rehabbed and businesses began returning to downtown Grand Rapids. Courtesy of Guy L. Bazzani.

housing stock is considered to be affordable, some of it protected by long-term controls and covenants.[12]

Heading South

Not long ago, Chattanooga, Tennessee, was a town in trouble, judged to be the dirtiest city in the nation because of extreme air pollution. Sometimes things have to get very bad before serious change can occur, and that's just what happened in this town just north of the Georgia border. Like so many others in the early 1970s, this city of 170,000 people had largely traded clean air and a healthy environment for jobs and economic growth. Once confronted with this fact, however, Chattanooga's response—and its future—were quite out of the ordinary.

It began with a mandate to clean up their smokestacks to meet new emission standards passed by the U.S. Congress as part of the 1970 Clean Air Act. Chattanooga did this, but it also turned pollution control into economic development by working with local companies to build some of the scrubbers and other needed equipment. This helped set the pattern that was to follow: wherever possible, turn problems into opportunities, with local companies and organizations the first choice to fill those needs.

As Chattanooga began to bring its industrial emissions under control and air quality improved, the next frontier was in transportation. Two electric buses were purchased in a pilot effort to bring more people downtown, while continuing to clean up the air. After some initial success with this pilot effort, the city decided to expand the fleet to sixteen electric buses, and a local company formed—Advanced Transportation Systems (ATS)—to manufacture them. Over the next several years, ATS and the city worked in tandem to steadily improve the design of the buses, making them easier to operate and maintain.[13] The electric buses now transport nearly 1 million passengers each year,[14] with buses available every five minutes to take people along the 3.5-mile downtown corridor. While there have been challenges, residents and visitors alike frequently cite the clean, reliable—and free—downtown transit as one of the city's most important features. With maintenance and fuel costs running between one-fourth and one-third that of the city's diesel buses, there is also significant cost savings.

More recently, clean transportation has been expanded with the launch of Bike Chattanooga. More than three hundred bikes are now available and can be picked up or dropped off at any of thirty-three docking stations downtown.[15] The increasing number of bikes on the road is complemented by efforts to make the city more walkable as well. The Walnut Street Bridge, which had become unusable a generation ago, has been thoroughly restored and now represents the longest pedestrian bridge in the nation.[16] The extensive urban tree planting that began in the early 1990s helps to make travel for bikers and pedestrians that much more pleasant.

Of course, if people are to come downtown, the city center needs more

Investment in the Walnut Street Bridge overcame disrepair and made it central to the "walkability" of Chattanooga, Tennessee. Author's collection.

than a good way to get around; there must be things to do and see, and places to work and live. The twenty-three-mile-long River Walk is certainly one of the key attractions, part of a larger network of greenways that are making the city more walkable while also restoring the health of the Tennessee River and its tributaries.[17] An expansion of farmers markets, CSAs, and restaurants buying locally has enhanced the downtown while helping to support farms both within the city and nearby. There is also a strong local art scene, promoted both publicly by Public Art Chattanooga and privately by a steadily growing base of artists. The Chattanooga WorkSpace, essentially an arts "incubator," has helped cultivate and support local artists of all types by providing low-cost studios, a gallery for exhibition, and event space. They have been at nearly 100 percent capacity since opening in 2013, with a wide range of artists settled in the top three floors of the renovated building.[18] Every floor has a shared lounge as well as a kitchen, small design steps that help cultivate collaboration and innovation among the artists.

Such shared work spaces, with available support and a culture of innovation and collaboration, are not limited to the arts but also include facilities such as Society of Work, Concierge Office Suites, and Chattlabs, a so-called shared "maker space." These informal and dynamic workplaces are particularly attractive to young people and seem to promote the innovative entrepreneurialism for which the city is becoming well known. CO.LAB, founded in 2010, is among the most important of these innovation hubs. An outgrowth of a business-planning program called Spring Board, CO.LAB has grown to include a wide range of training, support, and business acceleration programs, with links to alternative capital sources and investors. This holistic support system is helping launch a diverse array of local businesses while steering them toward ideas that capitalize on emerging trends and markets. The theme of their 2014 annual business pitch competition, for instance, was "Outdoor Recreation and Sustainability."[19]

Chattanooga's historic place as a major manufacturing center in the Southeast is gradually being reclaimed, but this time with much more of a focus on cleaner, more sustainable, and well-paying companies. Some of the biggest of these are certainly not local, with Volkswagen the most notable among them. But the VW plant is nevertheless a leader both in high-efficiency vehicles and as a good corporate neighbor. Their LEED-certified building is in fact one of the only manufacturing facilities in the world to achieve Platinum status, the highest ranking available for sustainability and energy efficiency. Leadership in Energy and Environmental Design, or LEED, is an international certification system that promotes green design, construction, and operation of commercial, professional, and public buildings. The VW plant is one of twenty-three LEED-certified buildings in the city, ranging from manufacturing facilities to hotels, banks, and a movie theater. With twenty-four more structures awaiting LEED approval,[20] and scores of other sustainably focused building and housing developments in place, Chattanooga has one of the highest rates of green building per capita in the country.

Many local companies are counted among the one thousand manufacturers in the Greater Chattanooga area, altogether providing more than twenty-nine thousand jobs.[21] The Orange Grove Recycling Center is one of those, a private business that removes more than 1 million pounds of recyclable materials from the waste stream every month. And they don't do it with imported industrial sorting equipment, instead employing about one hundred mentally challenged people for whom the job provides a decent wage and help toward living independent lives.[22] It is another example where Chattanooga's leaders and business folk first look to build on their own strengths rather than immediately seeking to bring things in from outside.

And, of course, there is Chattanooga's almost legendary fiber optic system, providing among the very fastest Internet speeds in the country, roughly ten times faster than the nation's average. This didn't just happen but resulted from a decision early on in the city's renewal to facilitate innovation, attract creative people and businesses, and make it a great place for younger people. The sophisticated fiber optic network has indeed attracted high-tech entrepreneurs and has also made it possible to create a "smart" energy grid that reduces overall fuel consumption while increasing the reliability of power to its customers. The business that operates the network, the Electronic Power Board, is owned by the city, not by a giant cable company.

Of course, there are gaps and problems in Chattanooga like anywhere else. Yet this is a town truly reborn, shaped and led by its own citizens, increasingly building upon its own unique local strengths.

Into the Rust Belt

Like so many cities in the Northeast and mid-Atlantic regions of our country, Buffalo experienced an extraordinarily steep decline beginning in the 1970s, when its role as a major distribution hub for grain, and its steel and other traditional industries collapsed in the face of disinvestment and international competition. A staggering two hundred thousand jobs were lost over a twenty-year period. One of the areas worst hit by these changes was the West Side, which declined amid deteriorating housing, increases in vacant lots and buildings, and rising unemployment. In many ways, it was the story of so many older cities in our nation.

In 2004, a newly formed organization, PUSH Buffalo, emerged with a fire to turn things around, using a strategy that was both local and "green." PUSH, which stands for People United for Sustainable Housing, got started with scores of conversations among community residents to identify their most important concerns and priorities. This old-fashioned community organizing step led to research that uncovered one of the main reasons behind the area's inability to deal with its large number of vacant houses. The New York State Housing Agency, rather than working to rehabilitate these properties, had instead taken ownership of the property liens and then sold them on Wall Street (to Bear Stearns, to be exact) to generate revenue. Incredibly enough, the agency charged with helping maintain and expand affordable housing was instead using the decline of communities like the West Side of Buffalo to make a buck.

Thus was born PUSH Buffalo's first major campaign aimed at holding public institutions accountable. The results came surprisingly quickly, assisted by a change in leadership in the governor's office: the State of New York relinquished its ownership of the properties, turning them over to the City of Buffalo and launching a major funding stream to assist with much-needed renovations. PUSH, meanwhile, had continued its organizing efforts, including countless community meetings and a "Community Planning Congress," the first of several. All of this led to the decision to create a Green Development Zone in a twenty-five-square-block area, focusing on business development and job creation based on affordable and energy efficient housing and the transformation of vacant lots into productive green spaces, including community gardens, rain gardens, and public parks.[23]

One of the PUSH Buffalo housing crews, taking a break from a green infrastructure job. Courtesy of Aaron Bartley, PUSH Buffalo.

Along the way, PUSH has forged critical partnerships with other organizations, ranging from the Massachusetts Avenue Project's urban farm to a nonprofit developer, the Buffalo Neighborhood Stabilization Project. Among the most important of these partners has been a network of local contractors committed to training and hiring from within the community, to good pay and benefits, and to green building principles. In this way, rehabbing older buildings and improving their energy efficiency is not only saving people money but also becoming a key driver of a new green economy. To date, more than 450 homes have undergone energy-efficiency retrofits, along with eighteen multifamily apartments and six commercial buildings. This has enabled contractors to hire thirty-five people from the community, providing the needed training and support to make these high-skill, livable-wage jobs.[24]

Four men who were formerly incarcerated, "ex-cons," are now foremen on the construction crews undertaking the housing rehab and weatherization work in the community. Not only are they earning a living doing this, but they've also become board members of PUSH and well-respected leaders in the community. They are "pillars in the community," says PUSH Buffalo codirector Aaron Bartley.

In addition to affordable and green housing, another central "push" in Buffalo's West Side has been the reclamation of vacant lots into community gardens and other green spaces. Twenty such lots have thus far been reclaimed, as community gardens, "rain gardens" that capture water for irrigation, and a small urban farm. This is part of the "green infrastructure" PUSH is building as a means to reclaim land, reduce runoff and water contamination, and put people to work.

These parcels are part of a larger inventory of more than one hundred lots held in the Community Land Bank. Decisions about their use are governed by PUSH's Community Development Committee. The recently opened Massachusetts Avenue Park exemplifies another critical element of the revitalization under way, that is, creating green spaces for the community to gather, celebrate, and connect. These spaces have proven instrumental in reclaiming the community's *space*. This is a major shift from just a few years ago, when vacant lots and buildings were controlled by the state government and used to generate revenue on Wall Street. Now that space has been reclaimed as a community asset, with a playground for young children, ball fields, basketball and handball courts, and a large green space popular for community events.

According to Aaron Bartley: "There's food growing everywhere you look in our neighborhood, infinitely more than there was twenty years ago. We've steadily increased population density by filling in formerly vacant housing, with vacancies declining from 30 percent to 8 percent in less than 10 years." PUSH has also instigated commercial-scale composting, helping to transform produce waste from nearby supermarkets into much-needed soil building for vacant lots. All told, more than one hundred people who were previously unemployed or underemployed now have good jobs, focused on various aspects of bringing their community back to life. In this part of Buffalo, they didn't ask, "Where are the jobs?" but instead, "What is the work that needs to be done?"

Heading West

If you've ever been to Bellingham, Washington, you likely sensed the vitality of the community almost immediately. It wasn't always that way. In the second half of the twentieth century, as coal mining died out and the timber industry declined, the city of eighty thousand people seemed to be headed the way of most midsize U.S. towns: losing its center, struggling to find jobs or industries to replace long-standing manufacturing, unsure of what if anything could be done to the reverse the decline. In the 1970s, hippies and other free spirits began to take up residence in and around the town, bringing back-to-the-land ambitions and a spirit of openness to new ideas. Mingling with longtime residents, they helped pave the way for the emergence of one of the most sustainable midsize towns in the country in the first decade of the new millennium. In 2003, a newly formed organization, Sustainable Connections, began to mobilize both residents and businesses around a plan to make Bellingham super energy-efficient, a leader in green building, and a community committed to renewable energy.

The founders of Sustainable Connections, Michelle Long and Derek Long, decided to take advantage of the somewhat "greener" demographic of Bellingham, laying down two major "challenges" to residents and businesses alike. First came "Toward Zero Waste" in 2005, followed by the "Community Energy Challenge" in 2007. The strategy was all about carrots rather than sticks, with a feel of friendly competition, especially among local businesses. Both campaigns clicked, eliciting broad participation and helping to build a culture of sustainability.

The mix of businesses undertaking the Zero Waste challenge has been extraordinarily diverse, from the public library, which reduced trash headed to the landfill by 78 percent, to the Bellingham Farmers Market, whose waste dropped more than 80 percent. The farmers market replaced trash cans with recycling stations, required prepared food vendors to shift to compostable plates and cutlery, and provided education to vendors and customers alike. Small businesses in town, from retail shops and microbreweries to professional service providers, realized marked reductions in waste and, as a result, significant savings. Architects, builders, and a local church also came on board. And several midsize manufacturers took the challenge: Louws Truss, which manufactures building trusses, achieved an extraordinary 90 percent reduction in waste, diverting 100 tons per year from the landfill and generating thirty thousand dollars in annual savings; Samson, a high-performance rope manufacturer, realized a 50 percent reduction within just the first few months, amounting to twenty thousand dollars per year in savings.[25]

The Community Energy Challenge has been equally if not more successful. With Sustainable Connections at the center of a mix of non-profits, public agencies, and local businesses, the initiative was designed to demonstrate the multiple benefits of energy efficiency and clean energy, and to provide the technical assistance and business support to make the shift relatively easy. This includes professional energy audits, along with readily available products and services needed to reduce energy use or shift to renewables.

While the Zero Waste challenge focused on businesses (and some organizations), the Clean Energy Challenge encompasses businesses and households. In its first six years, the results have been impressive. In excess of four hundred local businesses are participating, with the number buying green power increasing by 20 percent annually, to more than 240. The number of solar systems on residential and commercial buildings grew from fewer than 20 in 2008 to more than 350 in 2014. The number of households getting an energy audit rocketed from fewer than 50 in 2010 to 1,550 in 2014, and of

Bellingham-based Itek Energy donated solar panels to help make this thirty-home Habitat for Humanity development greener and more affordable. Courtesy of Adam Simmons, Habitat for Humanity, Kitsap County.

these, more than 1,100 have had some sort of "energy retrofit" (an improvement in energy efficiency) performed.[26] All of this has encouraged the local utility, Puget Sound Energy (PSE), to begin to get serious about renewable energy, with wind power having increased from negligible amounts to 773 megawatts during this same period. That's enough to power 200,000 homes and makes PSE the second-largest utility wind generator in the nation.[27]

Bellingham has done a good job ensuring that the benefits from all this savings in energy, landfill waste, and other resource conservation also accrue to the local economy. More than twenty-five energy-efficiency contractors now work in Bellingham and Whatcom County. By adding energy retrofits to their services, they've been better able than some other contractors to weather the recession and housing downturn. Because of the entrepreneurial approach taken and the strong involvement of the local business community, environmental gains have been made not at the expense of businesses but very much to their benefit.

In 2012, Itek Energy opened its doors in Bellingham, the first manufacturer of solar photovoltaic (PV) panels in the state. The groundwork done by Sustainable Connections to build broad community support for clean energy, complemented by strong state incentives for solar, has helped propel dramatic growth in the company's short history. In just three short years, Itek has grown from twelve full-time employees to nearly eighty. Their output of PV panels has increased even faster, with more than 70,000 produced and shipped thus far. This local production—supported by incentives from Washington State—has in turn helped grow the solar industry throughout the state, with 129 companies employing approximately 2,400 people in 2015.[28]

Bellingham's local food scene is among one of the most developed in the nation, with the Bellingham Farmers Market at the center. This market is one of six farmers markets in the county, a doubling over the past decade. Independent restaurants have also helped drive the market for local foods, with both the number of restaurants and their purchase volumes increasing steadily. Surveys done by Sustainable Connections show that from 2012 to 2014, the number or restaurants buying from local farms more than doubled, from thirty-three to sixty-eight, and that the proportion of local sourcing increased as well, from an average of 33 percent to 43 percent.[29] Compared to many communities around the nation, these numbers demonstrate a very strong commitment on the part of Bellingham chefs. In addition to direct purchases from local farmers, some are now sourcing through an emerging network of small food hubs. This network is evolving to include three different "aggregation sites," or places where farmers can drop off their food, linked to a web-based ordering system that connects farmers with chefs and other buyers. Though still in its early stages, the hub is working with farmers and buyers alike to design a workable system.

Out to Sea

Brendan Smith started commercial fishing when he was only fourteen years old, moving around from his home place in the Northeast all the way to the Canadian West Coast. Over the ensuing two decades, he witnessed firsthand the steady decline in most of those fisheries, and along with that, the decimation of thousands of livelihoods up and down both coasts. Returning to his native New England thirteen years ago, Brendan combined his wide-ranging practical skills and his substantial intellect to create an entirely new and sustainable approach to harvesting the ocean's bounty. He calls it "3-D ocean farming," as it utilizes the entire water column in a thoroughly planned and highly managed system of regenerative aquaculture. If you're like me, the term "aquaculture" might conjure images of genetically modified salmon or Asian shrimp farms destroying native ocean habitat. In Brendan's case, it's precisely the opposite.

Brendan's system encompasses 20-acre "plots" of ocean water, immediately adjacent to the shoreline. His farm is in the Long Island Sound. These plots are traversed by a series of ropes laid horizontally, six feet below the water surface. From the ropes to the surface, two types of seaweed grow, kelp and a sea grass. From the ropes hang "socks" growing mussels and nets containing scallops. Farther down the water column are cages for oysters and clams. One space, four different types of native species of seafood, all clean, delicious, and highly marketable. Additionally, the kelp is harvested for use in everything from kelp noodles to animal feed and fertilizer for farms, for which its abundant nutrients make it very well suited. More recently, experiments have begun to extract fuel from the kelp, and the results are encouraging, with yields of 2,000 gallons of fuel derived per acre of harvested kelp.

To beat it all, sports fisherman can and do fish the surface of these very same waters, as the combination of abundant seaweed and water-cleansing oysters and other species make for an ideal fish habitat. Five high-value "crops," completely compatible with traditional fishing, all assembled together to preserve the ocean commons while providing a major carbon sink (the seaweed is twenty times more effective than grasslands in sequestering carbon from the atmosphere). "More than anything else," says Brendan, "I'm a climate farmer. This system helps us mitigate climate change, by pulling carbon out of the atmosphere, and it also helps us adapt to the changing climate and ocean conditions."

He is exquisitely "solving for pattern," in Wendell Berry's words; he's "stacking enterprises," to quote Joel Salatin.

Ecological sustainability was not the only goal of this unique system. Of equal importance to Brendan was economic potential and affordability for rank-and-file fishermen. He's certainly accomplished the latter: setting up the self-sustaining system requires about a thirty-thousand-dollar investment— very modest by commercial fishing standards—and a boat. Because the system uses no inputs once operational, it is both environmentally sound and financially manageable.

The economics of 3-D ocean farming are still being worked through. There is no question as to the productivity of the system; the diverse bounty it yields with no inputs and minimal operational costs have led five other fishermen to set up the system thus far, with literally hundreds of inquires coming Brendan's way every year. But like all farming, "there are good years and bad years" along with the challenge all farmers face—how to secure a good enough price and to capture enough of the value of product, including its processing, to achieve sustained profitability. Brendan is part of a marketing cooperative that is grappling with these challenges. He also set up one of the first Community Supported Fisheries (CSF) in the country as a means to reach consumers directly and to help them share both the bounty and the risk. His system has already proven its productivity and extremely high levels of sustainability, so much so that his work is both a research and educational partner with the likes of Yale, the University of Connecticut, and Woods Hole Oceanic Institute. The next step for Brendan is turning these intellectual collaborators into full partners in the development of markets, infrastructure, and support needed to revitalize the region's ocean-based livelihoods.

Common Characteristics of Bottom-Up Economies

Five features consistently emerge as communities, cities, and regions move from a dependence on trickle-down to an economy built from the bottom up:

1. **They are diverse,** usually along several dimensions:
   a. *Economic sectors,* including almost always a strong presence of food- and farming-related enterprises and retail businesses, but also involving increasing activity related to energy efficiency and clean energy, affordable and green building, arts, music, and culture, innovative manufacturing, and other sectors. This trend toward diversity is growing, even in southwest Virginia and Appalachia, a region long dominated by just a handful of industries.
   b. *Business size and age.* While there is always a relatively high proportion of newer and smaller enterprises, experience from Athens, Grand Rapids, and most other communities also shows a healthy blend of older, more traditional businesses with start-ups and new businesses; with the presence of mentoring and microfinance programs, the business size ranges from very small home-based enterprises, to midsize, multimillion-dollar companies.
   c. *Ownership,* representing both an emerging reality and a gap in these economies. Compared to business ownership on the whole, enterprises in local living economies appear more likely to be owned and operated by younger people and by women, as well as to pioneer new forms of ownership, from cooperatives to Benefit corporations. The evidence for this is anecdotal at this point and merits examination. Business ownership among blacks and Latinos nevertheless appears to lag within the local economy sector.

2. **Typically, though not always, there is a "signature" to the local living economy,** a defining event or a sector of the economy for which the community is becoming known, and which is drawing in both visitors and new or returning talent. In southwest Virginia, it is Appalachian music, artisanship, and culture, melded with food and farming; in Bellingham, it is the innovation in green building, energy

efficiency, and clean energy; in Chattanooga, it is the high-speed fiber optics and the smart grid and high-tech start-ups that has enabled. In all of these cases, these represent but one component of the emerging local economy. In some respects the "branding" that occurs around such lead sectors might shortchange other businesses and sectors, but in the short run at least, it appears to help put these communities on the map for visitors, public agencies, and investors.

3. **Many of the businesses grow out of community needs more than individual wants.** For much of the consumer economy, the driving motivation is to create new things or, more often, new versions of old things that will capture people's attention, pretty much anywhere and everywhere. Global retailers, be they of the brick-and-mortar or Amazon persuasion, have helped facilitate this wants-based economy. It is characterized by cheaper, disposable items with no connection to any particular place. Local living economies have their share of silly stuff for sale, but they are much more inclined to create businesses and jobs that address fundamental needs and challenges in their place, as PUSH Buffalo has done with affordable, energy-efficient housing work, as has happened in southwest Virginia in creating alternatives for tobacco farmers, and in the Long Island Sound in response to declining fisheries. They tend, in other words, to ask, "What work needs to be done?" rather than exclusively focusing on, "Where are the jobs?"

4. **A culture of innovation, rooted in place and with strong local support, pervades.** In Athens and southeast Ohio, this began with the launching of the ACEnet kitchen incubator but has continued and expanded to include additional ventures, such as the produce auction, a furnishings "reuse" store, a local mill using ancient varieties of grains, and more. The innovations derive less from the desire to create novelties or "the next big thing" that storms the market than from the hope of finding better, cleaner, more pleasurable ways of getting things done. Electric buses and bike sharing in Chattanooga, 3-D ocean farming, manufacturing bins from recycled plastic in Grand Rapids, and deploying businesses and organizations to dramatically reduce energy costs across local businesses all represent this needs-based innovation.

5. **Many of the individual businesses, and the local economy networks of which they're a part, utilize "full-cost accounting" in order to**

avoid externalizing their costs. The traditional approach to aquaculture in the oceans has followed the factory model of maximizing output (or sales) while minimizing costs to the business. Part of that "cost minimization" occurs when the bad things that happen as a result of the business—habitat destruction for native species, for instance—are not included in the cost of the product and are instead "externalized" for someone else to pay. Brendan Smith's 3-D ocean farming internalizes its costs by accounting for all inputs and all outputs, not just the primary "product." In many respects, the best organic and sustainable farming systems do this as well. In-fill development in Grand Rapids provides another example, as the reclamation of a building becomes part of the cost, as opposed to sprawl development which engenders additional, usually externalized costs.

Analysis of Transition Two

Small businesses, family farms, bustling downtowns—all of these have been part of our history and our cultural imagination for generations. To this day, most Americans prefer the idea of family farms, friendly hometown banks, and mom-and-pop businesses.[30] The challenge here is not in convincing people that these things are good but in persuading people that they are possible. And for policy makers and economic development professionals, many of whom consider this to be little more than nostalgia for bygone days, persuading them that bottom-up economic development offers real potential is a far greater challenge.

There are some good reasons for the skepticism. First of all, the globalization of commerce, the advance of franchises and big boxes in almost every sector of the economy, and the rise of gargantuan financial institutions have been swift and wide reaching. When hundreds of interstate exits, from New Mexico to North Carolina, become indistinguishable from one another, the idea of place-based economies is pretty hard to conjure. When local banks close or are bought out by ever-larger banks, and bookstores and record stores fold as Amazon's stock prices rise, the whole thing begins to feel inexorable. Unstoppable. Just the way it goes. So you can't exactly blame the mayors and economic developers and county supervisors who feel that "getting their share" of this global largess may be about the only option they've got.

But as we saw in chapter 1, the rise of "big, global" and the decline of "smaller, local" has been based neither on the inherent superiority or greater efficiency of multinationals nor on some "invisible hand" guiding the economy. Instead, these companies have used their economic resources and political clout to strengthen their position and tilt the balance in their favor on everything from tax and trade policy to subsidies for doing business. We'll talk more about this later in the chapter, but when you understand just how unlevel the playing field has become, the emergence of local living economies from the bottom up becomes far more impressive.

The first thing to note about the examples I've highlighted above is that none is completely consistent or comprehensive in its embracing of a bottom-up economy. All still depend, to varying degrees, on a significant number of larger, nonlocal businesses to provide both jobs and tax revenues. While the number of locally owned, independent businesses has grown substantially in all of these communities, they still represent a relatively small portion of the economy, overall. This is true across the country, even in places where localism is very strong, like Bellingham, Athens, and Austin. Can we conclude from this that local, independent businesses, especially those focused on "living" economies, will always remain but a small part of the broader economy? The boutique shopping that tourists love? Some analysts and pundits certainly have.

There's a very different way to see this, though, and I'll use a story from my own experience to illustrate the point. Eighteen miles south of my hometown of Abingdon is Bristol, a town bisected by the state line. When you walk down State Street, you can hop back and forth between Virginia and Tennessee. Once a pearl, State Street and most of downtown Bristol were in bad shape just fifteen years ago, with many empty storefronts, buildings in decline, and a handful of pawn shops and antique malls comprising most of the commercial activity. By 2014, however, State Street, and many of the small arteries feeding into it, had become a very different place. It is a center for live music and cultural and musical heritage, including Rhythm and Roots, one of the premier music festivals in the nation. It is building an increasingly strong retail sector and a growing base of independent restaurants, including a twenty-four-hour bakery and coffee shop and half a dozen live music venues; and it has once again become a mixed-use neighborhood, with loft apartments and condos taking the place of previously empty second and third floors. Part of that mixed use also includes the beautiful Bristol Public Library, right downtown, a facility with many green features, including sustainably sourced local hardwood floors. A lot of folks have worked hard to bring State Street back and to encourage "place-based" businesses and entrepreneurs, and, to a significant degree, it has worked.

In September 2013, the local paper, the *Bristol Herald Courier,* ran a small story on the very back page of the front section, announcing the winner of the Entrepreneurship Prize for that year, one of several ways in which local leaders encourage homegrown businesses. The prize is five thousand dollars, along with assistance with marketing and other noncash support. On the front page of that same edition, the *Herald Courier* ran a story about a different sort of prize: regional economic development leaders and elected officials proudly announcing a deal to ensure that Cabela's, the national outdoor sports chain, would locate just 5 miles from downtown. Its cost? More than $50 million in government subsidies. In case your math is not too good, that is ten thousand times greater than the local entrepreneurship award.

This story—and there are hundreds more like it in towns and cities across the country—at least begs the question: What might happen if such subsidies for large, nonlocal companies were dramatically reduced, with the funds instead routed to homegrown, living businesses? Surveys consistently demonstrate that access to capital is one of the biggest impediments to start-up companies, especially small to midsize enterprises. In the case of Bristol, $50 million could have capitalized hundreds of small independent businesses. Let's be more precise: *for the same amount of money offered to one large national chain, five hundred local businesses could have received an average investment of $100,000* in some mix of grants, loans, and tax abatements. If you're a local businessperson, those kinds of numbers are pretty astonishing. Farm subsidies follow a similar pattern of extreme concentration at the top, as illustrated by the graph below.

What happens when local leaders decide *not* to fight for outside companies using huge taxpayer subsidies but instead pursue a homegrown development strategy? One striking example comes from the west central region of rural Minnesota and the work of the West Central Initiative. In the mid-1980s, this part of the state had been hard hit by farm foreclosures and a slow but steady decline in the region's manufacturing base. Population was declining, especially among young people, two-thirds of whom were leaving the area the first chance they got. The West Central Initiative (WCI), led by John Molinaro, looked at the potential for recruiting outside companies and decided to instead pursue a strategy of supporting the small to midsize manufacturing businesses they already had. They called it "growth from within." Most of these companies, which included metalworks, plastics, equipment manufacturers, and food processors, were struggling to stay afloat. In 1986, WCI began working with them to identify and address their most important challenges: the need for

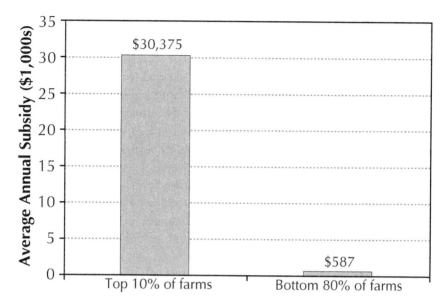

Federal subsidies by farm size, 1995–2010. Federal farm subsidies in the United States are concentrated among the largest farmers, who on average receive more than fifty times as much subsidy as small to midsize farmers. Two-thirds of U.S. farmers receive no subsidies. (From Ecological Working Group, "Farm Subsidy Database: The United State Summary Information," www.ewg.org.)

plant expansion and modernized equipment, but a lack of access to affordable financing; updating the skills of their current workers and training new workers with the right skills; and overall assistance with business planning and management. That's where WCI focused its efforts.

The results of this "growth from within" approach were incredible. The manufacturing companies, most of which were locally owned, began expanding and modernizing their plants, sharing the cost of training workers, and growing the markets for their products. Over the ensuing twenty years, they more than doubled the number of manufacturing jobs, from 4,350 to nearly 10,000, even as the nation as a whole lost one-third of its manufacturing employment. Wages increased by more than 20 percent on average. Employment as a whole across the region increased by 30,000 jobs, as many other companies started or grew to meet the needs of the expanding manufacturing workforce. The population decline reversed, adding twenty thousand people. Young people, who had been leaving at the rate of two out of every three, were now staying in the region at that same rate.[31]

And they didn't spend a dime on subsidies to woo outside corporations.

The issue of the imbalance in financial support for the local versus nonlocal economy is just one of several challenges they face. These notwithstanding, the expansion of local living economies is taking place in many parts of the country. Because of the relative newness of this approach to economic development, data and "metrics" (the new way of saying "ways to measure things") are difficult to come by. Nevertheless, we can begin to see certain trends that illuminate both the strengths and challenges of this new economic approach. We'll focus on four of these trends.

Food and farming are consistently at the forefront in most places where a local living economy is beginning to take hold. Thus far, this has mostly been a strength, for several reasons: Primarily, food is essential to our health and well-being, and we've neglected that fact for a couple of generations. Eating better, along with other lifestyle changes, offers a reasonably good chance to improve our overall health, and with that, increase our productivity and happiness while reducing our spending on diet-based health problems. The growing concern about health has helped to propel a thirty-year-long growth in the market for organic foods, where annual sales now exceed $30 billion. And the desire to eat better, long considered a luxury of the well-heeled, increasingly encompasses ordinary people, working folks, and those with limited incomes. This is substantiated not only by the steady increase in the use of EBT—formerly known as food stamps—at farmers markets and CSAs but also by studies showing that lower-income consumers continue to purchase at farmers markets even after incentives come to an end.[32]

Second, **sufficient economic return is critical if farmers are to maintain—or in some cases, restore—land, soils, and water.** If we want to preserve farmland, as most of us say we do, we've got to figure out how to make farming reasonably profitable, and part of that lies with getting farmers much more of the consumer dollar. So, most Americans need to eat better, and at the same time, we all need our farms, forests, and waterways to be productive and fully functioning in their ecological roles of cleaning our air, purifying water, and providing habitat for other species. In many communities, the local food movement has helped in both of these respects, providing more, often healthier food to consumers while providing a better return to farmers, especially those utilizing soil building, sustainable practices. It's the proverbial "win-win."

To boot, several studies have shown the catalytic role that farmers markets often play in downtown revitalization and overall economic development. A survey of eight hundred farmers-market shoppers nationwide, done by the Project for Public Spaces, found that 60 percent of people only came to town on market days, and of them, nearly two-thirds stuck around and visited other local businesses nearby.[33] So farmers markets draw people into town, and if there's much else going on, keep folks there, thinking and buying locally. With in excess of 8,100 known farmers markets nationwide,[34] along with a range of other food businesses, eateries, breweries, and wineries, it's clear that what we eat and drink is reclaiming its critical role in our communities and economies, this time with more attention to how things are grown and raised.

The local food (and now, drink) economy brings one more strength to the broader local economy movement—it provides a relatively easy point of entry for a very broad group of people. Unlike renewable energy, or green building, or even the arts, the appeal of good-quality food is very broad. On a given Saturday morning at Abingdon's market, the line at our booth will include liberals and conservatives, libertarians and social activists. This not only means that the market is broad but that people of all kinds are congregating and talking, something increasingly rare in our society.

On the other hand, many communities with relatively well-developed local food systems are also beginning to realize "plateaus" in the demand for local food, and with that farmers are facing increased price competition and/ or a stagnant or even declining market. Bellingham, Abingdon, Grand Rapids, and Athens are all reporting this along with communities as different as Lawrence, Kansas, and Minneapolis, Minnesota. A recent USDA analysis supports this as well: From 2002 to 2007, direct-to-consumer sales, mostly through farmers markets and CSAs, increased by 32 percent, while the number of farmers selling this way increased by 17 percent. From 2008 to 2012, however, direct-to-consumers sales did not increase, even though the number of farmers selling this way continued to grow.[35]

For years, supply trailed demand, as more and more people began to shift their eating and buying habits. While that's still the case in many communities, increasingly the local food movement must also face this new challenge: It is time to reach beyond the locavores and earth mommas and figure out how to reach the next tier of potential consumers, a group that I've taken to calling the *vaguely concerned and sporadically motivated* food shopper. This will be an essential part of continuing to build economic opportunity, and to do so in such a way that supports stewardship of farmland and decent incomes for farmers, entrepreneurs, and workers in the food system.

Third, **the transition to bottom-up, local living economies generally builds upon the first transition, that of increasing productivity and self-reliance in households and communities.** The movement toward greater self-reliance and the emergence of more diverse, locally rooted economies share an important foundation: They reduce vulnerability and dependence on faraway things over which communities have no control, whether these be shifts in global markets or Wall Street–fueled corporate buyouts. Local living economies built from the bottom up mirror self-reliant households and neighborhood associations in their focus on adapting to their place, including its assets, limits, and challenges. The customers at the Chesterhill Produce Auction in southeast Ohio include chefs and retail buyers but also many individuals who buy in bulk to can, freeze, and put food up for the winter. The folks weatherizing their homes through MACED's Kentucky $mart program or PUSH Buffalo's energy retrofit program no doubt have a range of views on the environment, but all share the desire to save money and reduce their dependence on utility companies and volatile energy prices. All of these initiatives help equip people and communities to live more frugally, with less resources coming in and less waste going out. We used to call that being "conservative."

As mentioned in chapter 2, people pursuing self-reliance in their households often come to see the economic benefit of what they are doing, and from that some launch home-based businesses. Nearly all local living economies include a range of organizations, networks, and funding sources designed to nurture small and "micro" enterprises. Those that begin at home as a way to save a little money, help family or neighbors, or reduce dependence on the bigger economy can sometimes be nurtured into independent businesses serving the broader community. ACEnet's Food Ventures Commercial Kitchen has incubated scores of home-based enterprises, with many becoming successful small and midsize businesses. Farmers markets around the country also serve the role of incubator, according to a study from Cornell University, in large part because they provide a space to test new products and gradually build a market, in most cases with minimal investment.[36]

The bottom-up economy's roots in self-reliance sometimes also limits its broader potential, though not without good reason. Many in the organic movement view the fate of Stonyfield Yogurt and Cascadian Farms as cautionary tales, as these once homegrown businesses were bought out by giant food conglomerates and, in the process, lost much of their connection to local communities and farms. The anxiety of what "success" might do is not without merit. In fact, the popularity of organic foods has put it more or less in the mainstream, and this in turn has led to the same sort of "bigger is better" consolidation—one of the "six myths" I described—as the conventional food system. As one example, a 2013 study by Dr. Phil Howard of Michigan State University determined that the number of independent processors of organic foods had declined from eighty-one to just fifteen, as most of the smaller companies had been bought out by a few large ones.[37]

At the other end of the spectrum, previously mentioned studies of home-based businesses in the informal economy show that many such entrepreneurs are reluctant to go full-time with their businesses. For some, they simply can't take the risk or access the capital needed, but for others, the reluctance stems from the fear of losing their independence, of becoming saddled by the demands of the market, creditors, or the government. With the local economy movement comprised of many such alternative thinkers, there will remain for some time a tension between maintaining their integrity and independence versus reaching a scale big enough to have impact on the broader economy.

Fourth, **the close connection to place and the inclination to create businesses that address real needs has led to a strong foundation of triple-bottom-line businesses in the bottom-up economy.** "Triple-bottom-line" businesses, you may recall, are those that seek to be financially profitable while also providing both environmental and social benefits. Such businesses work hard to internalize all of their costs rather than leaving problems behind for someone else to clean up (and pay for!). For some companies, the triple bottom line is built into their most basic purpose, in some cases even their corporate structure. So-called "Benefit corporations," or "B-corps," provide examples of this, as do many cooperatives and a range of socially responsible or green businesses. (Though no broad assessment has yet been done, anecdotally it appears clear that bottom-up economies include a much higher proportion of cooperatives, B-corps, and similar alternative business forms than does the broader economy.) Other businesses gradually come to embrace the second and third bottom line, both as good business practice and as part of a commitment to better stewardship and neighborliness. The success of Bellingham's Zero Waste Challenge provides a good example here, with everyone from boutique breweries to more traditional manufacturers making waste reduction an important part of their business.

On the other end of the spectrum, big multinational corporations argue against "internalizing" the human and ecological costs of doing business, claiming that the law *requires* them to "maximize shareholder return," which is to say, short-term profits. As Lynn Stout demonstrates in *The Shareholder Value Myth,* this pervasive view is based on a misreading of a single court case from 1919 and is not supported by any other legal precedents: "It has become routine for journalists, economists, and business observers to claim as undisputed fact that U.S. law legally obligates the directors of corporations to maximize shareholder wealth. Business reporters blithely assert that 'the law states that the duty of a business's directors is to maximize profits for shareholders.' . . . There is one fatal flaw in their reasoning. There is no solid legal support for the claim that directors and executives in U.S. public corporations have an enforceable legal duty to maximize shareholder wealth. The idea is fable."[38]

Few "fables" have had such profound impact on people and communities as this one. As triple-bottom-line enterprises, place-based small businesses, and Benefit corporations grow in number, it may well become more feasible to challenge this widespread and destructive belief.

The Green Development Zone in west Buffalo provides an example where strong social outcomes, in the form of well-paying jobs with potential for advancement, and increased community food self-sufficiency, combine with environmental goals—community green space, reduced energy use and emissions—as the fundamental goals of a community-wide economic strategy. PUSH Buffalo's strategy, and in many respects, the work of Sustainable Connections in Bellingham, of Evergreen Cooperatives in Cleveland, and of ASD in Central Appalachia, reflect a belief that all three elements of the triple bottom line are not only equally important but potentially synergistic; that is, they can enhance and strengthen one another. This, in fact, is one of the foundational ideas of BALLE, the Business Alliance for Local Living Economies, about which we'll talk more in chapter 5.

It is nevertheless more common among those promoting local economies that the social and environmental benefits of economic development are secondary to economic revitalization and job creation, often cast as "something to work toward." The recent and now strong cache of "local" can propel this, as the local brand becomes a substitute for, or embodiment of, sustainable, healthy, better. While there's much to like about local, it is a mistake to automatically equate it with sustainability or better social outcomes. We know, for instance, that farming practices—that is, *how* food is produced—are of far greater importance in terms of carbon emissions and other ecological impacts than is the distance it traveled, so-called "food miles."[39] We know, too, that

The Summit City Café, formerly an abandoned building, is now a gathering place and musical venue, especially for young people, in Whitesburg, Kentucky. Courtesy of Amelia Kirby.

small businesses are less likely to provide health insurance to their employees than larger corporations,[40] though many of the latter are dropping or greatly shrinking health care coverage for their workers. Of course, small businesses pay an average of 18 percent higher health insurance premiums and face triple the administrative costs of big businesses, making it much more difficult for them to offer these benefits.[41]

Another result of the triple-bottom-line influence in local living economies is the culture of innovation that emerges. ACEnet's Food Ventures incubator, Chattanooga Chattlab's shared maker space, and farm incubators in Bellingham, Charleston (South Carolina), Vermont, and other places are but a few of the examples of the concerted support for nurturing new ideas, generating better solutions. This culture of experimentation and innovation is almost surely one of the reasons that so many young people are coming to, or coming back to, places where living economies are developing. Sometimes that support is deliberate and relatively comprehensive, as with the Food Ventures in Athens, or Chattanooga's CO.LAB.

In other instances, innovation is spawned more by example, completely informally. The Summit City Café in Whitesburg, Kentucky, a tiny town in the heart of the coalfields, is just that kind of space. Great coffee, interesting food, and live music six nights per week have made it one of the premier gathering places, especially for younger folks and those with new ideas. Launched and owned by Amelia Kirby and Joel Beverly, a young couple from the region, Summit City is not only a delightful place to hang out but a spot where new ideas are often brewed up as well.

In many parts of the country, historic industries are in steady decline, whether from trade policies and overseas competition, shifts in consumption patterns, or stronger health and environmental standards. One of the most important features of bottom-up economies is their culture of innovation, which now needs to be brought to bear on creating new manufacturing opportunities that utilize the skills of laid-off miners, steel workers, construction workers, and others.

Most fundamentally, local living economies must build the foundation for a just and livable world. This means that triple-bottom-line businesses and bottom-up economic strategies alone won't work if they, too, depend on endless growth, something our ecosystems can't accommodate for much longer. Nor can current levels of wealth concentration continue. Local living economies must focus on meeting real needs and equipping people and communities to live well, while living within the limits of our places.

As bottom-up economies take root, the central challenges revolve around three big questions: *scale, price, and ownership.* What is the appropriate scale for these businesses and the economies of which they're a part; and how can farmers, green builders, and other "high road" businesses make a decent living while providing their goods and services at a price most folks can afford? And who can and should own these businesses for them to be most viable and beneficial?

As local economies begin to mature, they typically move beyond the boutique nature that might have characterized their early stages of development. Funky, quirky businesses remain—thank goodness!—but they are joined by more "normal" companies as well, such as builders and contractors, hardware and building supply, pharmacies, grocers, transportation services. Many of these companies are filling traditional needs but using new means of doing so. We've seen some examples of this, including bike-sharing and car-sharing businesses, cooperatively owned restaurants, green building enterprises, and new, integrated forms of ocean farming.

As these and countless other businesses grow to meet emerging demand, the question of *scale* becomes critical. And it is a much more complex question than would normally be the case. For traditional economic thinkers, the answer is pretty straightforward: Get bigger. If you get big enough, you can go national, possibly even franchise your business, and at some point, cash out. Think Ben & Jerry's, Chipotle, Cabela's, even Walmart. All started out small and local, and for a variety of reasons, grew into national chains with billions of dollars in sales and thousands of employees. What's wrong with that?

For those working to build more resilient communities and local living economies, *appropriate scale* is rarely so clear or simple. First, the businesses must make enough money to pay a fair wage to employees and provide a reasonable return to the owner and any investment partners. This often means at least some growth to allow for greater purchasing power, to establish a consistent presence in the marketplace, to capitalize new ideas and improvements. Village Bakery, which started out in the Food Ventures incubator, now has better than twenty employees and $1 million in yearly sales.[42] Yet it continues to source many of its ingredients from local farmers, pays above-average wages, and gives considerable time and money to the community. The same can be said, even more so, of Casa Nueva. Are these businesses now at their optimal scale, or should they grow considerably larger?

Determining appropriate scale is also a question for producer and business networks, as we'll see in chapter 5, and for bottom-up economy strategies more broadly. As one example, the proliferation of farmers markets has helped revitalize many small towns and create wonderful options for healthy eating in multiple neighborhoods of larger cities. Grand Rapids has fourteen markets; Oakland has fourteen, New York City, more than fifty.[43] Most everyone is encouraged by the recent emergence of farmers markets in lower-income neighborhoods, a sign of both untapped markets and the desire to make "good food" accessible to all. But if you talk with farmers in some communities, they'll tell you that there are now just too many markets. The result in these cases has been a dilution of the market, with farmers and vendors spending more time for the same or declining amounts of sales. Not long ago, the attitude was "the more the merrier," based at least in part on our notions of ever-growing pies and rising tides. It turns out that scale is an important issue here as well.

The challenge of *price* parallels the issue of scale. We've seen it most acutely in the local foods movement, as this has been the first segment of local living economies to move into the mainstream. Price issues around food are both real and perceived. The perception that local food, especially organic food, costs much more is often exaggerated. In 2011, SCALE, Inc. (my consulting firm) gathered prices of everyday foods at twenty-five farmers markets in six Appalachian and southeastern states, comparing them with supermarkets nearby. In three-fourths of the cases, the local food was at or below the cost of comparable items in the supermarket. The comparison held for organic foods, even more so.[44] The point is not that healthy local foods are usually cheaper, or even that they should be, but rather that the *perception* of their much higher cost is often misplaced.

Perceptions, whatever their basis, also influence who is participating in local economies, both as businesses and as customers. A 2013 survey conducted for Local First Grand Rapids showed a clear and consistent correlation between education, income, and race, and the levels of awareness of and support for local businesses. In a nutshell, the higher your education level and the greater your income, the more likely you were to "support local." It was also true that white people were more involved than black folks and other people of color, with the interesting exception of Native Americans.[45] Though this is but one survey, it is likely that the results would not diverge greatly in other places where the local economy has emerged. The questions it raises, about perception for sure, but also about types and locations of businesses, the form of support offered, and the availability of capital for investment, all need attention.

Of course there are also very real issues of price, around food, renewable energy, green building, and more. Solving these won't be easy and will almost surely require new and open collaborations between those of us producing the goods and the larger group of folks buying or hoping to buy them. In an era of stagnant wages, declining job benefits and security, and extreme pressure on government to tighten its belt, this search for solutions to the challenge of price and affordability could not be more important.

The ownership of businesses and infrastructure is both a challenge and opportunity within the bottom-up economy, an issue we'll focus on in chapter 4.

Public Policy

The work of Stacy Mitchell and the Institute for Local Self-Reliance, as well as the Sustainable Law Center, are among those at the cutting edge of creative, practical proposals for policy in support of local living economies. The final section of this chapter draws heavily from that work, but only to provide a small sampling of what is wrong with most current policy and a taste of what our public policy could be. We'll look at policy from three perspectives:

- Leveling the playing field (between big, nonlocal and smaller, local)
- Integrating critical social goals—health, equity, environmental conservation—with economic goals
- Investment in areas of critical need and/or promising opportunity

Leveling the Playing Field

Five policy changes stand out here:

1. **Dramatically alter subsidies for economic development.** Currently, local, state, and federal subsidies to attract and retain large companies exceed $100 billion per year, dwarfing the budget of the Small Business Administration and all other state and federal agencies providing support to small and midsize companies. As we saw in the example of Bristol, the real-world consequences of this are enormous, providing very large corporations with dramatically more support than home-grown businesses. What's more, in spite of Abingdon's victory in keeping Walmart out of town, the county where Abingdon is located offered incentives of nearly $1 million in 2014, making it likely that the big box will be built just outside of the town limits. As we saw earlier, the trend holds in federal agricultural policies, where the biggest 10 percent of farms and agribusinesses averaged more than $30,000 per year in taxpayer support from 1995 to 2012, while the bottom 80 percent of farms averaged just over $600 per year. Approximately two thirds of U.S. farms received no federal subsidy.[46] Subsidies for multinational firms flush with cash, and for very large commodity farms should be scaled back dramatically, reserved only for those larger firms doing pioneering work in new systems or technologies with clear public benefit. Some of the money saved could instead be invested in small to midsize farms and businesses with the result being increased innovation and more jobs per dollar invested. A recent study demonstrated that for every $10 million in sales, independent retailers employed fifty people; for the same volume of sales, Walmart employs twenty-one people and Amazon, just fourteen.[47]

2. **When outside companies are recruited, link subsidies or incentives to Community Benefits Agreements.** Now being utilized in Philadelphia, Atlanta, Pittsburgh, Denver, and several other cities, Community Benefit Agreements are legally binding agreements between a developer and a citizens group to provide a range of benefits in

exchange for public support of the development. These typically include commitments to employ specific percentages of local people in all phases, to pay fair wages, to provide adequate training for these jobs, to help finance community infrastructure or affordable housing, and to respect community priorities.[48] This makes the promises that developers often put forth both specific and binding. In some cases, most notably Detroit, local leaders are considering making CBAs mandatory for developments of a certain scale.[49]

3. **Make regulations "scale appropriate."** At present, a small community bank faces essentially the same limits and requirements as those placed upon huge Wall Street financial institutions. This is entirely counterproductive, not to mention silly, as it has led to policies that allow the big financial institutions to continue to gamble with investor money while creating reporting burdens and collateral limits that seriously handicap community lenders. This has helped spell the demise of nearly one-fourth of local banks over the past six years alone.[50] We must remember that community banks and credit unions lend four times as much money, dollar for dollar, to home owners and small businesses than do the big Wall Street banks. In Bellingham, the community banks are providing the capital needed for new solar installations and many other local enterprises. We should be freeing them up to do more of that, and in doing so need not give a free pass to Bank of America or Wells Fargo. A parallel argument holds for small farms and small businesses generally vis-à-vis their giant competitors. Everything from food safety requirements to small business licensing requirements should be made more scale-appropriate.

4. **Eliminate tax advantages for companies that off-shore jobs or move corporate headquarters to tax-friendlier places.** It's bad enough that they do this, but to reward them for it is nothing less than stupid public policy. In our current political context, we regularly hear about the need to lower corporate tax rates in order to stimulate investment and job creation. In actuality, the current corporate tax rate of 35 percent is well below the 50 percent rate of the 1950s, a time when our economic growth rate was more than double what it is now. And because of the loopholes and incentives in both tax and trade policy, the effective corporate tax rate averages 27 percent, and is often far lower for the biggest multinational firms.

5. **Devise procurement policies, primarily at the state level, that**

encourage local or in-state procurement of goods and services. Small to midsize companies already do much more local procurement per dollar of sales, even in the absence of such policies. Contracts undertaken by public institutions—schools, universities, parks and state agencies, hospitals—should give preference to local farms and businesses, both to secure and stabilize markets and to improve the quality of products and services. When Chattanooga awarded its contract for the manufacture of electric buses to AVS, a local company, they not only helped create local jobs but got a partner close enough to them to work through problems quickly, collaboratively and effectively. Washington State and Minnesota both have incentives for solar installers to use PV panels manufactured in-state, and in both cases, this has helped propel a rapid growth in business and jobs.

6. **Reduce the barriers and burdens—licensing, fees, regulations—on home-based businesses, start-ups, and businesses launched by young people and minority entrepreneurs.** In my experience, a growing body of young folks want to try their hand at entrepreneurship, as do women and people of color. In most communities, a fairly substantial number are already doing this, but under the table. A number of things keeps most of these folks from fully launching their business ideas, and one of those is the number of hoops they have to jump through.

Integrating Social, Economic, and Ecological Goals

Four policy changes, all driven by the goal of promoting triple-bottom-line businesses and those that internalize rather than externalize their costs:

1. **Reward businesses that pay well, that provide benefits and opportunities for advancement, and that invest in their workers,** especially through Employee Stock Ownership Programs and similar means of investing in the workers. Most current economic incentives turn on one factor, the promise of job creation. Rooted in notions of growth and trickle-down prosperity, these policies support business investment, expansion, and even relocation largely based on the number of jobs they promise. Putting aside the fact that many of these promises often don't materialize, we should be focusing public dollars and incentives on good jobs and good companies, as PUSH Buffalo has done with "high-road contractors" committed to good jobs with good pay.

2. **Make it easier to form cooperatives, B-corps, and other forms of enterprises that strive to integrate economic, social. and environmental objectives.** Several states now allow for B-corps, but the majority do not. Outdated notions, like Milton Friedman's oft-quoted statement that "the only socially responsible requirement for business is to maximize its profit," still hold sway with too many legislators.

3. **Ease restrictions, bond requirements, and other obstacles to speed the conversion of vacant land, unused buildings, and idle or endangered land to be brought into productive use.** From Grand Rapids to Bristol, mixed-use and in-fill development have helped regenerate urban centers while bringing businesses and homes closer together, to the benefit of both. Vacant lots in Detroit and Buffalo are being converted to gardens, farms, and parks. Policies that reward such conversion and others that make it expensive for absentee landlords to allow lots to continue to decline both help spur this critical transformation.

4. **Create both the incentives and means to transfer farm, forest, and other productive land from retired or older farmers to the next generation.** At present, with the advanced age of most farmers, literally tens of millions of acres are at risk of conversion to "development." In fact, the acquisition of farmland for future speculation is well under way, with very wealthy investors adding "land" to their portfolios of assets. Policies that help maintain land in its productive use, such as Purchase of Development Rights, land trusts, and land banks, need to be dramatically expanded and adequately funded if we want to avoid a massive shift and concentration of farm and forest land.

Invest in Areas of Great Need as Well as Those of Great Opportunity

Three policy areas offer potential to hasten development of new, sustainable businesses and technologies, particularly in regions dependent upon industries in steep decline:

1. **Provide direct public investment, incentivize private investment, and build critical supports for communities and regions undergoing major economic shifts,** including those historically dependent on tobacco, mining, timbering, commercial fishing, and other such industries. In Virginia, North Carolina, and Kentucky, state economic development agencies are working with federal agencies, such

as USDA and the Appalachian Regional Commission, and Tobacco Settlement funds to help diversify the agricultural base in response to a 70 percent decline in the number of tobacco farmers since 2002.[51] This has meant direct investment in promising new farming enterprises, in regional aggregation and processing facilities, as well as entirely new economic sectors, most notably music, culture, and nature-based tourism. While these investments have helped, they need to be wedded to procurement policies that help build large and stable markets, and with policies that remove obstacles to starting small businesses.

2. **As the transition to cleaner, renewable energy continues, fossil fuel-dependent regions must not be abandoned, but enabled to build a much more diverse and sustainable economic base.** From the coalfields of Appalachia and the Powder River Basin to coastal fishing communities, the very people who supplied the nation with so much cheap energy and food are largely being ignored. Public policies should encourage and support the development of promising innovations in these areas, from Brendan Smith's 3-D ocean farming, to efforts to reclaim vast areas of stripped mine land with native hardwoods, which have potential to generate income while restoring, to some degree at least, degraded landscapes. In my area, someone described the effort needed as "a Marshall Plan for the mountains."

3. **Support emerging businesses and technologies that better equip us to live within our means in the coming years,** from community solar arrays in Colorado to facilities turning by-products from animal and vegetable processing into truly clean fuel. Not far from Abingdon, in the town of Radford, Virginia, ACME Panel builds Structurally Insulated Panels that reduce energy use by 50 percent in homes, offices, and commercial buildings while also making these structures far stronger in storms. Owner Joe Fortier built his business in a refurbished vacant schoolhouse, adding enough solar panels to provide nearly 75 percent of the energy used in their manufacturing process. Policies should include investment in research partnerships for waste reduction, alternative energy, soil carbon sequestration, and other cutting edge tools for sustainability; local procurement preferences in universities, hospitals, and other "anchor institutions"; and direct public investment in community based infrastructure.

Transition Two: Recap and Looking Forward

Bottom-up, living economies are emerging in cities, towns, and rural areas across the country as more and more communities quit waiting for jobs and prosperity to trickle down. In spite of tremendous disadvantages in tax, trade, and economic policies, and comparatively minimal resources with which to work, much progress has been made. Key lessons from this transition include:

1. Local living economies build on and emulate the transition toward greater self-reliance in their emphasis on more diversified, locally focused economies that address real needs, build capacity for innovation and frugality (making the most of what you have), and reduce dependence on outside inputs or single large employers. More self-reliant, less dependent households are also a source of innovation and entrepreneurship that can feed into local living economies.
2. The close connection to place and the inclination to address real needs in bottom-up economies have also propelled more triple-bottom-line businesses, that is, those that measure and value their social and ecological "profits" as well.
3. The bottom-up nature of these economies—based on place, led by local people—is one of their fundamental strengths. However, it can also limit their development when being "local" translates to a neglect of a strategy for broader recognition, investment, and supportive public policy. "Leave us alone" works up to a point but is ultimately self-defeating. Emerging local economies must be linked, regionally and nationally.
4. Local living economies are emerging in most areas of the country, from urban centers to small towns and rural communities. It is nevertheless true that in most cases, the preponderance of business owners, local leaders, and consumers supporting these emerging economies are mostly white or somewhat more affluent. There are plenty of exceptions to this, in Buffalo, in Philadelphia, in Oakland, and in some small towns. But at this point they remain exceptions to the rule. The experiences and strategies taking hold in these communities should be highlighted, supported, and adapted much more widely.

Up next: The second transition, from *trickle-down problems to bottom-up economic solutions,* will not on its own solve our biggest problems. But it dovetails very well with the first transition to *more productive households and self-reliant communities,* and with the third, toward *broadly shared prosperity and far greater worker and community capital,* which will be discussed in chapter 4. Together, these three transitions can form the basis for an economy that works for people, their communities, and the environment.

Further Reading

Flaccavento, Anthony. "Is Local Food Affordable for Ordinary Folks? A Comparison of Farmers Markets and Supermarkets in Nineteen Communities in the Southeast." SCALE. November 1, 2011. www.ruralscale.com.

Mitchell, Stacy. *Big Box Swindle.* Boston: Beacon, 2006.

O'Hara, Jeffrey K. "Market Forces: Creating Jobs through Public Investment in Local and Regional Food Systems." Union of Concerned Scientists, August 2011. www.ucsusa.org.

Shuman, Michael. *Local Dollars, Local Sense: How to Shift Your Money from Wall Street to Main Street and Achieve Real Prosperity.* White River Junction, VT: Chelsea Green, 2012.

Stout, Lynn. *The Shareholder Value Myth: How Putting Shareholders First Harms Investors, Corporations, and the Public.* San Francisco: Berrett-Koehler, 2012.

4

Building Broadly Based and Durable Prosperity

From Concentrated Wealth and Widespread Insecurity to Worker Ownership and Community Capital

The reality of democracy is far from ideal—but still the democratic values of liberty, justice, and equality remain our ideals. Where are the corollary ideals in the world of the economy? . . . It's time to dream a deeper dream, the dream of an economy that is built around ideals like fairness, community, and sustainability—an economy that in its normal functioning tends to create fair and just outcomes, benefits the many rather than the few, and enables an enduring human presence on a flourishing earth.
—Marjorie Kelly, *Owning Our Future*

We need to steer money . . . towards life, towards the enterprises that enhance the quality of life, that preserve and restore fertility, biodiversity and the health of bioregions and communities and the households that live in them, and away from enterprises that degrade quality in the name of quantity. . . . We need to start thinking about money . . . as irrigation for the field of our intentions.
—Woody Tasch, *Inquiries into the Nature of Slow Money*

In the latter part of the 1990s, there was a lot of talk in southwest Virginia and neighboring states about the steady decline in tobacco farming in the region. It would be five more years before the federal tobacco program came to an end, but both the amount of tobacco being raised and the profitability in doing so had been falling sharply for some time. Part of this had resulted from the decline in tobacco use in the United States, but it was also due to cheaper overseas tobacco. Martin Miles, mentioned in this

A former tobacco barn, previously owned by Martin Miles, was converted to the Appalachian Harvest produce packing and aggregation center. Author's collection.

work's introduction, had seen his "allotment"—the amount of poundage he was entitled to grow—drop from nearly 100.000 pounds to just 12,000, or about 6 acres of production. That's a big part of why Martin was looking for alternatives, and part of why he offered to let us use his barn as a packing shed.

Martin's barn was in Stickleyville, a tiny town in rural Lee County, Virginia. This is the hinterlands of Virginia, 350 miles from Richmond, more than 400 miles from Washington, D.C. In fact, the western edge of the county is due south of Detroit. Even though it was far from population centers in the Northeast, Martin's barn was relatively close to farmers not only in Lee County but in Scott County and parts of Tennessee as well. And as it turns out, a manageable distance from markets in Asheville, Abingdon, and even Atlanta.

The barn itself was fairly typical, about 7,000 square feet, in decent condition, with a small loft in one area, full of assorted farm-related junk. By the time we had begun to look at the barn, we had a handful of farmers more or less committed to growing organic produce, and three supermarket chains more or less committed to buying it. There were more "maybes" than solid agreements, but enough of them to give it a try. The missing piece was a place to bring it all together before loading the produce onto the truck. Oh, and there was no truck, either.

In the early spring of 2000, a handful of farmers and a couple of staff people from Appalachian Sustainable Development (ASD) began the work of turning the barn into the central packing facility that would link small farmers with large buyers. We had only part of the barn to work with, as Martin still needed a portion of it to hang his tobacco come September. We selected one bay, 16 feet wide by 96 feet long, and with help from the local Job Corps, we cleaned and leveled it, poured a concrete pad, cut some larger doors, and fashioned something of a loading dock. The Kroger store in Abingdon was upgrading its coolers, so we got the old one, which we took apart, moved to Stickleyville, and reassembled at the back end of that bay. We bought a secondhand compressor to complete the cooler. We then purchased a small washing and grading line for about four thousand dollars, and a couple of pallet jacks to move things around. We cleared a space in the loft to make room for the produce boxes we'd soon be ordering.

Not long before the produce started coming in, we bought a small refrigerated delivery truck with more miles on it than we cared to think about. By that June, with the hard work of several volunteers and an investment of roughly twenty-five thousand dollars, we had us a "packinghouse." Within a few years, ASD had purchased the barn from Martin—he'd basically been loaning it to us, even as we built on and around it—converted the other bays to packing areas, built a 3,000-square-foot addition, doubled the cooler space, and added two more grading lines. And a couple more trucks.

While ownership of the facility transferred from one local individual to a community-based non-profit organization (ASD), it remained tightly bound to the local community. By that time we were moving many tons of local, organically raised produce and free-range eggs to supermarkets, most of which were within 150 miles of the farms. The packinghouse had become, in essence, a piece of "community capital," a facility that created access to large, relatively well-paying markets for farmers who could not afford to set up their own washing, grading, cooling, and shipping facilities. And though we invested far more than twenty-five thousand dollars over the years of expansion and upgrading, the total cost remained dramatically less than what it would have been to individually equip the nearly one hundred farmers who sold through Appalachian Harvest over the first several years. No less important, it helped create a relatively tightly knit group with a sense that "we're all in this together." That's no small thing among farmers.

The examples below will allow us to explore three different ways in which communities are building the foundations of wealth and capacity, beginning with the idea of *community capital*. We'll also look at *cooperatives* and other forms of worker ownership and, finally, at ways to keep wealth from "leaking" out of communities, what I'm calling *retained capital*. All three approaches are critical to the emergence of the third transition *from concentrated wealth and widespread insecurity to worker ownership and community capital*. But first, a few words about capital.

What Is Capital?

We all know the old saying, "Give a man a fish and feed him for a day. Teach him how to fish and feed him for a lifetime." There's no doubt some truth to this, but the saying always made me want to ask, "What if he doesn't have nets, or a boat, or access to the water?" This question is more than hypothetical, because for many people in economic hardship, it is not only or even necessarily a lack of knowledge or skill that keeps them in poverty but rather a lack of capital—the boats, the nets, and the access to resources. This gap in access to productive resources has, in many cases, impacted whole communities, particularly urban communities of color but certainly including predominantly white, rural places as well. This is one of the reasons why our "rising tide" of economic output isn't "lifting all boats."

Capital, properly designed, makes us more productive. It takes many forms, from a farm tractor to a solar pump that increases access to underground water. Tools, equipment, technologies, structures, and facilities are all types of capital. (So are land and other natural resources, but they're a bit different, so we'll come back to them in a moment.) Capital expands possibilities and makes human labor more productive. Ten years ago, I bought a "bed shaper" to pull behind my tractor. This simple but well-designed piece of equipment enables me to make raised beds, put my irrigation in place, and lay down mulch, all in one pass. A 100-foot-long raised bed now takes me about two minutes to make, compared to an hour or more of hard work when I did it all by hand. (The first time I ever used my bed shaper, I looked back at the perfectly formed bed emerging behind my tractor and thought I'd died and gone to heaven!) This little piece of capital has made my small, rather low-tech farm operation considerably more productive, and this phase of the work dramatically less physically demanding.

Capital also can be used to change the form of something from a raw material to a useable product, whether that is converting coal into steam and then into electricity, or turning blemished apples into cider. It is also used to process and extend the life of things (canning, freezing, drying) and to create access to more places, markets, or opportunities.

In recent years, we have increasingly confused *money* with *capital,* much as we've done with money and wealth. Having a net worth of millions of dollars certainly gives you the means to purchase or build capital, but it is not capital in itself, in spite of what you might find in the textbooks. If a flood devastates your town and you're trapped on the roof, a boat would be much more valuable to you than a wad of cash. A working-class neighborhood where lots of folks heat with wood is likely to come through an ice storm–induced power outage better than an affluent suburb, at least in the immediate aftermath. Money, including stocks and bonds, is not productive in and of itself.

"Ecological capital"—soils, forests, grasslands, lakes, rivers, oceans, etc.—are even more important to human survival than human-made capital, as they provide the ultimate foundation upon which our lives depend. Ecological capital is essential to our survival as both "source" and "sink," that is, the source for stuff (oil, wood, food) and the sink for our wastes and leftovers. Regardless of whether we're discussing "renewable" or "nonrenewable" resources, it is possible to use any form of ecological capital too fast, and to clog nature's sinks with too much waste. Excess carbon in the atmosphere, for instance.

The common characteristic shared between ecological and human-made capital is that *both represent a form of savings:* They can grow in value over time or depreciate; they can enable us to invest and create additional wealth; and they can be used for income when things are tight. Capital can be "drawn down" too quickly, just like people can use up their savings too fast. If it is not replenished or maintained, this inevitably happens. Buildings and equipment must be maintained, added to, and periodically fixed if we want them to last, just as soil must be maintained and replenished with organic matter and good farming practices. And almost invariably, it is less expensive to do this upkeep than to deplete things and then try to fix or replace them. As one example, it takes between 150 and 300 years to generate an inch of topsoil in nature, so letting it wash away or degrade is very costly.

While you may have checked out of Economics 101 when the distinction between "savings" and "income" was being made, it is actually enormously important, for two reasons: First, when capital is treated as savings, our current tax and business laws allow companies to save money by claiming "depreciation" of their assets. This is certainly abused at times, but it stems from the fact that capital, as a form of savings, gets used up over time. That depreciation is a cost for the business, and by extension, its customers. So, we tend to place a lot of importance on the value of capital. The problem is that ecological capital is *not* treated as savings, not as an asset that can depreciate over time, but only as a onetime input cost. So, we tend to use our land, water, and other ecological assets more like income, rather than treating them as savings; that is, far beyond rates of natural renewal.

There's a second problem with how we treat capital. At the other end of the spectrum, human-made capital is now so favored over income by our tax code and economic policies that people who have lots of it can readily accumulate more and more, "store it away," so to speak, at minimal cost. As just one (of many) examples, tax rates on income from dividends and capital gains are far lower than middle-income tax rates, meaning that if you make money from the stock market or from owning and selling buildings and other capital, you pay much less than doctors, teachers, and plumbers. Meanwhile the vast majority of people depend on *income,* which is less secure, much more heavily taxed, and, over the last three decades, stagnant or in decline.

For capital to benefit the economy it must be put to use, widely and thoughtfully. By "thoughtfully," I mean to solve real problems, to create broader prosperity. Recent experience clearly demonstrates that when the vast majority of capital is held by a handful of people, it is not used widely or thoughtfully, but primarily to benefit those who already have it. This perpetuation of the advantages of capital is clearly demonstrated in both the economic realm, where the share of all wealth held by the very richest continues to increase, and in the political realm, where both legislative and court decisions increasingly favor the very wealthy (much more about that in chapter 7). This is why we need to "capitalize" producers, workers, consumers, and communities as one part of the strategy for overcoming the great concentration of wealth in our nation. Let's look at how that's being done in a variety of places.

Emerging Examples of Community Capital and Local Wealth-Building Strategies

Community Capital

Into the Great Plains

Martin's barn, retrofitted into a produce packinghouse, is one very simple form of community capital, as it is owned by and built for the benefit of small farmers in the region. It effectively "capitalizes" scores of farmers at a fraction of the cost. Such aggregation centers, sometimes called "food hubs," have emerged in many parts of the country, from Philadelphia to Wisconsin. We'll look at another innovative example from eastern North Carolina later in this chapter. But first, let's take a break from food.

In the small town of Galesburg, Illinois, the Sustainable Business Center (SBC) emerged in 2010. There had been some previous efforts to cultivate entrepreneurship and small businesses, but this was the first to focus on triple-bottom-line businesses. For a midwestern town of a little more than thirty thousand people, this was a bold step. Galesburg had seen its manufacturing base sharply decline, and one of the last of those was a regional manufacturing and distribution center for Carhartt. To its credit, when Carhartt closed its doors, it donated the building to the Seattle-based Human Links Foundation, which then gave it back to the community as an incubator.

The Center is located on 10 acres of land, nearly 2 acres of which are under roof. The facilities were refurbished after the donation, with improved efficiency in heating and cooling, lighting, and other features. The Center's mission is to cultivate and support the development of sustainable businesses, focusing on the following sectors: renewable energy, energy efficiency, conservation, and local and sustainable food. Nearly two-thirds of the money it took to develop and launch the Center came from the private sector, including businesses and individual investors.

Like most all business incubators, the SBC provides affordable rental space, strong IT services, basic office and business support services, and a wide range of training and technical assistance to strengthen basic business practices. They also encourage and assist businesses in moving toward greater sustainability. A small portion of the space is for offices, while more than 90 percent is designed for manufacturing, warehousing, and product development. A commercial kitchen incubator opened in 2011 to help food entrepreneurs test and develop food products made from sustainably sourced ingredients; an on-site restaurant, "En Season," allows for test marketing of some of these food products, while also featuring produce and meats from local farmers.

The Sustainable Business Center is not yet at capacity, but some of the enterprises using their facilities include:

- Intellihot Green Technologies, the first U.S.-based manufacturer of high-efficiency tankless water heaters. In addition to saving energy, the system they've developed enables the user to have hot water immediately rather than the usual wait with such heaters.
- Pennycress Energy Company, which is building markets for bio-diesel made from pennycress, a low-input winter cover crop that can maintain the soil quality on small farms while also providing a source for biodiesel and jet fuel.
- Sitka Salmon Shares, which connects consumers in the Midwest and other parts of the country with sustainably harvested, wild-caught salmon from southeast Alaska.
- Jerry's Mojo, a local coffee roaster that is the first to also create a mobile coffee shop, focused on organic and Fair Trade coffees.
- One business has "graduated" from the incubator. Lamboo, which makes building materials out of bamboo, is now on its own and growing rapidly.

The Center is not without its share of challenges. According to Cindy Teel, the facility manager, it takes a great deal of community outreach and education to overcome some negative connotations around "sustainability" that are common in rural communities (believe me, I know!), as well as the perception that they are a government agency, which they are not. They have also struggled to strike a balance between promoting environmental responsibility while promoting use of the facility. The requirement that food businesses use only organic ingredients as a condition of use of the kitchen incubator has, unfortunately, proven to be a major obstacle for local food businesses and is being reconsidered.[1] Even with the challenges, the Sustainable Business Center has nevertheless helped incubate several successful companies that are not only creating jobs but are helping to build the "living economy" discussed in the chapter 3.

Down to the Gulf

The Propeller Social Innovation Center grew out of the desire to cultivate successful small businesses that would in turn create jobs, while simultaneously supporting people working to address some of New Orleans's social and environmental challenges. Linking the goals of economic development with improvements in the community's social and ecological conditions was fundamental to the vision of founder Andrea Chen. A former teacher as well as a trainer of teachers, Andrea began discussions with Morgan Williams in 2006 about how to build on the emergence of community-oriented businesses they saw as part of the recovery from Hurricane Katrina. Like the Sustainable Business Center in Illinois, Propeller's founders and investors were convinced that "jobs versus the environment" was a false and counterproductive choice; they instead adopted the mission to "help launch social and environmental ventures to address local challenges."

Launched in 2009, Propeller has built a unique and holistic system to support emerging "social enterprises." This includes, first of all, a business incubator with space tailored for enterprises at almost any stage of development. The 10,000-square-foot facility, formerly a car rim shop, is LEED-certified, indicating that good environmental, energy, and waste-reduction features are built into the design. It includes private office space for from $600 to $770 per month, all the way down to a "ten-day pass" for $80, allowing people to try the space out, meet others starting social ventures, and learn more precisely what they might need. In between those two ends, one can rent a "co-working desk," sort of an "un-cubicle," as these spaces put creative entrepreneurs in proximity to one another in a very open area with natural light, business and IT support, and free coffee or tea. Propeller's leaders are clear that they want to provide more than high-quality space at below-market prices; they want to help nurture the creative, problem-solving energy that New Orleans—and so many other places—so urgently needs.

In addition to the incubator, Propeller also hosts its "Accelerator," an intensive training and mentorship effort designed to build the capacity of emerging social entrepreneurs. The Accelerator Fellowship program, begun in 2011, is at the center of this work. Each year a group of a dozen or so social entrepreneurs are selected from among many more applicants. Their enterprises can be of many kinds, but they generally fall within one of Propeller's four target areas: (1) healthy food access and local food economy; (2) water management, including conservation, water quality, and coastal erosion control; (3) public health, especially focused on communities or people with limited access; and (4) public education.

Examples of some of the "social enterprises" that have been launched with help from Propeller include:

- Youth Rebuilding New Orleans, begun in 2012, which purchases and rehabs dilapidated buildings, using primarily volunteer labor. The buildings are then sold to teachers and others at very affordable costs, helping to repopulate neighborhoods devastated by Katrina and its aftermath.
- The Justice and Accountability Center, which since 2012, has worked with 1,500 nonviolent offenders, helping them find and keep work rather than return to prison.
- The Farm City Initiative, launched in 2013, which has facilitated 120 agricultural redevelopment projects throughout New Orleans.

Accelerator fellows receive twelve months of concerted support, including one-on-one mentoring from consultants with expertise in their area, access to a network of more than one hundred business professionals; regular classes and training opportunities; and help learning to deal with regulatory and public policy challenges their businesses may face. The latter includes building their confidence and skills in advocacy for appropriate changes. They also receive free space at the incubator during their training, followed by a 50 percent discount rate after completing the training.

In its first three years, the Propeller Accelerator has incubated thirty-five new social ventures, which together have created more than one hundred full-time and part-time jobs. More than $6 million in investment and external financing has been generated for these enterprises.[2] Similar accelerators have begun to emerge in other communities, including Accelerate Appalachia, an Asheville, North Carolina, initiative focused on nature-based businesses in western North Carolina. Under the leadership of Sara Day Evans, Accelerate Appalachia is helping to launch and grow triple-bottom-line enterprises, many with strong connections to the region and its land.

Back to the Mountains

Although it grows in many parts of the United States, there is something about the wild ramp that seems particularly well-suited to the Appalachians. Like other "wild edibles"—think of "dry land fish" (morel mushrooms), pawpaws, or creasy greens—the wild ramp has a very strong, distinctive flavor, a limited season for harvesting, and devoted followers. Maybe that's why Gail Patton and other local leaders chose that name for their local food store in Huntington, West Virginia.

When the Wild Ramp Local Food store opened in July 2012, it seemed like quite a gamble. Retail, especially retail food, is a tough business with very small margins. People have become accustomed to the seeming ubiquitous abundance of foods, especially in supermarkets where you can get just about anything, anytime, anywhere. How can a small local store, carrying *only* products from its local area and region, possibly compete with that? Well, first, the Wild Ramp did not come out of the blue but followed nearly a year of community conversations, discussions with farmers, and

The Wild Ramp, the town's only "all-local" grocer, moved into the old Central Market as it outgrew its first site in Huntington, West Virginia. Courtesy of Shelly Keeney, the Wild Ramp.

visits to and from other community food initiatives. There seemed to be a clear demand for more availability of fresh produce and meats, which the city's farmers market alone was not able to meet.

Wild Ramp is structured as a non-profit enterprise, a business that can earn revenues, but where any "profits" must be put toward their social mission, not accrue to the board of directors. They set up the business to create good markets for local produce, meats, cheese, and other food products while dramatically increasing both the season and hours during which consumers could buy these products. Most farmers markets, even the very good ones, are only open for one or two days each week, and then typically for about half a day or so. Wild Ramp is open six days per week, from morning to early evening, year-round. All of their products come from within 250 miles of Huntington; three-fourths come from within just 50 miles. Farmers and food entrepreneurs sell their products on a consignment basis, keeping 90 percent of the sales price, which they set themselves. The store helps with displays and signage, provides cooling and freezing, and offers feedback on pricing, packaging, and other things that will help producers increase their sales. Consignment is riskier for a farmer, especially those with perishable products like produce, and may not work for everyone. But selling into most mainstream grocers and supermarkets means that you're likely to get half or less of the final sales price, not 90 percent of the value. That makes this risk worth taking for some farmers.

In just over two years since opening, Wild Ramp has paid out in excess of $600,000 to nearly 160 farmers in the region. In a town of fewer than fifty thousand people, in an area not known for its "foodies," this represents an impressive launch for a new and different type of community business.[3] The growth has been so strong that the Wild Ramp has already had to move to a larger location, a 2,500-square-foot space in the town's historic Central City Market building.[4] And 2,500 hundred square feet is still quite small, well under one-tenth of the typical modern supermarket. Nevertheless, it clearly represents a critical piece of community capital that is energizing farmers, entrepreneurs, consumers, and local leaders.

These four examples of community capital—a barn turned into a packing shed, a sustainable business center with a commercial kitchen, a social enterprise incubator and accelerator, and a small, all-local grocery store—have each contributed to the broader wealth and capacity of their respective communities. And many other forms of capacity-building community capital are emerging as well, including Chattanooga's high-speed fiber optic network, attractive especially to younger entrepreneurs with innovative ideas. These and many other types of community capital nurture farms and businesses through lower-cost access to equipment and space, through vibrant training and technical assistance, through access to markets and additional investment. And they do what capital is supposed to do, making enterprises more productive and better equipped to meet their own needs while contributing to the well-being of their communities.

Another way of capitalizing local people and communities is through cooperatives, to which we'll now turn our focus.

Cooperatives and Worker Ownership

Chilly New England

Conversations about sustainability, organic food, and the like often get bogged down around one of two charges: they are too pricey for working folks and lower-income families; and the emphasis on environmental conservation or higher wages ends up costing jobs and shutting down businesses. From its very first days in 2002, Co-op Power was determined to refute those claims.

Based in Massachusetts and southern Vermont, Co-op Power is a multiracial, multiclass, consumer-owned cooperative with a mission to foster economic development that works for the environment and for people and communities who've largely been left out of past economic strategies. They do this through a series of *local organizing councils,* of which they now have six. With help from Co-op Power staff and its wide base of skilled professional volunteers, the councils conceive, design, and help launch businesses in their communities, including cooperatives, non-profit businesses, and others that can demonstrate a clear community purpose and foundation. Co-op Power's focus is on energy-related businesses, including alternative energy, energy efficiency, and energy services.

Energia, based in Holyoke, Massachusetts, provides one example of the type of business Co-op Power has helped foster. Begun in 2009, Energia provides energy audits, weatherization, and high-performance insulation to commercial, community, and residential buildings, including many affordable housing developments. In 2010, the business completed energy and insulation improvements on roughly one hundred homes with a couple of small crews. By 2014, the company was employing twenty-eight people, who weatherized more than six hundred single-family homes, and an even greater number of multifamily, apartment, and commercial units. The employees, who average just twenty-four years of age, many with little or no work history, have an ownership share in the enterprise. In 2014, they saw their first profit-sharing payments, with dividends ranging from $500 to $1,500.[5]

Additionally, Co-op Power and two other community-based organizations—Nuestras Raices and Nueva Esperanza—have ownership stake in the company. In this way, Energia is helping to capitalize both workers in the community and some of the local organizations doing critically needed work. This has helped build the company while making homes and businesses in the community more comfortable and more affordable.

To get Energia and other businesses off the ground, Co-op Power has built its own base of capital, with three streams of funds: $320,000 in member equity (that is, the membership contributions of its 450 members); $800,000 in member loans, which return an average of 4.5 percent; and another $850,000 in financing from local banks and financial institutions. In a community generally considered to be "poor," they have found and mobilized a considerable amount of local resources.[6] In addition to Energia, Co-op Power has worked with its other local organizing councils to capitalize and launch several other community-based businesses, including five solar-panel installation companies, two electricians with a green focus, and a company that manufactures and retrofits windows to improve energy efficiency. In each case, community needs and interests were matched with the investment resources of Co-op Power and its extraordinary network of resource people, including lawyers, accountants, green building professionals, engineers, and many more. In each case they asked, "What work needs to be done?" rather than, "Where are the jobs?"

Two other ventures illuminate the resourcefulness of Co-op Power and its willingness to take some risks in partnership with its members and their communities. The community solar program was started in 2012, when Co-op Power joined forces with the Brattleboro Food Cooperative to build a community solar array, similar to the community solar systems we've discussed in Colorado and elsewhere. Since they got their feet wet with this project in southern Vermont, the community solar program has expanded, now having installed fifty solar hot water systems and twenty-five renewable energy systems in communities throughout their area.[7]

Perhaps their most ambitious enterprise of all is set to open in 2016. In the works for nearly eight years now, Northeast Biodiesel will soon be processing waste oil from hundreds of restaurants, dining halls, and institutions into as much as 3 million gallons of biodiesel each year. The development of Northeast Biodiesel has been complex, from obtaining licenses from the Department of Transportation and EPA, to lining up "suppliers" of the waste oil, and an efficient means to collect it. The nearly $4 million cost has been funded in part through Co-op Power's own, member resources, but outside investment has also been required. It is a testimony to the persuasiveness of Executive Director Lynn Bandener and to the support for Co-op Power that these external investors agreed to provide nearly two-thirds of the total funds, but hold only a 25 percent stake in the company.[8]

The Flatlands of North Carolina

Eastern Carolina Organics (ECO) was founded out of the desire of farmers and local food activists to build large, well-paying markets for organic farmers in North Carolina. Begun with help from the Carolina Farm Stewardship Association in 2004, ECO grew quickly, from less than $200,000 their first year to nearly $4 million in sales in 2014. Considered by many to be one of the most effective and successful food hubs, ECO is an extraordinary example of bootstrapping. After an initial grant of just $48,000 from the Golden Leaf Fund, ECO and its farmers have been entirely self-funded for a decade. Like many food hubs, ECO retains 20 percent of every sale to cover aggregation, distribution, and marketing, but unlike most others, they were able to use that small percentage to be self-sustaining within the first two years of operation.

ECO capitalizes its farmers in a number of ways, but we'll focus here on two. First, like Appalachian Harvest and its facility, ECO has from the outset maintained an aggregation and distribution center—a "packing shed"—to which farmers bring their products, from where it is used to fill the orders of its customers. Some of these are pretty good-size farmers, while many more are small to midsize growers. All of them contribute to filling the orders from more than two dozen buying clubs, scores of restaurants, and a number of grocers and large supermarkets. Because all of their produce is certified organic, they have been able to build a consistent market presence and to maintain pretty good prices. The 80 percent that farmers keep ends up being substantially more than they would be able to get in almost any other wholesale outlet, in part because that's a much higher percentage than farmers usually get, and also because of the better end-price for high-quality organic food.

The facility itself is part of the key to their success. As the volume of produce ECO was selling and distribution steadily expanded, they soon outgrew their original facility. In 2012, they bought an old metal shell building with loans from the Self-Help Credit Union and the Natural Capital Investment Fund. By the 2013 season, they had readied the large building—26,000 square feet—for their own use, and to accommodate other local and sustainable enterprises.[9] The facility includes abundant cooler and freezer space, a large "common" warehousing area, loading docks, and office space. The partnership between ECO and its tenants has helped them generate funds to help pay off their loans (the first loans since their founding), while also providing a quality, lower-cost space for businesses with similar social and environmental goals. In many ways they resemble both the Sustainable Business Center in Illinois and the Propeller Incubator in Louisiana, except that the building owner itself uses a portion of the facility to operate its own business. It all adds up to ECO creating and steadily expanding market access, at almost no cost, to farmers of all sizes, much as Appalachian Harvest and other food hubs are doing.

The other major way in which ECO capitalizes its community is through its own co-op-like structure. Legally, they are an LLC, a Limited Liability Corporation. But in their case, 40 percent of the ownership is held by a group of about a dozen "anchor farmers," while the other 60 percent is owned by the staff, making it fully owned by the folks who supply and operate the business. The governance is by a board of directors that includes farmers, staff, and other stakeholders.[10] This hybrid structure seems to have worked very well, not only in making ECO profitable in a low-margin business but in ensuring that the business is truly locally rooted, and that it uses its resources, including the facility, to the benefit of the community. It is similar to Employee Stock Ownership Programs, or ESOPs, in that it returns not only "wages" (in this case, the farmers' sales and the staff salaries) but also a share of the profits. There are more than eleven thousand companies in the United States that have used ESOPs to provide complete or partial ownership to employees, and like cooperatives, these businesses are more productive and longer lasting than those without employee ownership. Worker ownership isn't just good for the workers; it's good for the community and economy as well.

The Great Southwest

The first couple of times I visited New Mexico, I was struck by its beauty, the amazing colors in the rocks and mountains, and the soothing quality of the ever-present adobe homes and buildings. It also hit me how much less green there was than back East. I was amazed that folks, especially farmers, could make it work in a place with so much less water. I imagined that they were probably a pretty resourceful lot, frugal, accustomed to making the most of what they had. Like the more self-reliant communities described in chapter 2.

No doubt that way of thinking had something to do with the founding and success of La Montañita Cooperative. Starting out, like so many other "buying clubs," in someone's basement, La Montañita is now the biggest consumer-based cooperative in the Southwest, with more than seventeen thousand members. Six different store locations make it possible for thousands of people to buy local and sustainably produced foods in Albuquerque, Santa Fe, and Gallup, New Mexico. The stores do some of their own purchasing but are primarily supplied by La Montañita's central warehouse, the Co-op Distribution Center (CDC), based in Albuquerque. The 18,000-square-foot facility has helped all the stores increase their product offerings and find a more reliable

Chile peppers, an important part of traditional cuisine in New Mexico, dry outside of the La Montañita facility in Albuquerque, New Mexico. Courtesy of La Montañita Cooperative.

and consistent supply of healthy foods. For farmers, the central facility enables them to deliver more volume to one place rather than having to deliver to multiple stores. The CDC's first priority is to supply its six member stores, though it also sells to more than one hundred additional outlets, including restaurants, schools, and other grocers.[11]

La Montañita works with more than one hundred farmers and food entrepreneurs and is New Mexico's biggest retail buyer of local farm products. Most of the farms from which they buy use organic or sustainable production practices, along with humane treatment of animals for ranchers and livestock producers. Along with most of the standard fruits, vegetables, and meats you'd see in a mainstream grocer, the co-op puts special emphasis on foods particular to their region, such as the famous New Mexico chili peppers.

In addition to the six retail stores and the Co-op Distribution Center, La Montañita also operates a micro-loan fund, financed entirely by member investment contributions. Through a partnership with the New Mexico Educators Federal Credit Union, member contributions provide collateral, enabling the credit union to extend loans under the terms and conditions specified by La Montañita. The fund, known as LAM (short for La Montañita), is focused on farm- and food-related businesses based in New Mexico, with a commitment to ecological stewardship and fair labor practices. A committee appointed by the Co-op's board reviews the loans and makes decisions, while the credit union actually administers the loan. In the two and a half years since its establishment, seventeen sustainable food businesses have received loans through the LAM fund, in amounts ranging from $400 to $27,500. All of these funds come from cooperative members.[12] According to Robin Seydel, who manages membership for the Co-op, repayment rates on these loans have been excellent, with few defaults thus far.

La Montañita is an especially well-developed model of community capitalization, encompassing all three of the types of local capital we are considering. Their six storefronts provide access to healthy local foods and other necessities in both urban and rural communities, while the central warehouse creates substantial market access for local farmers and food entrepreneurs. All of these facilities are clearly examples of community capital. La Montañita is a consumer- and worker-owned cooperative, helping to capitalize more than seventeen thousand individuals, many of whom would otherwise have limited means to accrue savings and capital. And the LAM loan fund is an example of our third form of local wealth building, retained capital, to which we now turn our attention.

Retained Capital

The idea of "plugging leaks" has long been central to folks involved in home weatherization and other energy-efficiency efforts. A drafty house, we all know, "leaks" its warm air to the outside, increasing the amount of heat—and therefore energy and cost—that needs to be constantly added back. This is why energy audits, which identify those leaky areas, are always a first step before weatherization work is done or new heating and cooling systems are introduced. The warm air in your house is an asset that you've paid for in some way, whether that's the monthly electric bill or time spent cutting wood. It's common sense to try to hold on to as much of that asset as you can.

As Michael Shuman and others have pointed out, the same principle applies in a very real way to local economies. When Shuman speaks of economic leakages, he is talking about economic opportunities and assets that are allowed to dissipate, to leak out of the community. They then must be replaced by additional resources from outside the community. When young people with creativity, energy, and education leave their home communities because they see little opportunity, this represents an enormous leakage of talent and potential productivity. This is a common problem, especially for rural areas. Similarly, when young people of color are incarcerated for non-violent and petty crimes at double the rate of middle-class white kids, as is the case, this is a major leakage of potential from those communities. (Contrary to most media portrayals of this issue, many of these young folks are holding down jobs, are pursuing a trade or education, or are trying to be responsible parents when this occurs.) Not to mention the hardship on people and their families and the injustice to which so many are subjected. (For an in-depth look at this issue, see Matt Taibbi's *The Great Divide* and Michelle Alexander's *The New Jim Crow*.)

When we buy books, computers, toys, kitchen appliances, and other things from Amazon, sales to local businesses leak out of the community with virtually no economic benefit staying behind. When entrepreneurs or small businesses leave a community because it lacks the infrastructure they need, or because markets are not accessible, or because their neighbors are buying from Amazon, that, too, is economic leakage. I think you get the point. And yes, I hope you'll think twice before you order from Amazon again.

The leakage of money from local economies to Wall Street financial giants is a major loss for local economies. Michael Shuman's *Local Dollars, Local Sense* explains this fully and comprehensively.[13] We won't go into that detail here but will focus instead on a couple of interesting efforts to address this problem.

The Lovely Berkshires

In western Massachusetts in the lovely valley known as the Berkshires, resides a small non-profit organization called the Schumacher Center for New Economics. The original Center was formed more than two decades ago in the hope of expanding the public's understanding of the ideas put forth by E. F. Schumacher in his famous book *Small Is Beautiful.* The Center is a think tank of sorts, with a strong learning and teaching focus, but it is something else as well: a catalyst for experiments in new economic strategies and models. Over the years, they've been involved in some of the first land trusts in the United States, early efforts at Community Supported Agriculture, and, more recently, the development of a community-supported scholars program. It's an overused term, but I'd call these folks "cutting-edge."

In 2006, the Center launched an experiment in local currency, that is, a form of legal tender useable just like dollars but based in and limited to a place. This initiative built on earlier efforts to keep money circulating locally, including both a farm and a restaurant that issued promissory notes to hundreds of very small investors. These businesses raised local investment for needed expansions by offering ten-dollar notes, redeemable later on for the food and meals they were producing. This novel approach to raising needed investment has worked in other places, from North Carolina to Edmonton, Canada. The strong community support for these earlier efforts helped persuade the Schumacher Center staff that the time was right for a local currency that could support not one but hundreds of local businesses.

Aptly called "BerkShares," the new local currency first appeared in September 2006. Available in denominations of one, five, ten, and twenty, BerkShares have expanded steadily. By 2014, participating local banks had issued the equivalent of 5 million of them, an extraordinary number considering that the main area where they are used, the Berkshire Valley, is home to only nineteen thousand people.[14] BerkShares are not the first or only experiment in local currencies in the United States, but because such efforts are still largely unknown, let's take a moment to explain how this works.

Four locally based banks participate, making the BerkShares available to anyone who comes into one of their seven respective branches. Each BerkShare is worth 5 percent less than the equivalent amount of dollars, meaning that you get one hundred BerkShares for ninety-five U.S. dollars. This

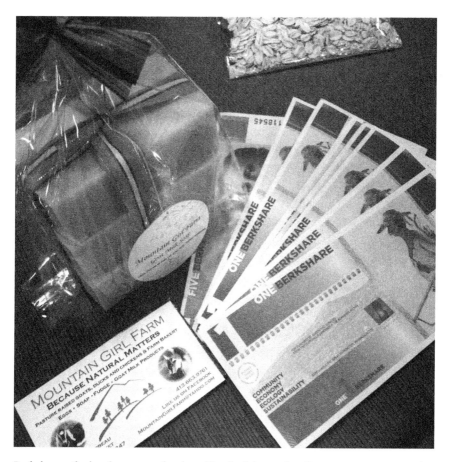

Berkshares, the local currency developed by the Schumacher Center, are now accepted by more than four hundred local businesses. Courtesy of Alice Maggio.

"exchange rate" does not fluctuate as it does between other currencies like the dollar and the euro. Should you want to "cash out" your BerkShares, you can readily do it at any of the banks, though at that point your one hundred Berk-Shares will trade for ninety-five dollars.[15] Part of the simple brilliance of local currencies is that you get a small bump in value when you first purchase them, and after that, it makes more sense to keep trading with them rather than cashing them out, because *their value in trade is equal to the dollar, but is slightly less at the bank.*

The BerkShares are redeemable only with participating businesses throughout the region, along with some in southern New York and a small part of Connecticut. Getting enough businesses on board is one of the challenges that local currency initiatives face, especially in their early years. If you are unable to sign up many businesses, and a diverse array of businesses, the local currency is less appealing, less valuable. For BerkShares, they've met both of these challenges quite well, adding sixty businesses this past year to bring the total to just over four hundred.[16] And the diversity of businesses is amazing: restaurants, farmers, jewelers, auto parts, hardware and building supply, tree trimming, furniture and cabinet makers, attorneys, accountants, and other professionals, grocers, retailers of all types, chiropractors and other health and wellness practitioners, and many more.[17] This wide base of businesses is undoubtedly a big part of why BerkShares continue to grow.

Once they complete the relatively simple process to join, participating businesses get listed online and in a print directory, along with a "We Accept BerkShares" sign for their business. And they benefit as well from the good publicity and general promotion of "local buying" that the Center undertakes.[18]

It's important to note that while businesses can place certain limits on the use of BerkShares in their store, most do not; a one-hundred-dollar item can be purchased with one hundred dollars, one hundred BerkShares, or a combination of both. Think about what that means in terms of keeping money circulating locally. If you sell one hundred dollars' worth of merchandise in BerkShares, and then go to the bank to get dollars, you'll get only ninety-five dollars back. But if you use those same one hundred BerkShares to pay your accountant, or fix your laptop, or buy food for the office party, it will trade for its full value. Very clever!

Getting to the Root of Things

Though farmers and gardeners have been saving seeds for millennia, over the past one hundred years the practice had been in steady decline, especially in the United States. The availability of hybrid seeds, which sometimes perform better or more reliably, persuades countless growers to stop saving and start buying seeds, every year. While you can save seeds of a hybrid variety, you won't get the same thing when you plant it the following year. Seed saving is instead for "open pollinated" varieties. If you're one of the millions of folks who've come to love "heirloom" tomatoes, an heirloom is simply an open-pollinated variety that's been maintained and passed down for several generations.

Southern Exposure Seed Exchange (SESE) formed in 1982 to help reinvigorate seed saving among farmers and gardeners, and to provide a simple system to share and exchange these seeds. The husband and wife team of Jeff McCormack and Patty Wallens had already started and managed a small solar greenhouse business in Charlottesville, Virginia, when they decided to take on the challenge of helping to preserve the genetic richness of our food crops.[19] At that time, seed saving in central Virginia, where they're located, was uncommon, especially among commercial farmers. The burgeoning interest in heirlooms, and in better-tasting fruits and vegetables more broadly, convinced the founders of SESE that the time was right to start the exchange.

In 1999, Jeff and Patty sold SESE to a community-based cooperative, Acorn Community. This is both an organization and a place, a worker-owned cooperative and a working farm. Most people who work for SESE live on the Acorn Community farm, sharing work, chores, decision making, and profits.

Fewer than two hundred orders came in that first year, this small group of customers choosing from among just sixty-five varieties. Things grew steadily from there. By 2014, sixty farmers were growing out seeds for SESE, providing nearly eight hundred regionally adapted varieties.[20] Most of these farmers also grow produce for farmers markets or other outlets but have found that seed production diversifies and increases their farm income. One of those is Richard Moyer, a professor of biology who traded in most of his academic career (he still teaches part-time) for full-time farming in Russell County, Virginia, about thirty minutes from Abingdon. Over the past few years, Richard has expanded the variety and quantity of seeds he produces for SESE, providing additional farm enterprises for his children and family. The seed business also complements the Moyer family's frugal, resilient lifestyle: When the seeds are extracted from tomatoes or peppers, the flesh and pulp is then cooked into sauce that they can, eat, and sell.

Complementing the farmers growing under contract for SESE, about 5 percent of the seeds they sell are grown on the Acorn Community farm. While SESE is still very much a community-based, locally owned enterprise, their sales now exceed $1 million annually with approximately thirty-seven thousand customers spread around the Southeast and parts of Appalachia. The seed business, along with other small farm enterprises, provides a living for the worker-owners of ACORN and have generated enough net income to allow them to make steady improvements to both the farm and its infrastructure, all without taking on debt from banks or others.[21]

Southern Exposure Seed Exchange is a very successful example of a growing trend of regionally based and heirloom seed companies that have emerged primarily over the past ten to twenty years. SESE, Sow True Seeds, Fedco, and several others emphasize heirloom seeds and work with a wide range of farmers and gardeners who test and produce the seed stock for sale to other farmers and gardeners.[22] Nationally, the Seed Savers Exchange helps link these groups and provides up-to-date education and training. As part of this seed-saving movement, many communities are launching seed-saving libraries and "seed swaps," open to farmers and gardeners alike. While there is money to be made in producing seeds, other folks are using the seeds they raise as a form of currency to trade for other seeds or, in some cases, nonseed gardening supplies. Just as tool libraries enable people to better maintain their homes or gardens, seed-saving libraries empower folks to grow a more diverse array of food while helping to maintain the genetic diversity of our food sources. Janisse Ray's *The Seed Underground* provides both a personal look and a strong analysis of seed saving and its role in rebuilding genetic diversity (listed under "Further Reading" at the end of this chapter).

In addition to heirloom seeds and place-based currencies, many other forms of locally rooted financing networks are emerging across the country, from crowd-funding platforms for everyday folks to LION clubs—Local Investment Opportunity Networks—that connect people of means to triple-bottom-line businesses in their own areas. Typically these locally rooted funders channel their resources toward building or restoring real community capital rather than toward purely financial transactions. When the New Hampshire Community Loan Fund provided loans to residents of the Meredith Center Trailer Park in 1983, it enabled them to buy the land underneath their manufactured homes rather than be evicted to make way for a developer with no connection to the community. The residents paid their loans back, made improvements to their neighborhood, and in the process gave birth to the loan fund's Manufactured Housing Park Program.[23]

The "Slow Money" movement, founded by investor Woody Tasch, provides another fascinating model of community-directed investment. At this point, Slow Money chapters are focusing on sustainable food and farming businesses. They have emerged from New Mexico to North Carolina. These have taken a variety of forms, but they share at least two key characteristics with other local, triple-bottom-line investment strategies: they focus resources on ecologically sustainable and socially responsible local businesses; and they enable small, so-called "unaccredited investors" to put their modest investment dollars toward businesses they believe in rather than into Wall Street.

These pioneering efforts are beginning to challenge the field of "socially responsible investment" to go beyond investment in faraway companies that aren't too bad, and move toward support for local and regional businesses that are decidedly good.

And, of course, the role of community banks, community loan funds, and credit unions, the three main funders of small to midsize local businesses, is absolutely critical. While we touch on these a bit in the analysis and policy sections of this chapter, all of these emerging strategies comprise a book unto themselves. The good news is that several folks have already written "that" book, from Michael Shuman to Elizabeth U to Woody Tasch, whose work is mentioned in the "Further Reading" section below.

Analysis of Transition Three

The local food movement has been under way for close to thirty years, while concerted and widespread "local economy" efforts are perhaps fifteen to twenty years old at this point. Attention to issues and challenges around community capital by contrast are much more recent, most emerging within the past five to ten years. It is a new field, arising out of the recognition that how and where we spend our money, and how farmers and entrepreneurs can add value to their products, is in fact critical to community economic vitality. It's too bad we didn't figure this out sooner, but, as they say, better late than never. And right now, there is a ferment of both thinking and doing around community capital and wealth building with Michael Shuman, Elizabeth U, Marjorie Kelly, and the Business Alliance for Local Living Economies (BALLE) at the forefront. I've offered just a handful of the many emerging experiments above, in the hope of making a broader point: *We need to recapitalize workers, farmers, and producers, everyday consumers and communities as one piece of critical work to foster broadly based wealth in this country.*

It's important to note that in many places, especially African American communities, it is less about *re*-capitalizing and rebuilding wealth than it is about beginning to overcome hundreds of years of systematic wealth extraction, and deliberate policies to prevent the accumulation of assets. Such policies were not just the domain of southern states or racist city leaders. They were, in fact, built into federal housing policy across the nation, for decades, and impacted not only how federal housing loans were distributed but largely drove the discriminatory policies of private lenders and real estate agencies throughout most of the twentieth century.[24] It's an ugly truth but one we must deal with if we're going to effectively address poverty and disparities in wealth and income.

Of the three types of capital presented above, cooperatives are distinct in that they've been around for a very long time, well over a hundred years, in fact. And comparatively, they are also substantial in size and value. Cooperatives of all types—consumer-owned, farmer- or producer-owned, and worker-owned—held more than $3 trillion in assets in 2006, according to a study that year from the University of Wisconsin, and generated at least $500 billion in annual revenues.[25] In that same year, more than 850,000 people were directly employed by co-ops, while roughly 2 million jobs were indirectly attributable to them. The vast majority of cooperatives in the United States are consumer co-ops, numbering nearly 27,000. By comparison, there are just under 1,500 farmer or producer cooperatives and about 220 worker co-ops.[26] There are more cooperatives than most folks realize, and their total contribution to the economy is substantial. But do they offer more hope of "building broad prosperity" than traditional economic strategies and business structures?

Several studies have looked at co-ops at the micro level, considering such things as the wages and overall working environment they offer, their impact on a business's productivity and efficiency, and their ability to facilitate savings and wealth creation among members. A 2012 assessment of dozens of studies of worker co-ops found increased "productive efficiency" in worker cooperatives, particularly when workers are involved in the decisions about the business.[27] An earlier look at the plywood industry in the Pacific Northwest also determined greater output per unit of input for cooperatives as compared with privately owned manufacturers.[28] (Among the privately held firms, unionized companies performed better than nonunion.) Though few in number, worker co-ops in fact perform very well in terms of conventional economic assessments. But their benefits are much broader than that.

Beyond productivity, it is clear that co-ops generally do better in terms of building worker and community wealth and other "social" outcomes. Prospera, an Oakland, California–based community development organization, has helped lower-income, mostly Latina women launch five worker co-ops over the past fifteen years, all of which continue to operate. These enterprises mostly focus on green, eco-friendly house cleaning but pay far better than the conventional house-cleaning franchises, with wages as high as fourteen dollars per hour. What's more, the worker-owners have seen their own assets grow dramatically over time, from about $400 to $8,700 on average.[29] Studies show that ESOPs (Employee Stock Ownership Programs) achieve similar results, with one analysis finding workers in ESOPs holding more than double the assets at retirement compared with employees in traditional firms.[30]

In addition to better pay and higher savings rates, cooperatives appear to help stabilize local economies. In a study looking at thirteen years of data and thousands of businesses in Italy, it was found that during times of economic stress—recessions, sharp drop in demand, etc.—cooperatives were much more likely to maintain levels of employment by temporarily adjusting worker pay down, rather than laying people off, as happened in comparable private-sector businesses.[31] Thus it seems that co-ops tend to offer more security in an increasingly insecure labor market. The fact that they consistently generate more benefits for workers and communities *and* higher levels of economic productivity strongly refutes the myth that "looking out for Number One is best for everybody."

The role of community capital is more difficult to assess, though we do know that it has begun to expand in some sectors over the past decade. The number of food hubs across the nation has increased from fewer than fifty in 2000 to about three hundred in 2013, with quite a few more in development, according to a 2013 report from the Wallace Center.[32] Of these three hundred hubs, about two-thirds have built or otherwise developed some sort of centralized infrastructure in their community for aggregating, cleaning, packing, and other functions to increase the value and marketability of farm products. The report surveyed hubs across the country on other issues as well, including the number and type of farmers using the hubs, the sales volumes, ownership structure, and more. Though these numbers vary widely, the study found an average of about eighty farmers per food hub, meaning that nationwide, nearly 24,000 producers use them for at least some of their sales. Sales averaged just over $3 million per year at each hub, representing almost $1 billion in annual sales through all food hubs.[33]

The proportion of new farmers, minority farmers, and women farmers utilizing these systems ranged from 21 to 29 percent, well beyond the national average, indicating that *food hubs do appear to be creating access to farmers of lesser means.* That is to say, they are helping to capitalize them. Additionally, a high percentage of food hubs reported that many of their farmers were increasing their acreage under production (49 percent) and adopting more sustainable production practices (40 percent).[34] (These trends are consistent with my own experience working with food hubs in several states.)[35] For the 24,000 farmers currently using food hubs, a very modest estimate would be that it would take each one at least twenty thousand dollars to minimally equip themselves to be able to sell into larger markets, and that's assuming used equipment and a great deal of sweat equity. The reality is that most would not or could not make that investment. Hence the food hubs represent a form of community or collective capitalization, at least potentially.

The local food movement as a whole, including not only food hubs but farmers markets, CSAs, and farmer networks, has also helped build local capital by bringing younger people, women, and people of color into agriculture. This is happening in rural communities and urban areas, sometimes through formal internship and mentorship programs, other times through informal arrangements such as WWOOF (World Wide Workers On Organic Farms). The relatively widespread presence of farmers who can share knowledge, linked to markets, has helped to cultivate this new cadre of farmers and food entrepreneurs.

So-called kitchen incubators, like ACEnet's Food Ventures facility in Athens, Ohio, have been developing as a means of capitalizing not just farmers, but chefs, caterers, bakers, and many other types of food entrepreneurs. While Food Ventures is more successful than most other kitchen incubators, the numbers they've achieved show the extraordinary potential of this type of community capital: 25 or more new businesses launched every year, among nearly 150 with whom ACEnet is working at any one time; at least 300 businesses that utilized the facility now on their own and successful; millions of dollars in increased sales, and hundreds of food and farming jobs added to the local economy.

Nationwide kitchen incubators have had a more mixed history, often plunging ahead prematurely under the misguided notion that "if we build it, they will come." It turns out that in many cases, they don't, or at least not in enough numbers to keep the bills paid. Larry Fisher, ACEnet's director of finance, has found that most successful kitchen incubators have joined forces with other, established institutions, situating both their facilities and training and technical assistance efforts within the umbrella of these partners. These include universities, community colleges, Small Business Development Centers, and established community non-profits.[36]

It is clear that for food hubs, kitchen incubators, and small business incubators more broadly, the central business proposition makes it very challenging to reach financial viability. That's because all of these ventures have a social mission, typically including a focus on limited-resource, newer, and less experienced farmers and entrepreneurs as their core clients. As such, they attempt to make their equipment, facilities, and services as affordable as possible. Thus, they all operate on very small margins, working with folks who generally need *more* support to launch a successful enterprise. And for food hubs particularly, much of what they sell is into larger-volume markets where the expectation is for lower prices. So, it's a tough business, as illustrated by the failure of dozens of kitchen incubators and the struggle of nearly half of all food hubs to meet their costs. That struggle to be "price competitive" is very difficult for the farmers and food entrepreneurs as well, as Charlie Jackson, Brendan Smith, and others have pointed out.[37] But the value these facilities provide, economically as well as for the other two bottom lines, makes these strategies worthy of continued development and improvement, including candid discussions about the inherent challenges.

The idea of "retaining capital," though certainly not new, is only recently getting any significant attention from economic developers and policy makers. Instead, the focus has been on the *deficiencies* of local communities, rural and urban, rather than their assets. One of those deficiencies has certainly included money and capital, with almost all economic strategies built around "bringing new money" into seemingly poor areas. And that for sure is part of it. But what Slow Money, local investing and lending clubs, locally based credit cards, and small business lending by local banks and credit unions are all demonstrating is this: Even in these so-called poor areas, there is often a great deal more money available than we ever stopped to find, but almost all of it is leaking out—to credit card companies, to Wall Street, and to global retailers. Retaining that capital and circulating it in the local community must become an essential part of our economic development strategy, as part of the movement toward greater resilience, self-reliance, and bottom-up economies.

Local currencies are one of the more interesting ways in which we can stop this leakage of local money and refocus it instead on building up local businesses and capital. Of course, they have other benefits, too, perhaps most notably providing a platform and, typically, a directory that makes it much easier to find local products and services. Local currency can also help unite consumers and local businesses in a common purpose. Let's face it, folks of every political stripe should be able to get behind something that simultaneously thumbs its nose at Wall Street *and* the Fed! Unfortunately, to date, most local currencies have been relatively short-lived or have remained in operation but with very limited reach and impact. The key, according to University of Vermont professor Robert Costanza, is for these currencies to reach a significant scale, as BerkShares has begun to do. But that is the Catch-22, as getting a broad base of businesses on board while getting thousands of consumers to regularly use the new currency at designated local shops has proven quite difficult for these grassroots initiatives. They end up stuck in the "boutique" phase, according to Costanza, "functioning more like gift certificates."[38] Magnifying the impact of these local innovations through various types of networks, the focus of our next transition, may provide one means to increase their success and reach.

Public Policy

Money and finance represent an important tool in building the wealth and capital of workers, consumers, and local communities. Unfortunately, rather than trickling down, financial resources have been steadily sucked out of workers, local people, and local institutions, becoming extraordinarily concentrated at the top. A case in point: Caterpillar's profits reached $5.7 billion in 2012, and the company's CEO, Douglas Oberhelman, saw his compensation increase by 80 percent over the preceding two years. Yet he instituted a six-year freeze on wages for Caterpillar employees. Exemplifying the belief that "greed is good" and that "looking out for Number One benefits everybody," Oberhelman said in 2013: "I always try to communicate with our people that we can never make enough money. We can never make enough profit."[39] Mr. Oberhelman's apparent conviction has clearly worked to his advantage, and perhaps to the short-term benefit of Caterpillar's shareholders as well. But not for the thousands of workers who actually make the products.

The numbers in the banking sector are staggering. Over the past thirty years, the number of banks has shrunk by half, while the average size of financial institutions has increased by 400 percent.[40] During that same period, the U.S. population grew by more than 80 million, meaning that many more people were in need of loans and banking services. Yet most of the banks that disappeared were community banks, often swallowed up by the decidedly nonlocal megabanks, the biggest four of which now control almost 37 percent of all deposits in the United States. It's worth mentioning again that *this consolidation has nothing to do with efficiency or productivity, by any reasonable measure.* The megabanks lend dramatically less to small businesses and homeowners than do credit unions and community banks; they charge higher fees for their services; and they are the ones using federal taxpayer dollars by the trillions, not only when they get bailed out but as an ongoing source of extremely low-cost credit, money that helps them finance their risky speculations in the first place.

Let's remind ourselves that we are discussing *public* policy here. The people we elect and the laws they enact should always be for the public good. This certainly does not mean that such policies should be antibusiness or make it harder for the private sector or the market to function well. But it does mean that public policy should steer and at times constrain the private sector so that it better serves the public. It couldn't be clearer that our banking and financial sector public policies have failed this test than when the incoming chief economist of Citicorp says this: "Is the reality . . . that large private firms make enormous private profits when the going is good and get bailed out and taken into temporary public ownership when the going gets bad, with the taxpayer taking the risk and the losses?"[41]

The policies that might reign in the big banks, restore the Glass-Steagall Act's prudent separation of banking from Wall Street speculation, and simply place reasonable limits on the maximum size banks can attain are all being worked on by a range of public-interest groups. (Unfortunately these policies are a long shot in our present environment, in large part because of the out-of-control political influence of these megabanks.) *These policies are critically important and merit our strongest support.* For our purposes, however, we'll focus on the other end of that spectrum—how policy can enable building the resources of local communities and the financial institutions that serve them, from the bottom up.

Invest in Capacity-Building Infrastructure

In chapter 3, we raised the issue of the fantastically lopsided investment channeled to large, nonlocal corporations rather than local businesses. I suggested focusing a substantial portion of those local, state, and federal funds instead on locally based enterprises. As a cost-effective complement to this, it would also make sense to steer much more of our investment toward community capital, whether in the form of incubators, food hubs and processing centers, triple-bottom-line accelerators, or local research and development partnerships with community colleges, universities, and entrepreneurs. These kinds of funds already exist and have been utilized to help launch such facilities and initiatives. But many such funds have declined or are threatened. We live in an age where austerity is pushed by many in power, especially when it comes to long-term investments that could improve the lot of everyday people. We would do well to remember Angela Glover-Blackwell's observation that "we are not a poor country and we've got to stop acting like we are."[42] Instead of drastically cutting public investment, we should increase it and dramatically reorient it in three ways, toward:

- **Investments in local capacity,** that is, the ability of communities or regions to better meet their own needs. ACEnet's kitchen incubator, ECO's aggregation and shared-use facility, and community solar initiatives in Colorado and Washington, D.C., all offer examples.
- **Infrastructure that enables businesses to solve social and ecological problems,** rather than simply encourage consumption. The Propeller Incubator and Accelerator and Co-op Power's waste oil biodiesel facilities exemplify this standard.
- **Initiatives that broaden opportunity and wealth,** rather than further concentrate it, like the New Hampshire Loan Fund's Manufactured Home Loan program and the new markets for heirloom seed production being fostered by Southern Exposure Seed Exchange.

Encouraging Cooperatives and Worker Ownership

Interest in cooperatives has increased considerably over the past decade, in part due to their strong track record and in part because people are looking for creative ways to solve both economic and social problems. While consumer co-ops are widespread, worker- and producer-owned co-ops remain a very small part of the economy. A range of both policy and institutional changes could be implemented to dramatically increase the number of worker co-ops and to enable them to become a major part of the economy. Hilary Abell, who has instigated and worked in cooperatives for nearly a decade and has studied them as well, offers a range of ideas for accelerating and strengthening cooperatives in her paper "Worker Cooperatives: Pathways to Scale," published in 2014.[43] Some of the steps she advocates include:

- Increase capital available to worker co-ops, particularly "patient capital." This includes low-interest or deferred loans, equity investments, and grants that enable the co-op business to become established before facing overwhelming repayment schedules.
- Integrate cooperatives and the expertise needed to develop them into existing economic development programs and infrastructure at local, state, and federal levels. At present, very few economic development

staff understand co-ops, let alone have expertise to offer those considering or attempting to launch one. This capacity could be built with professional training and peer learning, in much the same way that Cooperative Extension has begun to build expertise in sustainable agriculture among its staff.

- Create co-op curriculum in public schools, community colleges and universities, and technical schools that will help build the "pipeline" of cooperative entrepreneurs, workers, managers, and support staff. Particular attention should be paid to economics departments and business schools.
- Strengthen regional and national cooperative federations, associations and support centers that work with cooperatives and provide technical assistance and training. Increased funding will be necessary to accomplish this.
- Expand existing tax incentives to encourage private business owners reaching retirement (and without an interested child or family heir) to sell their business to the employees as either a cooperative or through an Employee Stock Ownership Program.

Keeping Money and Capital Local and Supporting New Forms of Local Lending

"Localizing money," whether through local currencies or by creating investment clubs, networks, and platforms, is being explored and tested in scores of communities across the country. But it's a tough thing to pull off for a variety of reasons, including certain public policy hurdles. Local currencies like BerkShares probably face the fewest *direct* policy problems, but they are indirectly undermined by policies that dramatically favor franchises, big boxes, and big banks. When a community spends millions of dollars to lure a big-box chain, they've not only favored them over small businesses, but they've used that taxpayer money to create another place for people to shop that almost surely will not accept a local currency—because they buy most of their goods and services from outside the community! Similarly, when community banks and credit unions disappear due to the unfair advantages bestowed on Wall Street financial giants, the banking partners essential to local currency are also lost. It is challenging enough to build a strong local currency; a level playing field for local businesses would certainly help.

Another way to keep capital local is the "Foreclosure Fine Ordinance" recently adopted in Richmond, California, and intended to help reclaim vacant buildings. The ordinance requires owners of vacant buildings, often absentee banks, to restore their buildings to code and keep them that way or face up to one thousand dollars per day in fines.[44] Once restored, these old buildings have proven to be more marketable, whether for a private enterprise or for a community-based incubator. This represents the "stick"; other communities have used "carrots" such as tax incentives to spur reclamation of vacant buildings.[45] The key is to prioritize such incentives to support those enterprises committed to community prosperity, not further privatization of public assets, or concentration of wealth. If a community's "boats" are disappearing or are no longer seaworthy, what good will a rising tide do them?

Freeing up Local Banks, Credit Unions, and Loan Funds

Simply put, community-based banks and credit unions should not face reporting and regulatory expectations identical to the megabanks. Why? Because they utilize their assets to create broader prosperity among businesses and homeowners at nearly *four* times the rate of the big banks. Because they pose fantastically less risk to the overall economy when they do falter. And because they generate more jobs and economic impact per dollar invested, compared to the big guys. These banks, of course, should still be regulated to protect their customers and investors, but the current burden they face, developed by and for the big banks, is totally counterproductive to their role as community lenders and, in fact, is helping to put many of them out of business. We need genuine financial reform that tightens requirements on Wall Street investment firms while reducing unnecessary burdens for local banks and credit unions. That's almost the exact opposite of current federal policy.

Related to the above is the singular example of the Bank of North Dakota, a state-owned bank that for almost a century has helped community banks focus on community lending while keeping their costs of borrowing funds at a reasonable, nonspeculative rate. In this decidedly nonsocialist state, the Bank of North Dakota has withstood the test of time and proven that a public bank of modest scale makes smaller, private banks more competitive and more viable and increases community economic vitality by keeping funds circulating in the state. As Michael Shuman has described it, the bank "takes money that might have been placed in a multinational bank, where it might have done economic development work in, say, Singapore, and makes sure that the funds are doing that same work back home in North Dakota."[46] Multiple states are now looking at the North Dakota model, with Oregon closest to taking action. State legislators should be educated about the amazing success of the Bank of North Dakota and be urged to create a similar institution in their own state.

As in the early months of 2015, incomes in our country are extraordinarily lopsided, with CEOs earning on average more than three hundred times the wage of rank-and-file workers in their companies. And as we've seen, those supersized wages have not contributed to better company performance or to a trickle down of jobs and income. Quite the opposite, in fact. As bad as the wage situation is, it's even worse when it comes to savings and assets, where the vast majority of Americans have barely enough to get by for two or three months, where student debt is driving college graduates back into their parents' homes, and where for African American and Latino families, savings have plummeted to less than 10 percent of that of white families. Tackling this problem at the top will require, at a minimum, taxing investment income at least as much as earned income. Some of this money should then be used to build the assets of workers and to capitalize communities for long-term productivity and resilience. We already "redistribute" fantastic amounts of income and wealth, but most of it goes "up" to a tiny, ultrawealthy elite. We need instead to level this playing field and put public resources to work for the benefit of, well, the public. And in the process we need to put to bed the myth that looking out for Number One is good for everybody. Greed is greed, not good.

Transition Three: Recap and Looking Forward

By now you may be seeing some of the connections among the first three transitions, *building productive resilience, expanding bottom-up, living economies,* and *developing broadly based prosperity and wealth.* If there seems to be some overlap and repetition, that's because they are so deeply linked, both in the challenges they face and the opportunities ahead. Some of the key lessons from this transition are as follows:

1. For people to be secure and for communities to prosper, they need more than "jobs" and a stream of income; they need the capacity to meet their own needs, create livelihoods, and generate income. To do this, people and communities need to build capital and make sure it lasts.
2. Capital can and should increase the productivity of people, enabling them to meet needs, solve problems, and increase their independence.

Investing in place-based capital—the land and natural resources of a place, the art, culture, heritage, structures, and institutions—makes communities more resilient, stronger, and more distinct. It also enables businesses and communities to "plug economic leaks" and replace imported goods and services.

3. Unfortunately, tax incentives and most economic policy at present are strongly biased toward placeless capital, which in turn undermines local communities in favor of the highest and fastest financial return. Most public policy and many business practices also fail to recognize that land, air, and water are foundational, irreplaceable forms of capital.

4. Financial resources are needed to develop, build, and restore capital of all types, and for that reason, new forms of local investment and recirculation of financial resources are critical to building community capital.

The transition to broadly based and durable prosperity will require that we confront and dramatically reduce the wide array of tax, investment, and economic incentive policies that have enabled the richest people and biggest corporations to concentrate their wealth to ridiculous levels. We now know beyond any doubt that these policies are not lifting most people's boats. In fact, they are economically counterproductive and socially and environmentally destructive. Instead, a bottom-up strategy of investment in workers, people, and communities shows great promise in building strong, living economies that put more people to work and generate wider prosperity.

Up next: Communities are building resilience; local living economies are emerging widely; and investment in the capital of workers and communities is expanding. But all of these developments are badly underresourced and face major obstacles in both policies and the priorities and perceptions of public officials. The fourth transition, *from a thousand flickers of light to networks of learning, doing, and change,* is helping to strengthen and accelerate the first three transitions while beginning to build public support for this new approach.

Further Reading

Abell, Hilary. "Worker Cooperatives: Pathways to Scale." Democracy Collaborative. Takoma Park, MD. June 2014. http://community-wealth.org/content/worker-cooperatives-pathways-scale.

Deller, Steven, et al. "Research on the Economic Impact of Cooperatives," University of Wisconsin Center for Cooperatives. 2006. http://reic.uwcc.wisc.edu/sites/all/REIC_FINAL.pdf.

Jackson, Charlie. "At What Cost? Food Hubs, Walmart, and Local Food." March 26, 2014. www.asapconnections.org.

Kelly, Marjorie. *Owning Our Future: The Emerging Ownership Revolution.* San Francisco: Berrett-Koehler, 2012.

Ray, Janisse. *The Seed Underground: A Growing Revolution to Save Food.* White River Junction, VT: Chelsea Green, 2012.

Smith, Brendan. "Don't Let Your Children Grow Up to Be Farmers." *New York Times,* August 9, 2014. www.nytimes.com.

Tasch, Woody. *Inquiries into the Nature of Slow Money: Investing as if Food, Farms, and Fertility Mattered.* White River Junction, VT: Chelsea Green, 2008.

Taking Sustainability to Scale

From a Thousand Flickers of Light to Networks of Learning, Doing, and Change

Step by step and debate by debate, America's public officials have rewritten the rules of American politics and the American economy in ways that have benefited the few at the expense of the many. . . . The transformation of American government over the last generation has fundamentally changed what government does, and whom it does it for.
—Jacob Hacker and Paul Pierson, *Winner-Take-All Politics*

Despite all the important work accomplished by non-profit organizations over the last hundred years, significant growth or scaled impact has remained an elusive goal for most of them. . . . The inability to achieve scale—that is, to make a meaningful and sustainable impact by reaching greater numbers of people—has limited the potential of these organizations and the people and causes they serve. Simply put, society's complex and pressing challenges call for solutions with greater scale of impact.
—Catherine H. Clark et al., "Scaling Social Impact"

The first Saturday morning that Laurie and I set up our booth at the farmers market, we were one of about ten farmers in that rough old parking lot. There was a handful of very dedicated producers there every week, and a few who came and went. The quality and diversity of the products we were collectively selling could probably best be described as "okay." Customers ebbed and flowed too, some days far more than others. Certainly the most notable thing that happened at our booth that first year was when the author Barbara Kingsolver bought a couple of eggplants from us (which she still does today, on occasion).

Less than eight years later, we were one vendor among fifty, most of

The Abingdon, Virginia, Farmers Market on a Saturday in July. Author's collection.

whom now had space under the newly built Abingdon Farmers Market Pavilion. The range of farm and food products for sale—all locally raised—had increased dramatically, as had the overall quality. Some of that growth was due to good luck and good timing, but much of it came about because a small group of farmers and others worked hard to make it happen. By 2008, the market was one of the most important pieces of Abingdon's emerging local economy, a small-town market that visitors regularly proclaimed to be "one of the best I've seen, anywhere." Notwithstanding a population a thousand times smaller than New York City, we'd somehow built a vibrant, diverse, high-quality market.

As our market became better known around the region, community leaders from other small towns began looking for help. We had no magic formula to share, but we did have some pretty good ideas about what might work, what to watch out for, and how to build a base of customers and farmers at comparable rates. In 2007, Appalachian Sustainable Development (ASD), which had helped launch the market, formed the Appalachian Farmers Market Association, or AFMA, to better respond to these requests for help. This network of farmers market managers and leaders was quite small at the outset and remains so today, in terms of its budget and the part-time staff provided by ASD. Nevertheless, community leaders from St. Paul, Norton, and other small towns in the region have often cited AFMA as one of the keys to their success, helping them launch and build strong markets in places where they're not supposed to work: places with tiny populations and high poverty rates, where locavore sightings were a rarity.

Modest as it is, AFMA has worked because it is fundamentally a *network* of peers, a group that comes together to discuss challenges, share ideas and tips, and collaborate on joint projects better done at a regional level. The peer learning is "real-time," based on the unfolding experience of markets at various stages of development. It is augmented by an informal annual conference designed to bring new tools to leaders of farmers markets as well as farmers and vendors. And the joint projects of AFMA have resulted in concrete improvements in local markets, such as the development of simple systems to accept EBT cards (food stamps), along with better market promotion, customer outreach, and farmer training. With a very small investment of time and money, this network has helped strengthen farms and other small businesses, and the communities of which they're a part. It's a small example of the fourth transition, *taking sustainability to scale using networks of learning, doing, and change.*

The "thousand flickers of light" from which we need to transition may remind readers of George H. W. Bush's phrase of nearly thirty years ago, commending what he called "a thousand points of light." This was a reference to the countless volunteer, non-profit, and other local efforts to help people in need, to address a range of social problems. There was nothing wrong then with recognizing and supporting these efforts, nor is there today. People helping one another, often for no or minimal pay, is part of being neighborly, part of strong and resilient communities. The problem arises when that becomes the primary way in which we attempt to address complex and long-standing social and economic problems; the problem arises when we eliminate or whittle down public efforts in favor of purely private, localized solutions. I believe in the thousands of flickers of innovation, of adaptation, of caring that are under way across our country. But they're far too isolated and not nearly sufficient to meet the challenges. We need to bring these innovative solutions to scale.

What Are "Networks" and Why Do We Need Them?

People define networks in different ways, but here we'll keep it simple: A *network* is a group of individuals, businesses, or organizations that affiliate with each other, that "connect" in order to better achieve something they've not been able to do on their own. It might be as simple as greater buying power or market access, or it might encompass the desire to have more political influence. There are all shapes and sizes of networks, many entirely informal, with minimal rules and easy "entry and exit." These types of networks typically avoid formal membership categories and assume that people will come and go, depending upon how well the network is meeting their expectations. That describes the Appalachian Farmers Market Association pretty well. Other networks are more formalized with more specific goals and objectives and clearer expectations for those who get involved.

Over time, networks tend to gradually move toward this more deliberate approach and structure. Nevertheless, one of the most important characteristics of networks is their flexibility and responsiveness to the participants who comprise them. When they're functioning right, networks can offer the best of both worlds: the many advantages of a larger business or institution, without the bureaucracy, without being top-heavy and focused primarily on self-preservation. As we consider how to bring bottom-up, living economies to scale, we'll explore five other networks, beginning with those whose focus is local or regional, and concluding with examples of those working across many states, even nationally.

Networks are but one part of the emerging work to build a bottom-up economy, but they're critically important for a very basic reason: In spite of thousands of local "success stories" built over the past twenty-plus years, local living economies remain small, underresourced, and fantastically outgunned in economic and political clout. Here's one example: We have more than eight thousand farmers markets in the country now, nearly four thousand CSAs, and hundreds of grocers and supermarkets buying and selling local farm products of all kinds.[1] We've gotten to that point because thousands of dedicated people have worked to make it happen in communities from coast to coast. But when you add up all of the sales of local foods from all of these outlets—all of it—it amounts to less than a nickel for every dollar of grocery sales at Walmart.[2] Five cents on the dollar. Just compared to Walmart. So, we've got a ways to go, to put it nicely. Networks offer a potential means to help us get there, faster, smarter, and with better overall results.

We all know that Monsanto, GE, and a few hundred other corporations are really big, but there is more to it than just sheer size (although that is very important). For most modern corporations, they are big because they've gone *both deep and wide,* that is, they've vertically integrated, from raw material supplies to retail sales, and they've horizontally integrated through the acquisition of dozens of other companies, often businesses completely unrelated to their own industry. This kind of depth and breadth gives multinational corporations many streams of revenue, which in turn provides them with lots of "flexibility" in their business decisions. They can, for instance, sell off or close down entire businesses that are "underperforming," or use their vertical integration to reduce the cost of raw materials and ensure that every penny of the final sale price is kept in-house. More than anything else, such companies use their sheer size to expand their economic power—more control of markets, financing, pricing—while also increasing their political clout. Simply put, they make the rules by which every other business must play. Much of the economic and political clout they've amassed over the past few decades has been underpinned by the myth that *global trade makes everyone—consumers and businesses—better off.* This myth has bipartisan power, with many Democrats joining Republicans in their unabashed support for unfettered globalization.

Can networks accomplish much the same thing, even though they are fundamentally decentralized and made up of relatively small, locally focused, and independent businesses and organizations? Can the thousand flickers of light in the local economy movement be multiplied many times over, and soon, without compromising the values that make them different? Can this movement "get big" without forcing the local independents, the social enterprises, the organic farmers at its core to "get out"? Most difficult of all, can networks expand the reach and impact of local living economies in such a way as to also challenge the myth that endless economic growth is both desirable and possible? Well, let's have a look.

Emerging Examples of Networks

Weaving Together the Arts

In chapter 3, I briefly mentioned Heartwood, the regional "gateway" center for Appalachian arts, handicrafts, music, and food. This beautiful facility is located on the west side of Abingdon, within a mile of where the Walmart supercenter would have gone, had we not stopped it. Inside you'll find an amazing diversity of high-quality, locally made artisanal products, along with a fairly sophisticated yet user-friendly series of tools that allow you to interact with and locate the artists—or musicians, or farms—and go for a visit. The center provides a rich and interesting experience itself, but it was designed first and foremost to tie together a series of initiatives launched in an effort to build the "asset-based" economy of southwest Virginia.

It started with traditional, old-time Appalachian music. According to Jim Baldwin, who has been one of the driving forces behind this new economic approach, the original idea was to somehow connect the newly formed Ralph Stanley Museum in the mountains of Dickenson County with the Fiddlers Convention 150 miles to the east in Galax. Authentic old-time music had been coming out of these places and people for a long time, but in 2003, a small group of folks including Jim himself and Todd Christensen, who worked for Virginia's Department of Housing and Community Development, began to pull them together into a network called the Crooked Road. Jim is a native of the region. Having worked in community economic development his whole life, he had begun to see some of the limits of traditional, top-down economic development strategies. Looking for alternatives, he'd been one of the founders and early leaders of Appalachian Sustainable Development and was increasingly focused on bottom-up economic strategies.

The Crooked Road now includes nine major venues for traditional music, spanning mountains and valleys across southwest Virginia. There are an additional sixty "affiliated venues," including authentic old-time music festivals, musical gathering places, and luthiers and other instrument makers. The Crooked Road network lifts these musicians, instrument makers, and musical venues up through public education and marketing, and through investment in various musical venues and historical theaters, all of which have helped to build the Crooked Road "brand."[3] According to a 2008 analysis, this has produced well over four hundred jobs along with $23 million in annual economic benefits.[4] The Crooked Road is one of the region's most unique assets, and its musical heritage and those carrying it forward today are becoming a significant part of the economy.

Following the strong positive response to the Crooked Road, local artisan crafters began to organize with help from local and state leaders. This led, in 2004, to the formation of a second, closely related network called 'Round the Mountain (RTM). This assortment of weavers, wood-workers, blacksmiths, furniture makers, and other crafters has grown to nearly four hundred members from across a nineteen-county rural area in southwest Virginia. Like the Crooked Road, their work is highlighted through a series of events, joint promotion and publicity, and listing on the 'Round the Mountain website. Many of the members, whose work is jur-ied, also offer their products for sale through Heartwood. Additionally, RTM provides referrals from other galleries and art centers, and business and marketing training, often critical to helping crafters grow from a hob-byist to a small business.[5]

Heartwood emerged in 2012, in an effort to strengthen the Crooked Road and 'Round the Mountain, while also solidifying the importance of the emerging focus on asset-based economic development. This work had been under way for over a decade at that point, beginning in many ways with Appalachian Sustainable Development in the mid-1990s with its focus on sustainable food, farm, and forest enterprises. The inclusion of music, heritage, and the arts complemented the focus on natural resource–based economic development as both offered potential for long-term, "lower-impact" economic development than some of the region's tradi-tional industries. Todd Christensen, who was skeptical when he first vis-ited ASD's solar wood kiln and sustainable forestry initiative in 1995, has long since become one of Appalachia's most creative and persistent advo-cates for building asset-based economies.

Now that process has come full circle with the 2013 launching of Appalachian Spring, an outdoor recreation and trails network. The Appa-lachian Trail, the New River Trail, and Breaks Interstate Park are three of eight major outdoor destinations that are being linked together, along with numerous lesser-known trails and sites. Though still in its early develop-ment, Appalachian Spring shows promise as a major addition to the region's tourism and general quality of life, complementing the opportuni-ties in music, art, and cultural tourism. Taken together, the Crooked Road, 'Round the Mountain, and Appalachian Spring represent networks that are themselves networked together through Heartwood and the Southwest Virginia Cultural Heritage Association.

At the same time that the Crooked Road and 'Round the Mountain were emerging in Appalachian Virginia, another type of network was coming alive almost 2,000 miles to the west, led by an audacious entrepreneur.

Arizona Goes Local

Kimber Lanning was just nineteen years old when she opened her first business in downtown Phoenix. A musician herself and an avid believer in the arts, she started Stinkweeds Music Store in 1987 to sell new and used music and to provide a gathering place for local musicians. Stinkweeds has become, as they say, an iconic part of the city's musical and local business landscape. Not one to rest on her laurels, twelve years later Kimber opened Modified Arts, transforming a ramshackle building in a neglected part of town into a thriving art gallery to help rejuvenate the art scene. Her gallery served as a catalyst for urban renewal in the Roosevelt Row area, so much so that *USA Today* hailed this neighborhood as one of "America's Ten Best Arts Districts" in 2014.[6] Keep in mind, we're talking about Phoenix, Arizona.

Kimber Lanning exemplifies the entrepreneurial spirit in almost every respect. She is a risk taker, an innovator, and a believer in the power of small businesses, but with a twist: She sees the potential for community empowerment, even social transformation in everything she does. Based on that belief, she utilized her experiences with Stinkweeds and Modified Arts to undertake a new initiative in 2003, Local First Arizona (LFA). Kimber knew firsthand how to build a successful and innovative small business. And she knew many of the obstacles and challenges they faced. Even more than that, her experience demonstrated that when new entrepreneurs, small businesses, and community organizations join forces in practical, meaningful ways, the likelihood of success for all increases. In other words, having already cultivated, informally, a number of effective networks, she decided to make that her primary work.

When Local First Arizona got going in 2003, it was one of a handful of networks emerging around the country, loosely associated through the Business Alliance for Local Living Economies (which we'll discuss later in this chapter). Using some of the relationships she'd built as a small businesswoman, Kimber began "knocking on doors," as she puts it, of other small to midsize businesses in the Phoenix area with this basic question: What can we do together that will build up our individual businesses while at the same time strengthening the role of small businesses in the area's economy and among elected officials? Two other local businesspeople, Cindy Dach and Michael Monti, were among the first to work with Kimber to begin developing a strategy to make this work. Starting with fewer than 100 businesses that first year, LFA has grown dramatically and now includes more than 2,700 businesses spread across the state, encompassing retail, food and farming, music and the arts, builders, contractors, architects and designers, tech companies, small manufacturers, business services, banks and finance companies, and nearly every other part of the economy.[7]

Like all community-based networks, LFA puts its first priority on its business members, promoting them through marketing and creative community outreach strategies, and by encouraging them to buy and source from one another; strengthening them through seminars, educational webinars, and monthly peer-learning get-togethers; and building their profile through a host of festivals, campaigns, and events that attract many thousands of customers each year. Beyond trying to meet the general needs of their businesses, the network also provides customized training and other forms of assistance, including work with small farmers in northern Arizona, and a rigorous program of training, support, and access to capital for Latina entrepreneurs just getting started. This program, called Fuerza Locale, focuses on Latino and Latina men and women, providing extensive training, business mentoring, and access to small loans for business start-up or expansion.

The immediate needs of a small business owner or local farmer can be daunting, making it difficult to look much beyond tomorrow. For that reason, Local First Arizona also takes the long view, tackling problems and working toward broader changes that can help it meet its mission of building better communities by strengthening local businesses. Two key areas where they've successfully worked for "system-level" change include city and state procurement policies, and so-called "in-fill development," that is, utilizing existing lots and structures within the community, rather than flattening farmland or open land and expanding a city's footprint.

"Procurement" is important to the health of businesses, and to the direction of economic development, because public bodies buy a lot of stuff: hospitals and clinics, universities and community colleges, state parks, transportation authorities, and local, state, and federal agencies turn to the private sector from their first days—building their facilities— right through to everyday needs. This includes food and food service products, office supplies and stationery, office furnishings and equipment, IT hardware and software, laundry, recycling and waste disposal, and a wide range of other services and supplies. While some of this is done in-house, the vast majority is contracted out, usually by public bid. This represents a tremendous potential not only for small and local businesses but for those with better triple-bottom-line practices, like a "waste disposal" company that separates and utilizes recyclable and compostable materials.

Steering procurement toward locally based companies helps increase the overall economic impact in the community, as documented in several studies by the group Civic Economics. In a 2012 study, Civic Economics compared a local office supply company in Phoenix, Wist Office Products, with a national chain. They found that for every dollar spent at Wist, *nearly three times as much of it stayed within the local area* as compared to the chain.[8] More than simply providing a market for a local business, local or in-state procurement helps magnify the benefits by circulating the money first spent on procurement among other local businesses. LFA has been able to steer the City of Phoenix toward a focus on local procurement, though as yet they have not succeeded in bringing about changes at the state level. Even so, the changes in procurement policies in the city of Phoenix have already led to more than $3 million in new contracts for local independent businesses in just a few years.[9]

LFA's work to promote in-fill development began nearly eight years ago, driven by a simple but critical recognition: Phoenix—and other cities in the state—needed more high-wage jobs and high-skill employees, but attracting them to towns whose center lacked vibrancy was just not going to work. Part of revitalizing communities, whether small towns or large cities like Phoenix, comes from the presence and vitality of young people. This demographic, this group of people, are more likely to stay in or go to communities with microbreweries, live music, bookstores and coffee shops, farmers markets and a range of healthy and green businesses. And just as important, younger people want walkable (or bikeable) communities, neighborhoods where there is plenty to do and where you can do it without a car. By filling in empty buildings and spaces, downtowns and Main Street corridors become much more attractive and much more vital. And they save money on providing services and utilities since things don't keep spreading out.

Kimber began work on Phoenix's building code, which like many others, made rehabbing and "adaptive reuse" of old buildings both time-consuming and expensive. Within a couple of years, LFA had helped about a dozen small businesses to locate in vacant buildings in the city's center, saving them an average of more than four months and sixteen thousand dollars in permitting costs. With this success, and the new allies it had

An example of "adaptive reuse" by Venue Projects in Phoenix, The Newton transformed an 18,000-square-foot abandoned building into a bookstore, restaurant, home-and-garden store, and office and meeting space. Courtesy Andrew Pielage.

built, they were able to persuade local officials to change key elements of the building code, creating one of the most progressive policies in the nation for promoting in-fill and adaptive reuse. The results have been substantial, with at least ninety local businesses now taking root in what not long ago were empty, ugly shells, including some former big-box stores. Most of these fifty-plus "repurposed buildings" are in the downtown corridor and have helped reinvigorate the city center with hundreds of new jobs.[10]

The strength of Local First Arizona is inextricably tied to the dynamism, creativity, and persuasive power of its founder, Kimber Lanning. If you spend more than five minutes with her, you realize that she is a force of nature. But what is also clear from the Arizona experience is that diverse networks, built around businesses and groups that are rooted in their community, can not only help level the playing field for smaller, local enterprises but can become effective and influential in shaping the policies and priorities of their place as well.

Getting National with Local

Organic Valley is a brand that many people know, carried by almost every major supermarket chain in the United States, along with hundreds of cooperatives, health food stores, and smaller grocers. Unlike many other major organic brands of today, Organic Valley remains very tightly connected to the farmers producing their products through their cooperative, the Coulee Region Organic Produce Pool, or CROPP. What started out as a handful of local organic farmers near La Farge, Wisconsin, has grown into a national network of more than 1,800 organic family farms, producing and selling dairy and cheese products, meats, and eggs and a wide range of organic produce. Their annual sales in 2013 topped $900 million and at current rates of growth will reach $1 billion by 2015.[11]

Organic Valley has managed to grow to substantial size as a producers' network, without forcing its farmers to "get big or get out." They've been able to do this for two main reasons. First, they are owned by the farmers that produce for them and managed by people whom these same farmers elect to the board. This producer ownership is essential to their success, as Marjorie Kelly points out in her analysis of Organic Valley.[12] This is in direct contrast with so many organic and health-oriented companies that have been bought out by major multinational conglomerates once they'd become "successful." CROPP, however, has been protected from buyouts because of its cooperative ownership, and because of how they've drawn upon their members' resources to help finance needed growth.

This tight connection to its member-owners has ensured a second key factor in their success: They've never lost sight of what most farmers consider to be their single-biggest challenge, that is, *getting a fair price for their products.* Instead of trying to compete in the "high-volume, low-price" world that dominates retail grocery sales, Organic Valley has instead built its brand, maintained very high quality, and gradually educated consumers, well enough that a heck of a lot of us are willing to pay more for meats, milk, and produce with their label on it. This allows them to pay consistently better prices to their producers, most notably on milk, which has been a losing proposition for most farmers for more than thirty years. (Incredibly, as the retail price of milk has more than tripled since 1970, the price paid to farmers has barely budged.) Organic Valley has paid on average 60 percent more to their producers than other dairy farmers.[13] They've been able to do this by building a strong brand but also by "managing supply," which has included very careful production planning to keep farmers' output in sync with consumer demand. It has also included making powdered milk from raw milk when supply exceeds demand rather than pushing prices down for farmers, which is what usually happens.

Like all good networks, they come from the bottom up and exist not to become big, but to strengthen their members and magnify the benefits of what they do.

If you're wondering how a company that has both production and distribution nationwide can be considered part of the local living economy, that's a good question. In many cases, becoming national, or international, signals the end of connections to local communities, both those making things and those buying things nearby. Organic Valley has approached this very real challenge by organizing their farmers into six "regional pools." In fact, this regional orientation led to a change in their name in 2001 to "Cooperative Regions of Organic Producer Pools," still CROPP (never let a good acronym slip away!). In these six regions, what is being produced and in what quantities is largely driven by markets and consumer demand in that same area. Customers buying Organic Valley milk in Boston or meat in Philadelphia are very likely getting those items from farmers in the same region, rather than product shipped across the country.[14] This type of system is more complicated to plan and manage but helps reduce shipping costs and associated environmental impacts while also helping to maintain connections between farmers and consumers.

The regional system has other advantages as well. While Organic Valley maintains one milk-processing facility itself and recently developed its own logistics and shipping company, most of the processing and distribution is done through locally and regionally based companies. More than nine different independent milk-processing companies, from Washington State to New Jersey, process and package milk from Organic Valley farmers, while a number of other companies make it into a range of high-quality cheeses. Numerous independent distributors then get it to market, closely coordinated by the regional pools and networks.[15]

The network functions of Organic Valley don't stop with the brand recognition, access to very large markets, or the well-managed logistics (one of the biggest headaches for small farmers!). Organic Valley has also used its members' resources to help train, support, and, in some cases, finance new farmers or those transitioning to organic production from conventional practices. This support helps farmers increase their income and reduce costs through on-farm generation of renewable fuels, including methane from farm waste, wind energy, and solar power.

Farming is a tough business in many respects. One of the biggest challenges that small and locally oriented farmers often face is finding the right scale at which they can generate enough sales without giving up either their values or the chance to receive a fair price. Organic Valley, because of its cooperative nature and its use of regional networks within a national network, has proven one of the most effective at enabling farmers to find and achieve that optimum scale.

Taking Local Networks National

Probably very few national networks of any kind can trace their origins to two twelve-year-old boys, but that is the case for the Community Power Network. Moved by concerns about the environment and climate change, Walter Lynn and Diego Arene-Morley began talking with their parents, frustrated that adults seemed to complain a lot without doing much of anything to tackle these big problems. In response to the urgings of these two friends, Anya Schoolman, Walter's mom, and Jeff Morley, Diego's dad, sat down with them and began to work together to see what could be done. After more than a year of investigation and research, they decided to focus on promoting solar energy at the neighborhood scale, creating the Mount Pleasant Cooperative (MPC) with other community members in this Washington, D.C., neighborhood.[16] That was 2008. Within just a few years, the MPC had begun to "solarize" their community, with one hundred households installing rooftop solar panels, fully 10 percent of the homes in the neighborhood.[17] Bulk purchases saved individual households 20 percent or more on materials and installation, while newly adopted renewable energy policies from the D.C. City Council created additional financial incentives. Both resulted from the Cooperative's door knocking and grassroots advocacy.

The Mount Pleasant Cooperative's success generated interest from other D.C. neighborhoods, leading to formation of a wider group, DC SUN, or DC Solar United Neighborhoods. This localized network helped coordinate the work of solar co-ops throughout the city; by 2010, there was a solar cooperative in every one of D.C.'s eight wards. None had existed just four years earlier.[18] The remarkably fast rate at which community solar was spreading in the District appears to be related to the integrated strategy first utilized by Mount Pleasant Cooperative: grassroots, neighborhood-level work to build awareness and interest, and to create opportunities for more economical purchases of solar systems; and advocacy for better public policy, based directly on this growing base of community interest and demand. "Practice-driven policy," we might call it. Whatever the term, Anya Schoolman soon decided it was time to take this strategy national.

In 2011, the Community Power Network was launched, with Anya at the helm. In less than four years, the CPN has grown to include almost 130 local or regional affiliates encompassing thirty-nine states.[19] Many of these are non-profit organizations that themselves are building networks of local businesses, cooperatives, neighborhood associations, and renewable energy advocates. Some are cooperatives like MPC, the original group that Anya founded. These different groups are pursuing a range of strategies to make solar power more available and affordable in their communities, including group purchases of solar panels, development of community "solar gardens" similar to the approach of the Clean Energy Collective, public solar systems connected to churches, art centers, or other community buildings, and advocacy for public policy that will help make solar more widely available.[20]

As each community develops its own approach to expanding solar energy, the Community Power Network helps with a range of very specific tools they've created to help these groups accomplish their goals while strengthening their own local networks. CPN also helps local communities understand the policies impacting clean energy, and offers ways to increase their effectiveness as advocates for better policy. Beyond the tools they offer, CPN has created a national exchange among local solar energy groups, a peer-learning venue that some participants say has been instrumental to their own local success.

The foundation of the Community Power Network is certainly the base of independent local groups growing in number and diversity around the country. For this reason, much of CPN's energy and resources are spent in helping these groups increase their local impact, that is, spawning more solar energy systems owned by or rooted in local communities. But they also realize that local efforts alone simply aren't sufficient without some means to magnify and accelerate those efforts. That's why they are also changing the public discourse and public policies in order to foster a transition to renewable energy and more self-reliant communities.

A Network of Networks from Coast to Coast

Local First Arizona is an independent organization built from and governed by people from Arizona, just as Local First Grand Rapids is independently run by and for small business folks and community leaders in western Michigan. At the same time, they are among a growing number of independent business networks linked together through BALLE, the Business Alliance for Local Living Economies. The brainchild of Judy Wicks, a restaurant owner in Philadelphia, and Laury Hammel, a small business owner and activist from Boston, BALLE was formed with the goal of strengthening and accelerating small businesses in all parts of the country by building networks of support, learning, and innovation. Judy's experience with her business, the famed White Dog Café, had convinced her that small farms and small businesses were more competitive when they worked together on everything from sourcing the products they needed to building a scale of infrastructure suited to local businesses rather than huge international corporations.[21] She also believed that close collaboration would foster innovation and promote more socially and environmentally sound business practices. Laury had come to similar conclusions through his work in starting the Social Ventures Network a few years earlier.

There are now eighty BALLE networks around the country, up from just twenty in 2002. Some are in big cities, like the Sustainable Business Network in Philadelphia or the Sustainable Business Alliance in the Bay Area of California. Others are in rural communities and small towns, including High Country Local First in western North Carolina, while still others are in mid-size communities, such as Bellingham, Grand Rapids, or the Andersonville Chamber of Commerce, a community within the Greater Chicago area.[22] BALLE helped catalyze some of these groups, while others emerged entirely on their own, making the connection to BALLE sometime later. But all share the "dual network" nature. That is, each of these links together many local independent businesses and other core community organizations into dynamic networks adapted to their communities or regions; and each in turn is part of the larger "network of networks" that is BALLE. Local First Arizona counts more than 2,700 business members, while High Country Local First, a much newer affiliate, numbers fewer than 100, yet they both contribute to the more than 50,000 independent businesses connected through BALLE.[23]

From the outset, BALLE has focused on and encouraged experimentation and innovation, not only to make small businesses more competitive but to build better communities and solve social and ecological problems. They've done this in a variety of ways, from educational seminars, webinars, and conferences to building a research capacity to better understand what works and what doesn't, especially in the realm of community-based economic development. More recently, BALLE launched its "Fellows" program, selecting twelve to eighteen people each year whom they believe to be among the leading innovators in social entrepreneurship and triple-bottom-line businesses. (I should note that I was in the first cohort of BALLE Fellows in 2011 and 2012.) This group comes together five times over an eighteen-month period for shared learning and strategizing, for exposure to new tools and ideas, and to

Judy Wicks, cofounder of BALLE, speaks at the organization's annual conference in Phoenix in 2015. Courtesy of Business Alliance for Local Living Economies.

help build a stronger, more effective voice for local living economies in state and national policies.

BALLE's visionary, longtime executive director Michelle Long has helped create a culture of learning and innovation throughout the organization, contributing to making BALLE a national leader in both economic thinking and practice. A recent example of this was a two-day gathering in January 2015 at the Tom Cat Ranch in California. Farmers, BALLE network leaders, and funders came together to grapple with climate change, but from a different vantage point: how to expand sustainable ranching and farming practices that enable soils to sequester large amounts of carbon, helping to reduce atmospheric levels of carbon dioxide. The group saw these practices in action at the ranch and then discussed how to integrate this knowledge into their own work, education, and policy efforts.

Working with their local networks and with other regional and national organizations, BALLE has also pioneered a number of innovative approaches that move us beyond the "jobs or the environment" polarization that paralyzes so many regions. These have included:

- Promotion of Benefit corporations, structured to be profitable, not only in the financial sense but in their impacts on workers and the community. In that sense, Benefit corporations are much closer to the structure and purpose originally envisioned when corporations were created more than three hundred years ago. BALLE has worked with B Lab and others to expose many more enterprises to this unique legal structure and to make changes in state corporation laws to allow for this type of corporate structure. While still a tiny fraction of businesses overall, in fewer than ten years the number of Benefit corporations has grown to more than one thousand, with twenty-seven states having passed laws to enable this new corporate legal structure.[24]

- Helping to create and expand an array of training, support, and promotion/branding systems to increase the number of socially responsible enterprises, and those working to improve their environmental performance. The Sustainable Business Network in Philadelphia and the Social Ventures Network have been among the key partners there.
- Working with the Democracy Collaborative, Michael Shuman, and others to expand the field of Community Capital, including the tools and systems that help build more locally rooted wealth, democratized investment, and productive capital.
- Beginning to develop a clear, comprehensive and far-reaching policy platform that will help level the playing field for small to midsize businesses while building more resilient, sustainable communities. This work just got under way in late 2014 and is being led by the Institute for Local Self-Reliance, Demos, the American Sustainable Business Council, and BALLE.

Finding meaningful, useful ways to "network other networks" is not always clear and certainly not easy. The approach that BALLE has evolved over time attempts to strengthen local networks so that they can help their businesses while encouraging new, triple-bottom-line thinking, tools, and policies. As a national network with broad local roots, they appear to be well positioned to link the best thinkers and the most dynamic doers, something the bottom-up economy urgently needs.

Analysis of Transition Four

Networks come about for many reasons, most often in response to practical needs shared by a similar assortment of businesses or groups. This practicality is what grounds networks in the everyday challenges of their members and, hopefully, keeps them from becoming estranged or abstracted from the real world of their constituents. Some networks, however, grow to become more than the sum or their parts, that is, to not only strengthen their members but to foster other advances, other changes that might help create systemic change. In this sense, networks set out to change the rules of the game.

Just like Walmart, Monsanto, or Citigroup, but with different values, different "shareholders."

Our analysis in this section considers how well networks are doing this now, and examines their potential going forward. We'll explore whether they are able to gain some of the same advantages of vertical and horizontal integration as the huge international corporations have done, and whether they've been able to level the playing field in other critical ways. Ultimately, the question might be whether or not networks really are having, or are likely to have, substantial impact at state, even national, levels. But we'll begin by revisiting a local community where the impacts of networks seem abundantly clear.

Athens, Ohio, you may recall, is in the southeastern corner of Ohio, the Appalachian part of the state, where not that long ago, coal, iron ore, and other mining industries dominated. There wasn't much coal left to mine in that region in 1982, when June Holley, Roger Wilkinson, and Martha Zinn started the Worker Owned Network, soon to become ACEnet. Since that time, the development of food as an economic engine for Athens and surrounding communities has been unrelenting. Annual sales at the Athens Farmers Market are approaching $2 million,[25] spread across more than one hundred vendors, while sales from businesses using the Food Ventures Center reach $8 million annually.[26]

Much of this growth has been enabled by networks of learning, doing, and change. These networks encompass all components of the food system, from farm through processing to retail. And they include a number of key players not directly tied to the food system, including local bankers and other investors, non-profit antipoverty organizations, colleges, community colleges, and small-business support agencies. Nearly all of these are woven together by ACEnet and its longtime partner, Rural Action.

Several overlapping networks are at work here. One of the most important derives from ACEnet's Food Ventures Center, through which more than three hundred food-based enterprises have either been launched or expanded to the point of becoming stand-alone, independent businesses. Among the most successful of these are Casa Nueva, Crumbs Bakery, Village Bakery and Café (which also operates a market, a brick-oven bakery, and a second café), and Shagbark Mill and Seed Company. Together, these four local businesses alone have annual sales in excess of $5 million and employ about 110 people. These and scores of other local food enterprises, and dozens of restaurants in turn, purchase extensively from the more than one hundred farmers who comprise the Athens Farmers Market, along with some from neighboring counties. The purchases include not only organic produce and other fruits and vegetables, but milk, cheese, meats, honey, maple syrup, mushrooms, and even flour, grains, and dried beans. Slightly to the west, the Chesterhill Produce Auction provides a twice weekly wholesale market outlet for another one hundred–plus farmers. Both the Athens Farmers Market and the Chesterhill Produce Auction constitute essential networks of farmers, connecting them to each other and to better markets.

Snowville Creamery, less than ten years old in 2014, sells nearly $4 million of its milk each year, all derived from pasture-based cows in nearby Meigs County, and one other dairy farm in Racine, Ohio.[27] Snowville also makes the base for a gourmet ice cream, Jeni's Splendid Ice Creams, another local success story. Products from Snowville Creamery, Crumbs Bakery, Vino di Milo pasta sauces, and Shagbark Seed and Mill in turn are among the nearly 250 different local food products made by more than sixty different businesses that comprise Food We Love,[28] a branded network built to promote local foods at retail outlets. These are now available in dozens of local and regional outlets, ranging from the Athens Farmers Market and specialty grocers to several supermarkets in the area, including Kroger and Whole Foods. Sales through Food We Love were estimated at $5 million in 2014, providing both another outlet for local food entrepreneurs and a critical connection to consumers in these communities.

These networks of farmers and ranchers, of food manufacturers, and of restaurants and retailers have become so "dense" with diverse food businesses that ACEnet and its partners were able to create a local eating campaign based not on a 100-mile radius, but on just 30 miles. The 30 Mile Meal Campaign began in 2010 and now involves nearly 150 food businesses. This brings additional public attention and sales to local farms and food businesses in July, during the peak season for southeastern Ohio.

The layers of networks within and surrounding Athens have accomplished a number of critical things that illuminate the potential of networks as tools for building strong local economies:

- **Local sourcing.** In most communities in the country, you'll hear chefs, food service directors, and artisan food businesses talk about how they'd like to buy local, but "we just can't find a consistent supply." While they've not entirely solved this problem, the deep and multilayered networks in the Athens area have made local sourcing both much easier and far more common than in most other places. They've done this, it should be noted, without a food hub or some other form of centralized aggregation.

- **Filling gaps.** Shagbark Seed and Mill produces flours, dried beans, and a small line of corn chips and tortillas, using heirloom varieties of grains and locally adapted beans. They launched in 2007 because the founders, Michelle Ajamian and Brandon Jaeger, realized that, in spite of the vibrant local food scene, nearly all of the "staple food items" people ate came from far away. Their own research work, farmer experimentation, and support from Ohio University enabled them to focus on the best varieties, while one of ACEnet's facilities provided space for their mill and other processing equipment.

- **Research, education, and support of innovation.** Rural Action has built a partnership with one of the region's most dynamic and successful farms, Green Edge Gardens, to provide extensive, hands-on education to farmers, and even Cooperative Extension staff, in organic production, High Tunnel production, specialty mushroom cultivation, and other dimensions of farming. This is one of several partnerships that bridges research with real-time, farm-based education to support the growth in farms that the rapidly expanding markets have enabled.

- **Reaching beyond the choir.** Community Food Initiatives, a twenty-year-old antihunger organization that manages six community gardens, has brought another dimension to the historically white and middle-class local food scene with two critical initiatives: Donation Station works in the Athens Farmers Market and the Chesterhill Produce Auction to solicit produce donations from market vendors and cash donations from customers, the latter "recycled" immediately to purchase more produce from farmer vendors. All of this fresh produce—more than thirty thousand dollars' worth in 2013—is then donated to area food pantries.[29] Additionally, one of the six gardens that Community Food Initiatives manages is serving as a business incubator for low-income youth, through YEAH, Youth Entrepreneurs at Hope. These teens in turn get business training and support from ACEnet, including use of the Food Ventures incubator to develop their food product ideas.[30]

- **Changing the public discourse.** Since the early days of Athens's local foods movement, when mostly countercultural types were involved, the recognition of local food as a critical part of the local economy has broadened considerably. Now the discussion includes leaders from the public schools, Hocking College, and Ohio University, Extension and economic development staff, leaders in tourism, the arts and culture, and a much broader base of everyday people.

- **Impacting public policy.** Perhaps the most challenging thing faced by most local economy advocates has been to reach a point of impact and credibility where public policy, and the people who make it, can be influenced. Successful entrepreneurs and dynamic community leaders can impact public policy on their own. However, the experience from Athens seems to indicate that networks, by integrating and lifting up a rich and diverse range of businesses and community initiatives, offer a more effective and sustained voice for policy advocacy. This is evidenced by the increasing involvement of local and state elected officials in the region's food and farming economy, what ACEnet's Leslie Schaller has called "an incredible level of support." Additionally, one of the region's most successful food entrepreneurs, whose business was originally incubated at the Food Ventures facility, is now a county commissioner.

Public Policy

The potential for community-based, action-oriented networks to change policy is also seen in the Community Power Network's impact on the city council of Washington, D.C. Prior to the formation of the Mountain Pleasant Cooperative (which later spawned CPN), the District had almost no policies directly related to renewable energy, and certainly none that encouraged it. With the concrete experience of a local neighborhood starting to "solarize" their homes, and a growing, District-wide network pushing for support of community-based energy, the council passed two critical laws: a rebate program for the purchase of solar panels and a tax incentive related to renewable energy. With well over one hundred CPN affiliates in thirty-nine states now, the question will be whether similar changes can be brought to other states, eventually spreading nationally.

Local First Arizona accomplished similarly sweeping policy changes in regard to Phoenix's rules on use of abandoned buildings in the city, discussed earlier in this chapter. Again combining action on the ground with persistent advocacy through the LFA network, the city went from making it expensive and cumbersome to fix older buildings to creating what Kimber Lanning calls some of the best policies in the country in support of adaptive reuse. This policy change has helped to revitalize Phoenix's downtown center while maintaining the unique character of different parts of the city.[31]

The concrete success of farmers markets in the Appalachian region, some linked together through the Appalachian Farmers Market Association (AFMA), has also played a role in changing policy at both the state and federal level, as well as among land grant universities in the region. This effort has been far broader than just southwest Virginia or AFMA, but both have played a role by making the case, on the ground, for farmers markets as tools for economic and community revitalization. That has led to several improvements in policies from the Virginia Department of Agriculture and Consumer Services and the state legislature itself, including a new law, passed in 2013, that allows farmers to sell a wider range of preserved food items at farmers markets, without having to make them in a commercial kitchen. And overall, farmers markets, local food economies, and sustainable agriculture all receive both more serious attention and consistent support—staff time, research, marketing, funding—from every land grant university in the region, and virtually all state departments of agriculture. A similar shift in priorities, including personnel and funding, has been seen in the approach to other elements of the asset-based economy, including music, artisan crafts, heritage, and outdoor recreation. There is no doubt that the success of the Crooked Road and the broader networks built through Heartwood and the Southwest Virginia Cultural Heritage Foundation has been the primary catalyst for this change.

In spite of these and other encouraging successes at municipal, regional, and state levels, networks pushing to level the playing field for small businesses and local living economies are still overwhelmed by conventional trickle-down economic thinking and policies. Often such policies are pushed by the very same leaders who advocate for small businesses and healthier communities. This is frequently the case among local economic development leaders and elected officials who simultaneously support entrepreneurship and "homegrown businesses" while also aggressively wooing out-of-state companies with tax abatements, low-cost financing, and grants. This is sometimes called an "all-of-the-above" strategy for economic development, but the problem with it is twofold. First, as we saw in the example of Cabela's, the support for nonlocal corporations typically dwarfs what is provided to local businesses, both new and existing. You might recall that the incentive package offered to Cabela's in that case was ten thousand times the size of the annual entrepreneurship prize given to a local business. In practice, then, it is not so much an all-of-the-above strategy as a drop-in-the-bucket strategy when it comes to local enterprises.

Second, there are usually built-in contradictions to this approach. We know, for instance, that farmers markets tend to draw people into town, and that once there, about 60 percent of those same folks will visit other businesses close by.[32] So farmers markets, and vibrant town and city centers more generally, pull people into town. Most everyone agrees that's a good thing. Supercenters, on the other hand, are usually located outside of town or at least away from the downtown center. And they typically contain a big-box anchor store, along with a handful of restaurant franchises, often a big-box building supply store, and a variety of more specialized chains. In short, they offer a nearly complete set of buying opportunities, with food close at hand. So they draw people *out* of town. The basic issue is not, as people often argue, whether Walmart, Target, or Cabela's offers the same product line as Rita's Retail or the town farmers market. The question is, Where will the majority of people—busy, pressed for time—likely go to shop in the first place? If you want them to go to your downtown, why provide millions of dollars to companies that will almost surely draw them away?

At the national level, there is a host of policies that disadvantage local small and midsize businesses, some of which we've discussed in prior chapters. As it now stands, ever-larger corporations are able to use their size and their international nature to build a host of networks that further tilt the playing field to their advantage. They vertically integrate to gain the advantages of controlling "supply chains," but often with little regard for the "suppliers," be they U.S. farmers or Vietnamese textile workers. They spread horizontally, buying their way into a wide range of businesses and industries, and shedding them from their balance sheets when so-called shareholder value necessitates that action. They build and utilize these networks often with no accountability to workers or local communities.

Networks that grow out of local economies seem to offer real potential to help overcome some of these inequities and make bottom-up economies more widespread and robust. But to make this possible, several areas of federal public policy need to be completely rethought and dramatically changed.

Here are four areas of policy that could begin to level the playing field for bottom-up economy networks:

International Trade Agreements

At this writing, President Barack Obama is pushing heavily for the Trans-Pacific Partnership (TPP), an international trade agreement that would encompass twelve nations in Asia and the Pacific Basin. We don't know exactly what is in it, but the draft portions of the document that have been leaked are alarming for anyone trying to build healthy local economies or to reinvigorate our democracy. These parts of the TPP have been leaked because the entire negotiation process, ongoing for more than three years now, *has been kept completely secret from the public, including, to a large degree, our elected representatives in Congress.* It has not been kept secret from everyone, however, as nearly two hundred executives of large corporations have regularly participated in the process of crafting the plan. Let's pause here: a trade agreement that would affect almost every sector of the American economy and tens of millions of workers has been negotiated with no public input, except for the priorities of an elite group of corporate leaders. Not surprisingly, the material we have been able to see contains some remarkably bad ideas, from further consolidation of financial wealth and power over patents, to, and this is no joke, an independent, unelected court to which international corporations can bring suits against nations, states, or communities who "infringe" on their rights to do business. A state law protecting farmland could be grounds for a suit from a Chinese company wanting to buy it and build condominiums.

The Trans-Pacific Partnership is particularly bad, but the history of international "free trade" agreements and the international bodies connected to them has been a bad one for most working people and communities. As John MacArthur, editor of *Harper's Magazine,* has said, "All of these 'trade agreements' are really investment agreements that make it safer for U.S. corporations to set up shop in cheap labor locales."[33] Unfortunately, the myth that "global trade makes everyone—consumers and businesses—better off" still holds sway with the majority of elected officials, in spite of much evidence to the contrary (see chapter 1). At the very least, the TPP and all future trade deals should be required to be debated openly, with secret negotiations outlawed. It is not only unfair and undemocratic, but it is one of the main reasons why these trade agreements have usually been bad for ordinary people and local communities. Further, the goal of international trade should not be to enable international corporations to make even more money with fewer restrictions, but to improve the well-being of citizens, workers, and communities. Imagine that.

Eliminate Tax Preferences and Incentives That Serve No Public Interest

Stacy Mitchell of the Institute for Local Self-Reliance has calculated that *small businesses on average actually pay 6–8 percent more in taxes than multina-*

tional corporations because of the wide and perverse array of tax havens and loopholes that allow big businesses to avoid their tax obligations.[34] Consider that these megabusinesses, already networked to secure lower-cost labor, materials, and supplies, also pay far less income tax than their much smaller local counterparts. This is ridiculous, especially given the better performance of small to midsize companies in creating jobs, making innovations, and investing in their own communities. Eliminating all such tax-evasion opportunities for big businesses should be among our highest priorities. It would begin the process of leveling the playing field between big and small, international and local businesses.

Two other areas of tax policy stand out here. First, online sales should be taxed. While many consumers initially balk at this, the vast and constantly expanding world of Internet commerce makes it long past due that those retailing online also pay their fair share of sales taxes. In the absence of this, local businesses, which typically have relatively small proportions of Internet sales (with some exceptions), see customers leaving them in favor of the savings from tax-free sales at the tip of their fingers. A survey of more than two hundred thousand consumers across the country demonstrated that, indeed, the ability to buy things online without paying sales tax was an important part of why they were shifting their purchases away from local businesses. Recently, more and more states have begun to tax most online sales, including those through Amazon, with twenty-three states now collecting such taxes.[35]

Second is a rather obscure but very important piece of state legislation regarding business accounting practices. Known as "combined reporting," and already the law of the land in nearly half of U.S. states, this measure prevents companies from moving earnings, in say, Utah, to a subsidiary in Tennessee, in order to reduce its apparent earnings and, therefore, its income tax obligations. This tax avoidance, essentially the domestic version of overseas tax havens, costs states hundreds of millions of dollars of revenue every year. And it is yet another way that larger corporations can use their networks to unfair advantage against locally based enterprises, few of whom have the option of creating shell companies in the Cayman Islands or of opening subsidiaries in other states.

Tax policy can serve public ends, as when new technologies that promise greater efficiencies or healthier communities are given incentives for research, development, and investment. Tax incentives are essentially expenditures of public, taxpayer dollars, in the form of money not paid to the federal treasury. As such, the health and well-being of citizens and the places where they live should be the standard to which we hold such investments, not the private gain of the already well-off.

Internalizing Costs That Have Often Been Externalized

An eighteen-month investigation by reporters from the *Los Angeles Times,* released in December 2014, documented a horrific level of abuse of men and women working the giant tomato fields of Mexico.[36] Nearly all of these tomatoes are eaten by American consumers, either in restaurant chains or purchased from the shelves of large retail supermarkets. The *LA Times* article made it clear that the almost unimaginably bad living conditions, extremely low wages, and withheld pay are the norm in these fields, as it is to a somewhat smaller degree for migrant workers in the giant tomato fields of Florida. The poverty of these workers, the on-the-job injuries, the health problems for them and their children, all of these are "externalized costs." When we buy the ninety-nine-cent tomato or get that great deal at a restaurant, we pay for most of the costs of raising, shipping, and packing or preparing that tomato, but not all of them. The abuse of thousands of Mexican farmworkers and thousands of migrant workers in the United States are not included. Nor are most of the environmental costs associated with that production, whether it's nitrate poisoning of groundwater or pesticides weakening bee colonies. These very real costs are "externalized"; they're not paid for by the companies producing them, allowing them to keep products artificially cheap.

The problem of externalized costs is endemic in our globalized economy. While local businesses can and do externalize costs as well, it is much easier to find the source of the problem and to bring them to account. The labor abuses described in the *LA Times* story, by contrast, took place even though many of the U.S. buyers had fair labor standards built into their agreements with suppliers, including humane, decent housing standards for workers. In a globalized economy, where the original source of a product is so far removed from the final consumer, it usually takes an exposé of this sort to even begin to bring accountability.

This is why public policy should push businesses of all types toward so-called "full-cost accounting," making sure that all costs, including the health and safety of workers and protection of the environment in the communities where you do business, are included in the cost of the product. This is what organic and ecological farming attempts to do, though it, too, can externalize labor costs; and it is what triple-bottom-line businesses are fundamentally about. While it is difficult to mandate a triple-bottom-line approach for businesses, it is possible to strengthen policies and institutions set up to protect workers, like the National Labor Relations Board, or to ensure compliance with environmental laws. It is much harder to use these tools when, at the same time, tax policies encourage companies to outsource overseas (where such protections are often weaker) and trade policies, like the TPP, make it much harder for states or local communities to set and enforce their own standards.

The international networks of commerce and trade utilized by large corporations become tools to obscure, hide, or ignore real costs to workers, communities, and the environment. The awful truth is that for most of us, our lives depend on these global supply chains for much of what we need and buy. If public policy was used to level the playing field for local, bottom-up economies, we would be able to reduce our dependence on such businesses and stop supporting, unwittingly, practices we find deplorable.

Limiting Size, Reinvigorating Antitrust Laws

Antitrust laws are essential to ensuring that the "free market" remains free, that is, open and competitive for businesses, new and old, large and small. That is why it is so ironic that the steady weakening of such laws over the past thirty years has so often been pushed by people claiming to be free market advocates. In the absence of antitrust laws, banks and companies often become so large that they can exercise substantial control over the market, over prices paid to employees and suppliers, and over determining which consumers and which communities have access to the products and services. We have seen this, for example, in our agricultural conglomerates, with a handful of meat and poultry companies controlling as much as 80 percent of meat production and processing; and in telecommunications and the media, where more 24/7 availability of "communications" has been accompanied by declining choices about content and providers.

A renewed and updated Glass-Steagall Act is desperately needed in the financial industry, and stronger antitrust laws, backed by the courts, are essential to a reinvigorated, open, and fair market, for businesses and consumers alike. For workers, citizens, and communities, there is virtually no downside to stronger protections against monopolies, to separation of banking functions from Wall Street speculations. For local and regional networks to have a real chance of strengthening local, independent businesses and the communities where they reside, we'll have to dramatically scale back the tax, trade, and business advantages we've built for the biggest international corporations.

Transition Four: Recap and Looking Forward

Locally based small and midsize businesses are in many ways at a great disadvantage compared to huge multinational corporations. The "bigger is better" myth leads us to believe that this is due to the greater productivity and efficiency of very large enterprises. However, research and experience demonstrate that their advantages stem more from their propensity to externalize health, safety, and environmental costs, along with a dizzying array of tax, trade, and economic incentive policies designed by and for placeless global companies.

While renewed efforts to change these policies are slowly gaining traction, practical means to level the playing field for locally based farms and businesses are also emerging, most notably, networks. Some of the core lessons we've learned thus far from networks include:

1. Networks have emerged as very important tools to increase the competitiveness of small businesses and to foster learning, innovation, and economies of scale. In this way, networks help level the playing field against huge international corporations that have built their own networks of supplies, production, financing, markets, and influence.
2. Networks can also promote more vibrant community economies by identifying gaps to fill and increasing local business-to-business buying and procurement. Public institutions in communities—schools, hospitals, universities, etc.—can significantly boost this local procurement of products and services available from local businesses.
3. At this time, networks are limited primarily by the cash needed to sustain and grow, as many of their functions fall outside the scope of what funders and investors typically support. Those committed to building local economies, whether as investors or donors and philanthropists, need to recognize the essential role of networks.
4. The potential of wider regional and national networks to impact public policy is just beginning to be explored and tested. Because they are deeply connected to real people, real places and businesses, these networks offer a different voice to advocate for policy change than traditional advocates.

Policy changes that would enhance the effectiveness of networks and the bottom-up, local economies they serve have more to do with subtraction than addition. Limiting the size of megabanks and businesses by reinvigorating antitrust laws, reducing or eliminating subsidies and tax loopholes, and dramatically reorienting trade deals form their current focus on expanding the reach and power of multinational corporations.

Up next: The first four transitions together describe a path toward a more just, democratic, and sustainable economic system. More resilient, self-reliant households and communities (transition one) pave the way for diverse, local living economies (transition two); targeted investment in workers and communities to expand the base of local capital in these economies helps build much more broadly shared prosperity (transition three); and local, regional and national networks that tie these pieces together, accelerate their development and magnify their impact (transition four). These transitions are unfolding, in many places. But getting there is still hard, and takes far too long. That's because the public conversation and public policy are still largely bound by the "six myths," still controlled by the elites who benefit so much from the current system. That's why the final two transitions focus on changing the debate and building political power from the bottom up.

Further Reading

Farrell, John. "Anya Schoolman: Episode 1 of Local Energy Rules Podcast." Institute for Local Self-Reliance. January 16, 2013. https://ilsf.org. See also other Local Energy Rules Podcasts.

"Internet Sales Tax Fairness." Institute for Local Self-Reliance. December 22, 2014. https://ilsr.org.

Marosi, Richard. "Product of Mexico: Hardship on Mexico's Farms, a Bounty for U.S. Tables." *LA Times,* December 7, 2014. www.latimes.com.

Woodroofe, Natalie, and Leslie Schaller. "Reinventing Appalachia Ohio's Local Food System." ACEnet. October 2013. www.acenetworks.org.

Rebuilding a Meaningful Public Debate

From Debilitating Corporate Media to Energizing Civic Conversations

The idea that some areas of society and life are too precious, vulnerable, sacred, or important for the public interest to be subject to commercial exploitation seems to be losing its influence. Indeed, the very notion that there is a public interest, a common good that transcends our individual self-interest, is slipping away.
—Joel Bakan, "Corporations Unbound"

In order for people to turn away from the politics of denial that have overtaken the electorate . . . there needs to be a visible counter narrative about what else is possible here.
—Mimi Pickering, Appalshop, Whitesburg, Kentucky

Never forget that justice is what love looks like in public.
—Cornel West

In February 2011, I spoke to a group of about one hundred people in Blacksburg, Virginia's old downtown theater, the Lyric. My topic, "Economies, Community, and Love," offered lessons from my work in the Appalachian region, along with ideas about how to begin to rebuild community and restore love for our places, our environment, and one another. At the time, I had no plan for writing a book that in many respects would grapple with the same topics. Instead, I had been given the charge to make a presentation that drew lessons from my experience and from my place. Mine was one of the first talks in the new "Community Voices" series that had launched the prior fall under the care and guidance of Andy Morikawa. The range of topics in that series, which continues today, is extraordinarily broad, as are the backgrounds of the speakers. The common denominators are community, the lives and work of each presenter in their communities, and the potential that community can bring to restoring and renewing our world.

Andy knows a thing or two about the power of strong communities. I first met him in 1985, when he had just launched New River Self-Help and Resource Exchange, or SHARE. Building on the time-honored tradition of buying clubs, SHARE was a monthly food club for ordinary people, one that used bulk buying power combined with extensive volunteerism to make a thirty- to thirty-five-dollar box of good food available for twelve dollars. SHARE was not a government program, and there were no subsidies to bring down the cost of food. It required a very well-managed, carefully orchestrated few days of setup, packing, boxing, and loading once each month, typically with hundreds of volunteers giving their time. While SHARE was available to all people regardless of income, the great majority of participants were folks with limited or fixed incomes, particularly senior citizens, working folks, and young people needing to stretch their budget. SHARE required a community of people to make it work, and in the process helped further build and support that community. Not long after I first met Andy, we started a branch of SHARE in our area, about three hours southwest of Blacksburg, with Andy and his team guiding us through the process. At its peak, our two SHARE affiliates were providing more than five thousand boxes of food each month, all packed and paid for by the participants themselves.

Between his days with the New River SHARE program and his launching of Community Voices in 2010, Andy moved to California to become the national director of SHARE for eight years. But his heart never left Virginia's New River Valley, so in 1997 he returned to Blacksburg to jumpstart the Community Foundation of the New River Valley (CFNRV).[1] The foundation had actually started a couple of years earlier, but the initial leaders had concluded that there simply wasn't enough "wealth" in the region to build an asset base. Andy thought otherwise. With "community" central not only to its name and geographic boundaries, the CFNRV used a community-based strategy to build its board, identify the best projects to support, and develop its core financial assets. Building an extraordinarily wide base of partners and focusing on what Andy calls a "boundary-spanning" approach, the Community Foundation was able to create a substantial financial base along with a reputation for effective and innovative collaboration. Since its inception, it has provided more than $5 million in grants, mostly smaller ones to a rich range of non-profits and community groups. In spite of the relatively low median income prevalent in the New River Valley, they've built a $10 million asset base, entirely from the community.[2]

The foundation's deep roots in the community across class and race have also enabled it to help convene and sustain critically important community conversations around race and the impact of racism, providing a forum for discussion and leading to significant impacts in community policing, local government, and more. This work is ongoing.

By the time Andy began developing the idea for a Community Voices series, his nearly forty years of work in communities, with communities, and on behalf of communities was deep in the fiber of his being. Andy had been remarkably successful throughout his life, pioneering new ideas, launching new organizations, inspiring innovations among his peers. But he'd seen his share of setbacks and disappointments as well. Yet when we sat down to talk about my presentation, he still had that remarkable quality I'd come to see in so many past collaborations: an enduring hopefulness, based not on naiveté but on his own experience of working with people and building a better world, community by community.

Community Voices, and the foundation of experiences from which it builds, is one example of an emerging effort to "give voice" to ordinary people, often doing extraordinary things, within both the limits and the gifts of their places. We might think of these as "place-based public forums," for as you'll see in the examples that follow, they emerge from, and to a large degree tell the story of, particular places: their struggles, their responses, and their successes. Storytelling, community theater, and community-based media all represent pieces of our fifth transition, *rebuilding a meaningful public debate: from debilitating corporate media to energizing civic conversations*. So, too, do the physical spaces—parks and plazas, farmers markets and public markets, pedestrian corridors and vibrant downtowns—where people of all different stripes experience "actual physical contact!" to steal a line from *Ghostbusters*. We'll explore the intersection of these civic spaces with the media and storytelling efforts and examine how these together might reenergize our sense of common citizenship on a broader scale.

Telling the stories of ordinary people doing extraordinary things is not new, but I'd suggest that it is more urgently needed now than ever before, for at least two reasons: First, a wide and growing portion of the

American public has largely given up on politics and, worse yet, on the very idea of the public good or public action. Second, from Robert Putnam's *Bowling Alone*[3] to Benjamin Barber's *Consumed*,[4] it becomes clear that the trend of civic decline has been reinforced, perhaps even accelerated, by ever-more-autonomous consumerism. These two trends together have been further propelled by pervasive and highly effective marketing campaigns that equate "revolution," "freedom," "liberation," and "solidarity" with what you buy. Public, civic acts that one might consider on behalf of strangers or even neighbors have been largely subsumed within brands and market behavior. The self-actualized consumer, buying what he or she wants, when, where, and how they want it, is steadily replacing the engaged citizen. This has been disastrous for our democracy.

Second, and closely related to the above, is the general degradation of "public speech." As we'll see, the jury is still out on exactly why this is happening, what role the Internet may or may not be playing, and how much worse it is now than in past times. Nevertheless, several studies indicate that name calling and other forms of disrespect are now relatively commonplace not only among pundits and political elites but in the broader public debate as well. For instance, an examination of online forums connected to the *Arizona Daily Star* in 2013 found that over a three-week period, more than half of all issues debated contained at least one instance of degrading or disrespectful comments, and that more than 20 percent of all comments made were considered "uncivil."[5]

I'm arguing that we've created a perfect storm that is degrading citizenship, based on:

- the increasing prominence of autonomous consumerism in our lives;
- the slow but steady decline of broadly based civic organizations;
- a rapid decline of public spaces for gathering and interacting;
- the rise of "outrage speech" in both traditional and new media;
- a lack of trust in police, particularly in communities of color, and of authorities more generally; and
- record levels of cynicism about political participation based on the growing awareness that the priorities of everyday citizens have little impact on policies.

A lot of intelligent people are grappling with the problem of civic withdrawal and political alienation. Here, we'll look at how community- and place-based conversations, built around revitalized local living economies, might play a role in reversing this very bad trend. The myth that "looking out for Number One makes everyone better off" suggests that the decline of citizenship is not terribly important; that if we all simply pursue our individual self-interest, through the market, it will add up to more wealth and satisfaction for everyone. But as we'll see, for communities and society as a whole to function well, we need revitalized public spaces and meaningful public conversations every bit as much as we need vibrant local economies.

Emerging Examples of Civic Engagement and Community Media

In the Heart of the Coalfields

The first time I set foot in Whitesburg. Kentucky, was 1977. I was a student at the University of Kentucky, and I had traveled there to meet Harry Caudill, the famous author of *Night Comes to the Cumberlands.* Mr. Caudill was a relentless defender of the common man, and one of the coal industry's fiercest critics. My first of many teachers about the history and contemporary struggles of Appalachia, he was one of those rare people who had so much to say, yet who took an interest in a young stranger from well outside the region. Once he heard that my last name was "Flaccavento," he began to tell me tales of the Italian immigrants who had come a century earlier to help lay the bricks and build the bridges.

I didn't know it then, but not far from where Mr. Caudill and I were meeting, some other people who would one day also be mentors in my Appalachian schooling had formed a group to document and tell the stories of the region. Appalshop formed in 1969 in an effort to give voice to people, places, and issues largely overlooked. They continue that work today, one of the nation's longest-running and most innovative community-based media centers. Utilizing video and audio documentaries, written press and stories, and their flagship radio station, WMMT, this small but vibrant center reaches about 300,000 people in some of the most rural parts of southeastern Kentucky and southwest Virginia. With a staff of eighteen, they rely heavily on volunteers, particularly for programming on the radio station. In fact, nearly all of WMMT's programs are produced by volunteers—sixty of them—who range from high school students to senior citizens, from coal miners and truck drivers to college professors and envi-

Appalshop's office and media center in Whitesburg, Kentucky. Courtesy of Mimi Pickering.

ronmental activists. Appalshop and WMMT are truly community-based. Although not an affiliate of National Public Radio, they do share programs and stories with NPR and with community stations in other parts of the country through their participation in the Public Radio Exchange, a national network of community and public broadcasters.[6]

Much of the music broadcast on WMMT features bluegrass and other traditional music of the mountain region, including many local performers. Some of the younger staff—more than half are thirty or under—and volunteers bring other musical styles to the station, from rock to hip-hop. The focus on the region's music and culture, along with the diverse array of shows hosted by local volunteers, has enabled WMMT to reach a greater cross section of the public, including working folks and lower-income people, than does the typical NPR station. That is part of why Appalshop was well suited to help lead a new effort at public dialogue called Making Connections.[7]

Begun in 2013, Making Connections is part of a broader effort by Appalshop, Kentuckians for the Commonwealth, the Mountain Association for Community Economic Development, and others to help shape what is being called the "Appalachian Transition." The work to explore, develop, and build an economy beyond coal mining is long overdue throughout Central Appalachia, where mining jobs have been in sharp decline since the mid-1980s. Employment in mining and mine-related activities has dropped by nearly two-thirds since that time, the vast majority of that long before Barack Obama became president.[8] But one of the reasons that action has been delayed, and that support for emerging alternatives has been inadequate, has been the grave difficulty of talking about alternatives to coal mining. This has been true for a long time but was accentuated with the election of Obama and the coal industry's well-funded and largely successful campaign to label alternatives as part of the "War on Coal." (I experienced this in my own congressional campaign on more than one occasion, including a caller to a radio program in Grundy, Virginia, who asked me if I was "for the plans to build windmills on the sides of our mountains." When I replied that I didn't know about such plans, but that if they created jobs and provided locally generated energy, they seemed worth considering, she said, "That's all I needed to hear. You're for Obama and against coal!")

The truth is that a number of economic alternatives are emerging in Appalachia—several of which have been discussed in earlier sections of this book—but that few are well known outside of or even right here in the region. Making Connections is providing a vehicle to collect the stories of those local businesses, new technologies, and resurgent communities, and to use them to begin to change the public debate, moving it beyond the question of whether or not you are "pro-coal." It is an enormous challenge, to be sure. Developing alternatives for coal miners and their communities is a daunting task, similar to, but far greater than, the challenges faced in creating alternatives for tobacco farmers.

Yet there is reason to be hopeful. In Virginia, the work on local foods and sustainable farming, along with the newer focus on music, culture, artisan crafts, and trails has begun to generate public enthusiasm among local people and their elected representatives. In Kentucky, the combined effort of a Republican congressman, Hal Rodgers, and the Democratic governor, Steve Beshear, to tackle this issue led to the creation of SOAR—Strengthen Our Appalachian Region—that has put real alternatives on the table for the first time. And in West Virginia, the success of the Wild Ramp in Huntington, of the Coalfield Development Corporation in southern

West Virginia, and of the West Virginia Community Development Hub and its partners has many people talking about new ways to build good livelihoods.

For much of Appalachia's history, outsiders have largely called the shots. This pattern has held true not only for the railroad executives, timber barons, and coal company shareholders, but also for many of the people seeking to help change things for the better. With the deep roots of Appalshop and the strong ties to real, practical emerging alternatives, Making Connections offers hope of a much more bottom-up approach to building a new and better economy in the region.

Community Theater in the Deep South

Near the border with northwestern Florida and southeastern Alabama lies the small town of Colquitt, Georgia. Its two thousand residents share a history that weaves together cotton farming, plantation agriculture, and the racial challenges of so many towns in the United States, southern and otherwise. For Colquitt, that history and the personal stories behind it have become the key to economic and civic renewal rather than another way to separate into "us" and "them." It all started when one of the town's leaders, Joy Jinks, invited a theater director from Upstate New York to visit the town and hear some of the stories.[9]

By the early 1990s, Colquitt was in decline, economically and physically, with an increasing number of closed shops, vacant properties, and boarded-up buildings. When Joy heard Richard Geer speak about "the power of stories to renew a community," she invited him to her sleepy town to put the idea to the test. The result of this visit was a community play in 1992 and the creation of a new, community-based theater group named for a famed local dish—Swamp Gravy. The first play was held at the elementary school, and by 1995, Swamp Gravy had taken up residence in Cotton Hall Theater, which, fittingly, was a refurbished cotton warehouse. Their first production in 1992 sold out, as has virtually every one since, often months in advance.[10]

Community theaters take many forms, from Barter Theatre in Abingdon, Virginia, to the Flat Rock Playhouse in western North Carolina. Often they combine elements of professional theater companies—trained actors and directors, a playbill of old and new theater standards—with a variety of local subjects, writers, and aspiring actors. Barter Theatre, for instance, hosts an annual Appalachian Festival of Plays and Playwrights that pro-

Two of the local residents appearing in a production put on by Swamp Gravy at Cotton Hall Theater in Colquitt, Georgia. Photo by Richard Geer, courtesy of the Colquitt Miller Arts Council.

vides a venue for emerging writers and that complements the Barter Players, an ensemble of young actors learning the trade. Most of the directors of these theaters, and the local leaders in their communities, will tell you that they contribute more than just "arts and culture" to the community, and in Barter's case, well over one hundred jobs. They also help build community pride and help define the distinctive character of their particular places.

Swamp Gravy goes a step further. Although the people who write, direct, and choreograph the productions are all theater professionals, the substance of the plays comes from local people and the stories of their lives. This has helped build connections to their history, their culture, and the lives they are now leading. In a southern town, made up almost equally of blacks and whites, you might be a little concerned about the retelling of those personal stories. But Karen Kimbrel, who cofounded Swamp Gravy with Joy Winks, says it has worked just the other way, building bridges in the community while helping to open up a more candid conversation about the town and its past.[11]

In addition to the stories, Swamp Gravy relies on nearly one hundred volunteers who make up the cast and crew for most productions, and who also serve as promoters and ticket sellers, set builders and staffers for the theater's concession stands. In essence, the residents of Colquitt are truly making theater of and from their own experience, as storytellers and the actors who bring the stories to life. The professional direction and choreography helps ensure a very high level of quality, which is why people, both locals and tourists, keep coming back.

Swamp Gravy's success at community storytelling appears to have rekindled a spirit in a town many might have given up for dead. It has also been the catalyst for several related ventures, including the Market on the Square, which opened in 2001. Fixing up another old building, this Market provides space and essential services for twenty small businesses, some selling crafts and other things related to the community's growing art and theater scene. It has been at full capacity almost continuously for more than ten years now.[12] The Market on the Square and the Cotton Hall Theater also represent forms of community capital, discussed in chapter 4.

Colquitt's embrace of art as a community builder also includes murals depicting farmers and other occupations, along with important pieces of the town's history. Since the first one was completed in 1999, murals have grown to become a defining piece of both the look and the culture of Colquitt. With the walls of fifteen different buildings now adorned with murals, this town of just over two thousand people was chosen to host the Global Mural Arts and Cultural Tourism Conference in 2010. Karen Kimbrel has been quoted as saying that the murals "set the tone" for Colquitt, letting locals and tourists alike see how this place acknowledges and celebrates its place and its history.[13]

In the heart of Kentucky's coalfields, a similar community-based theater initiative emerged in 2003. Beginning with the collection of stories from local residents in Harlan County, Kentucky, Higher Ground put on its first production in 2005, focused on the epidemic of prescription drug abuse in mountain communities. Much as Swamp Gravy does, the small staff of Higher Ground connects to well over a hundred residents to listen to their stories, develop the play, and eventually put on the production. Their primary goal, as codirector Devyn Creech says, is "to open an honest dialogue about difficult issues, in a place where it's hard to have those conversations." This has led them to deal not only with drug abuse but with such hot-button issues as mountaintop removal and the economic transition beyond the coal industry, among the five productions they've put on thus far.[14] With miners among the participants as well as the audience, it seems that Higher Ground is making headway in cultivating honest discussions. This is a critical step in opening the door to new ideas and new approaches to building a healthy local economy.

Local Stories Shared Nationally

Few nationally broadcast radio and TV programs have given attention to local economic and community issues like Laura Flanders's *GRITtv*. Begun in 2008, her weekly program covers an extraordinarily wide range of issues spanning culture, politics, civic and community activism, political dissent, and the economy. The stories she features and the guests she interviews are consistently "out of the mainstream," precisely because most other media outlets provide few if any opportunities to hear from them. And while many of the stories grapple with some of the biggest issues of our time, Flanders seems to strive to connect these big-picture issues with grassroots efforts, with real people working locally to make their communities better. This local grounding has included communities in the Bronx, Appalachia, Iowa, Mississippi, and many other places.

GRITtv puts a particular emphasis on the people and communities working to build healthy, living economies. From thinkers like Michael Shuman and Vandana Shiva to leaders of local cooperatives creating jobs in neglected communities, the show provides one of the most consistent and thoughtful venues in which these alternative economic strategies are given voice. In addition to co-ops, which have been the subject on multiple occasions, other bottom-up economy initiatives featured on *GRITtv* include public banking, "shift your money" campaigns (from Wall Street to community banks), community wealth and care for "the commons," and several different grassroots economic development efforts and strategies. In this way, Flanders's program has helped elevate the importance and viability of the alternatives that are otherwise largely marginalized in the media. She has put "local" on the national map, albeit with more limited reach and influence than conventional media. Her work deserves to reach a much wider audience, and as it does that, it will help steer the public discourse away from trickle-down and its failures toward the success and potential of bottom-up economies and a revitalized grassroots democracy.

Community Space versus "Development" in Maine

There's an extensive backstory, wonderfully told by Jennifer Lunden of the *Portland Phoenix,* about the recent history of Congress Square Park.[15] Created in 1982 by a federal urban development grant, this small park embedded in Portland's most densely populated neighborhood had been a site for concerts, arts events, and much more during its first two decades. But over time, as both public and private funding dried up, the park fell victim to neglect, disrepair, and blight. Portland, being one of Maine's most family-friendly cities, according to surveys, had always prided itself on its open space for families, children, and community events. This time around, however, several local leaders, including the mayor, were initially persuaded by an Ohio-based hotel chain that most of the park should be sold and converted to a major "event center." That was 2012. It still might happen. But the story of Congress Square Park is, up to this point at least, a success story for those who believe in community control and the critical importance of civic space.

As neighbors and others began to mobilize to preserve and improve the park rather than sell it to a private developer, they furiously gathered signatures on citizen petitions, organized letter-writing and media campaigns, and steadily built a potent local political force. But very importantly, they also set about to show just how the park could once again be a vital part of the city's life and economy. With help from the Project for Public Spaces, based in New York, they launched a series of community events and activities, starting with a volunteer-led cleanup of the park, the donation of some movable chairs and furniture, and the presence of two food trucks, both local, selling meals, snacks, and refreshments. Working with a nearby business, they secured free Wi-Fi for the park. People started coming, to sit, to read, to work, to eat.[16]

Next they organized some simple but very effective events, including art contests, an evening of swing dancing, and a community gathering to view World Cup soccer matches on borrowed, wide-screen TVs. The diversity of events helped bring the community's own diversity out to the park, well beyond the middle-class professional crowd. With each event, word spread about the park's rebirth, and with that, more folks came to sit, read, work, or eat on a regular basis. It would have been understandable, and quite normal, for the folks of Portland to await the decision as to the sale of the park before investing their time, energy, and belongings into a space that might soon be lost. But they didn't wait, instead building a political force in support of the park through the experience of Congress Square as a vital, living part of the community.

The Friends of Congress Square Park, as the group called themselves,

A revitalized Congress Square Park, hosting a community viewing of the World Cup, part of the "Lighter, Quicker, Cheaper" strategy of revitalizing public spaces. Courtesy of Project for Public Spaces.

embraced a strategy developed by the Project for Public Spaces intended to make things happen without extensive assessment, cost, or bureaucratic compliance. Called "Lighter, Quicker, Cheaper," the approach taps entrepreneurial energy and helps galvanize a bottom-up approach to building better communities. Rather than wait for a new restaurant to open up adjacent to the park, they invited mobile food trucks to set up there on a regular basis. Instead of building permanent seating or tables, they set up temporary, moveable ones. Rather than wait for the town to budget staff time to clean and maintain the park, they do it themselves, voluntarily. While these steps are not a substitute for longer-term investment and commitment by the town itself, they serve the purpose of demonstrating what's possible and in the process build a broad and diverse group of people who become, at least on this issue, politicized; that is, who decide that they need to work for better policies regarding the park. This "action and place-based strategy" worked. The Friends of Congress Square Park and their allies introduced and won passage of a new law requiring a supermajority—8 out of 9—city council members to approve sale of any of the city's thirty-five public parks (and they did this in spite of considerable resistance and bureaucratic hurdles put forth by the city at that time). The connection between public space and citizen engagement could not be more clear.[17]

The Friends of Congress Square Park are not alone in leading a fight to make public places a key element of their city's life. There are similar stories with Market Square in Pittsburgh, Pioneer Courthouse Square in Portland, Oregon, Falls Park on the Reedy in Greenville, South Carolina, and many other parks and plazas in towns and cities of all sizes. Typically in these cases, a vacant or derelict spot has been renewed as a vibrant public space, often as an alternative to a planned private development. The fight to save these open spaces for public use helps build a grassroots base as the places go through a range of improvements, and as they begin to host music, art, theater, sports, and other events.

The stories of these public places vary, but there is little doubt that they help cultivate renewed energy, often as one of the last truly open public venues in increasingly privatized towns and cities. We know that public places are an asset to small cities like Portland, Maine, and bigger cities like Detroit and Buffalo. The question is, can they also help rekindle citizenship? Of equal importance, can we get it right this time and ensure that public spaces grow out of and serve all citizens, all communities? Can public spaces even become a force for social and racial justice in our communities? The pioneering work of Angela Glover-Blackwell and her organization, Policy Link, will surely be critical in this regard.[18]

Analysis of Transition Five

The sociologist Robert Putnam put the idea of "social capital" on the map with his 2000 book *Bowling Alone,* in which he looked at how civic organizations and informal networks of social relations impacted community cohesiveness and trust.[19] Putnam found that, overall, Americans' participation in voluntary associations and other civic groups had declined considerably over the past few decades, and along with that other measures of community well-being. Among the strongest reasons for this decline was the huge increase in economic inequality. Specifically, he found the highest levels of "social connectedness and civic engagement" during the post–World War II decades, when incomes were also much more equal, and a big drop in this social capital as inequality rose from 1980 onward. Eric Uslaner, a political scientist at the University of Maryland, reinforced Putnam's conclusion with his own findings that rising economic inequality led to declining levels of trust among the population.[20]

While some have contested Putnam's characterization of declining civic life in the United States, there has been, at the very least, a profound shift in the types of organizations available for people to join, in who is joining them, and what "membership" means. Theda Skocpol documents the widespread proliferation of voluntary associations from early in the nation's founding until the 1960s, at which time interest groups began to largely supplant the traditional organizations that had emerged among farmers, veterans, women, parents, and others.[21] She and her colleagues estimate that in 1955 the twenty largest voluntary associations in the country were so broadly based that from 3 to 5 percent of all adults were not just members but were serving in leadership roles. (Some of those organizations included the Veterans of Foreign Wars [VFW], the Elks, rural and agricultural associations like the Grange, along with PTAs and other primarily local associations. And, of course, trade unions were critically important for millions of working people, both as a potent political force and as a training ground for advocacy and civic involvement.) That is to say, a very sizeable portion of the population was getting on-the-job training in key elements of democracy, from managing debates and differences of opinion, to understanding parliamentary procedures and group problem solving. By contrast today, Skocpol contends, "there are too few opportunities for large numbers of Americans to work together for broadly shared values and interests. This leaves our public life impoverished."[22]

It goes without saying that these groups had plenty of flaws, most notably exclusion by race or gender. With the exception of labor unions, which sometimes bucked the prevailing exclusions of those times, most of these associations were surely complicit in the prevalent racism and sexism. The point is not to glorify these groups but to recognize some of the fundamental contributions they did make to our democracy and to see how those attributes might once again be built, albeit in a more inclusive form.

Among the core attributes that these associations brought to our civic life were:

- A sense of connection to neighbors and others in the immediate community, and to a larger process of discussion, decision making, and, in some cases, advocacy. The nature of many of these associations, national in scope, but fundamentally local and face-to-face in practice, cultivated a sense of how local actions could contribute to larger change. That's almost entirely lacking today.

- Empowerment (again in many cases, not for everyone) through meaningful processes that involved and required the building of knowledge, understanding of issues and skills of debate, dialogue, and leadership. Compare participation at that level with the modern "click here to make your voice heard" Internet world of political advocacy, and it is easy to see why so many of the current opportunities for expression of citizenship are so utterly dull and seemingly meaningless.

- Barriers based on race and class—and sometimes religious affiliation—were real and commonplace and no doubt contributed to some of our current problems in those realms. It is true, nevertheless, that compared to modern advocacy groups, which are both more narrowly defined and supported more by people of greater means and more formal education, many of these associations provided a meeting place across economic status and class. Local VFW chapters or PTA groups created places where blue-collar workers and business owners met on at least relatively equal terms. And according to Skocpol, there was typically broad "upward mobility" as people could become leaders on regional, state, or national bodies once they'd proven themselves at the local level.[23]

- The values these associations tended to cultivate were more of what today we might call "the common good," values of community service, of sacrifice for the greater good, and of fellowship. Again, recognizing that the common good was often not truly "common," there was nevertheless a general notion that the "we" was at least as important as the "me," that is, that being a citizen was as or more important than being a consumer. Today's interest groups, while focusing on critical issues, ironically may be helping to perpetuate the market's focus on "getting what you deserve."

The shrinking of voluntary associations where people of different backgrounds and means worked together has been accompanied by a decline in shared spaces where we congregate, that is, the commons. This has been the inevitable result of more than three decades of both privatization and commercialization. We have been selling formerly public spaces—parks, plazas, stadiums, sidewalks, bridges, etc.—to private corporations, while also expanding our sense of where it is appropriate to buy and sell rather than share. Jonathan Rowe states that "the appropriation of the commons for private gain has reached an epidemic level. New technologies, and the relentless appetite of the market, have resulted in a grab for every last inch of natural and social space."[24] This has both fostered and reinforced the concentration of wealth and the increasing segregation of America by class. And that's the way some people want it. Rowe quotes a builder of exclusive yachts as saying that the market for these very expensive boats is strong because "rich people can go to a beautiful hotel and pay $3,000 a night for a suite. The trouble is, when you go down the elevator you are in the lobby with people who paid twenty times less. My clients don't like that."[25] With extremes of wealth goes a desire to keep out the commoner, and that is facilitated by privatized rather than public, open spaces.

At the same time that voluntary associations and public spaces have been declining, both of which helped us mix and mingle across class, occupation, and ideology, the consolidation of our media has been staggering. In the early 1980s *fifty* different corporations owned roughly 90 percent of all media companies, already a relatively high level of concentration. By 2012, looser regulations from the Federal Communications Commission had led to only *six* massive companies owning 90 percent of all media outlets.[26] As we discussed in chapter 5, these companies went both "deep and wide" in developing their media networks. That is, they spread out geographically and across types of media, and they now own both the companies making the content and the ones doing the promotion and distribution. Bain Capital, a Wall Street investment firm with no history in media, now owns Clear Channel, which in turn owns more than one thousand radio stations across the country.[27] Bain also owns two major radio advertising firms, which then, of course, buy and facilitate advertising on many of those stations. Mitt Romney, you may recall, was a senior partner in Bain Capital.

There is growing evidence also that as consolidation makes media giants bigger, more national and global in their orientation, journalists and reporters are let go en masse, the depth of news coverage declines,[28] and locally developed or locally focused content declines.[29] There is a lot of money to be made in local TV news and local radio, but much more so if you trim your reporting staff and air primarily the same content, regardless of the community to which you're broadcasting. And that's exactly what is being done.

Less public space for gathering, meeting, and dialogue; far fewer voluntary associations that involve people of different backgrounds; and a media whose content is increasingly prepackaged, designed to sell particular products and specific points of view. On top of all that, we have low levels of trust, in politicians and even in our fellow citizens, spurred by unprecedented levels of inequality and the prevalence of outrage speech in the media (which often points the finger at minorities, the disadvantaged, immigrants, and other vulnerable people). It is no wonder that people feel disengaged, on their own, and cynical about the public sphere.

The examples we looked at in this chapter are challenging this homogenization, are reinvigorating local conversations, and are helping to spur more meaningful dialogue and analysis of real issues for and by real people. Strong local economies are emerging all over this nation, and along with them, more vibrant towns and healthier communities. Experiments in civic participation and public space are emerging. And community-based theaters and media companies are telling their stories. But there are not nearly enough of them, and this work can only go so far when the laws of the land so heavily favor extractive economies and giant, placeless corporations, including media conglomerates. If we are going to make the rules of the game fair, return them to their original purpose of supporting the general welfare of society, we must reverse the decline in civic participation and dramatically expand community-based discussion, participation, and control of our political process.

The good news is that more diverse, locally rooted economies have been shown to foster greater civic engagement, healthier, more resilient communities, and increased political participation. Multiple studies, beginning with the work of Walter Goldschmidt in the 1940s and updated by Thomas Lyson in 2006, make it clear that more, and more diverse, local businesses improve community health and reduce many negative, costly social problems, including obesity, crime and incarceration, teen pregnancy, infant mortality, and more.[30] A 2011 study found that a higher proportion of small businesses in a county correlated with a healthier population.[31] The Lyson study and another by Troy Blanchard also showed that a broad base of local businesses, compared to concentrations of a few large employers, strengthened overall civic participation, increased membership in local community groups, and increased voter turnout.[32]

Why does having more local, independent businesses make our communities healthier, stronger, more engaged? Part of the reason is surely trust and a sense of connection, what is often now called "social capital." And while not every local shop owner is either pleasant or civic-minded, as a group, local independent businesses on the whole are more connected to their communities, earning that trust. We've already seen how community banks make loans to homeowners and local businesses at a rate that is almost four times as high as the absentee banks. Here's another example: In the aftermath of Hurricane Katrina, Tulane University professor Richard Campanella found that local businesses reopened almost twice as fast as chain stores, making goods and gathering places available to the residents of the devastated city—in spite of the far smaller resources upon which they had to draw.[33]

Public Policy

At the time of the writing of this book, public opinion of the U.S. Congress, the president, and both major political parties are at near-record lows. People rightly believe that their needs, concerns, and ideas have little impact on the political process, especially nationally, but at lower levels of government as well. In the face of such widespread alienation, three different reactions are most commonplace: First are the people of all political stripes who have essentially given up on politics and are instead focusing on what they can do in their local places, and with their own consumer choices. Second is the group of people who have become outraged by this alienation, at their lack of real influence, and who express that outrage online, in letters to the editor, and sometimes at public debates and forums. And at times, even with violence or threats of violence. Although this is far more common for people on the right of the political spectrum (see the study by Sarah Sobieraj and Jeffrey M. Berry that found "decidedly more outrage speech on the right than the left"),[34] it does include all political persuasions. And third is perhaps the biggest group of all, folks who've basically said, "Screw it. There's no point." While some would call this a cop-out, their reaction to the present reality may well be the most logical and understandable of the three.

There are a host of reasons, good reasons, for this pervasive alienation and the growing cynicism it has precipitated. The powerlessness that most people feel leads to different reactions—parochialism, outrage, giving up altogether—none of which will get us where we need to be. Can vibrant local media and renewed public spaces, anchored in revitalizing local economies, provide the foundation for a renewed citizenship? Let's revisit Buffalo's West End, in the Green Development Zone formed by PUSH Buffalo, to begin to get a taste of how this might unfold.

Policies Related to Public and Open Space

The majority of decisions about the use of public space are made at state and local levels. A number of localities have enacted policies that protect public space from private development, including, as we saw earlier, Portland, Maine. In Buffalo, New York, PUSH Buffalo was already under way with turning vacant parcels into community gardens, parks, and public spaces when another battle for public space erupted along the city's famed Erie Canal. With their successful campaign to wrest ownership of vacant lots from the State Housing Agency and Wall Street under their belts, PUSH joined with four other groups in a fight to preserve this iconic downtown area. They found themselves fighting plans by the Erie Canal Harbor Development Corporation (ECHCD) to turn it over to private hands. When word got out that the ECHCD was negotiating with Bass Pro Shops, including $35 million in public financing for the national chain, citizens sprang into action. Mobilizing the community through public meetings and employing the "Lighter, Quicker, Cheaper" strategy to bring activity and vitality to the area, they managed to not only stop the Bass Pro deal but to launch a new chapter in the revitalization of Buffalo's downtown. Today, Canalside includes walking paths and re-created canal areas, an outdoor ice-skating rink three times bigger than the one at Rockefeller Center in New York, sitting areas and eateries, and hundreds of events throughout the year. And it includes the public, lots of people from all walks of life.

The Erie Canal Harbor Development Corporation, a state agency, has by all accounts changed its priorities and strategy, thanks to citizen mobilization and the development of creative alternatives. Now they are investing in public infrastructure and amenities that bring people—and local businesses—back downtown. Donn Esmonde, a reporter for the *Buffalo News,* says of the ECHDC that "its philosophy has done an about face," moving their thinking "from big box to outside of the box."[35] It can happen.

At the most basic level, both elected officials and staff (economic development, tourism in particular) need to be persuaded that open space, in the form of parks, plazas, greenways, gardens, community gardens, and similar sites are substantial assets for their community. We know that these spaces make towns and cities more livable for the people already there, more enticing for people considering moving there, and more likely to bring tourists back again. They are also essential for rekindling the shared sense of community that has been steadily eroded over the past two generations. The short-term economic boost of a major event center or high-end development should be weighed against lost opportunities for small, mobile businesses and micro-entrepreneurs, artists and cultural events, and, simply put, an inviting, *free* place for the community to gather.

It is also important to realize that preserving and enhancing (investing in) public open spaces is more likely to happen if localities also adopt policies that encourage adaptive reuse of old buildings and in-fill development as has happened in places like Phoenix and Grand Rapids. If we use the abandoned lots and buildings we already have—and nearly all cities have thousands of them—there is far less justification for filling an open space with high-end condos or converting a park into a convention center.

Maintaining or establishing vibrant, open public spaces can help communities maintain their character and foster the engagement needed for place-based development. But they can also become an amenity primarily for new residents and the better-off if community revitalization leads to gentrification, as it so often does. The "Equitable Development Toolkit," assembled by the research and action organization Policy Link and available online, highlights more than two dozen tools communities can use to fight gentrification while promoting stronger, better communities.[36] These range from land use and environmental policies to cooperative housing ownership and other affordable housing innovations. Given the frequency with which "renewal" leads to displacement of local businesses and residents, the "Toolkit" should be required reading for planners, economic developers, and community leaders.

Policies Related to the Media, Media Consolidation, and Ownership

Our laws and our traditions view the "airwaves" of television, radio, and now the Internet as part of "the commons," something that is a public good. Yet federal laws passed since the mid-1990s and the rules and rulings of the Federal Communications Commission increasingly treat them as if they were just another piece of private property, available to the highest bidder in unlimited amounts. Media companies have jumped on that change in policy to consolidate and concentrate their power and influence, from small-town radio stations to major urban newspapers. This has been bad for local communities, who've seen less and less content from and about their places and concerns. It's been bad for the quality of content, as more and more of it is produced to be mass-marketed, with less analysis, less variation, and less investigation in the first place; and it has been bad for public discourse, as the major media conglomerates focus on what makes money, that is, cheap, incendiary, often misleading talk radio and TV. If we wonder why our public debate has become so crass, so mean, or why we are generally less well-informed than prior generations, even as we live in the peak of the information age, we should, for one, look at what deregulation has done to the diversity and quality of our media.

Reversing two decades of deregulation won't be easy, but it is utterly essential if we are to open an honest and meaningful public debate about the critical issues we face. As Robert McChesney has quoted Jeff Cohen of Fairness and Accuracy in Reporting, "The current debate covers the spectrum from GE to GM."[37] For the average person, it may seem a somewhat obscure issue, but if you believe, as Jefferson did, that a democracy can function well only if its members are well informed, then this becomes a critical area for change.

To date, efforts at slowing the consolidation of media have been largely unsuccessful. However, one example of success is in the realm of low-power FM radio. Low-power stations are just that; with no more than 100 watts, they typically have a radius of just 3–5 miles. And they must be not-for-profit. This combination assures that they represent distinctly local voices and respond to community concerns and priorities. Some are associated with churches, while slightly more than half are run by community groups and non-profit organizations. According to a 2011 survey done by the Prometheus Radio Project, most are staffed by volunteers, with three-fourths having an annual budget of twenty thousand dollars or less. In the absence of overriding commercial pressures, they can focus on local issues well: 71 percent of these stations do public affairs programs, and 61 percent had programs specifically tailored for youth.[38] In this way, they represent a community asset rather than yet another way to stoke consumerism or rage.

The first wave of low-power FM stations came in the mid- to late 1990s, building up to an estimated eight hundred nationwide by early in the new millennium. With much bandwidth still available, Prometheus Radio Project and others worked to foster the next wave. After several years of work, the Community Radio Act of 2010 was finally passed into law in January 2011. This legislation removed a number of obstacles to low-power FM stations, enabling them to open in both large cities and small towns. In the two years following passage of the act, 2,800 non-profit and community groups have submitted applications for low-power FM stations across the country, potentially increasing community-focused broadcasting dramatically.[39] They don't have the reach or power of Clear Channel, but they do represent an important bottom-up response to media consolidation and capture.

Another important victory for public access to the airwaves came in the spring of 2015, when the Federal Communications Commission ruled in favor of so-called "net neutrality" deciding that the Internet should be regulated as a utility, with its access not allowed to be segregated by the ability to pay. Needless to say, that FCC ruling is being challenged by the media giants and their political allies in Congress.

Policies Related to Economic Concentration and Local Ownership

In prior chapters, we looked at policies that might help level the playing field between multinational corporations and small to midsize independent businesses. These ranged from elimination of tax incentives and tax havens that allowed these business giants to pay far lower tax rates than local businesses, to changes in local and state economic incentives that currently invest dramatically more in big out-of-town companies than homegrown businesses. I won't restate those here, but given the critical role that a vibrant, diverse, and locally rooted economy plays in civic participation, it is clear that *nurturing local living economies is one of the critical steps toward rekindling community and civic engagement,* the precursors to a revitalized citizenry.

I'll mention one more change that is clearly needed and warranted but only rarely discussed: changes in corporate charter laws. Corporate charters are the agreements that give corporations status as a legal entity. Every corporation, large and small, must first be incorporated in a specific state before it is allowed to start doing business. The original idea of a corporate charter was that it was more of a privilege than a right; it was fair to expect that corporations would offer something in return for this legal status and privilege, including proper care of its workers and the communities where it did business. To ensure that corporations were also "responsible corporate citizens," charters were limited in duration to just a few years and could be revoked, if a corporation was found not to be acting in the interest of its employees, neighbors, or communities.

National and international law has strayed so far from this original understanding, so much so that now trade agreements enable corporations to sue states and nations who diminish their profits because of laws designed to protect workers or the environment. In other words, rather than expecting them to be at our service and to follow reasonable laws and priorities of our communities, corporations can now go after us when we impinge on their profit making. This is as absurd as it is counterproductive. Trade laws need to eliminate such provisions, and citizens need to start talking about revoking corporate charters when they don't respect core community values.

Transition Five: Recap and Looking Forward

Rebuilding meaningful public debate through energizing civic conversations, the fifth transition, is an essential part of rebuilding our democracy and accelerating the transitions to resilient communities, living economies, and widely shared wealth and prosperity. Among the core lessons of this transition, four stand out:

1. Several factors have converged to degrade civic and community life and to even call into question the very idea of citizenship, including:
    a. a dramatic decline in voluntary associations and civic groups, particularly those that brought together people of different classes, occupations, and ideology;
    b. a loss of community and public space where people gather and build a sense of common experience and purpose;
    c. a relentless process of privatization and commercialization, increasing people's focus on "me" over "we," on being consumers more than citizens;
    d. extraordinarily high concentrations of media ownership, reducing local news and content, and marginalizing independent, alternative voices; and
    e. the rise of "outrage speech" encouraged by all of the above factors and by the anonymity and distance of virtual communication.
2. Efforts to rekindle citizenship and civic engagement are small but growing, including reclaiming and rebuilding public gathering places, growing community-based media, arts, storytelling, and other communications organizations, and efforts to reverse media consolidation and promote a wide base of independent local voices.
3. Diverse local economies clearly cultivate more vibrant community life and higher levels of civic engagement than do economies overly concentrated in a few big companies. Bottom-up economic strategies and community-based civic renewal are essential to one another.
4. As efforts to rebuild public spaces and public debate emerge, it is essential that this time the needs, wisdom, and voice of historically margin-

alized communities take an active role in the development and implementation of these ideas.

Up next: There are few things more fundamental to a vibrant democracy than a well-informed citizenry. This chapter looked at several examples in which communities have begun to reignite civic dialogue and the broader public debate through alternative media, the arts, and renewed public spaces. In the next chapter, our final transition considers new and creative approaches to cultivating more participatory democracy, and how these might help reinvigorate more traditional, tried-and-true means of political action on a broad scale.

Further Reading

Barber, Benjamin R. *Consumed: How Markets Corrupt Children, Infantilize Adults, and Swallow Citizens Whole.* New York: Norton, 2007.

Ehrenreich, Barbara. *Bright-Sided: How the Relentless Promotion of Positive Thinking Has Undermined America.* New York: Henry Holt, 2009.

"The Equitable Development Toolkit." Policy Link. 2015. www.policy.link.org.

Frank, Thomas. *One Market under God.* New York: Anchor, 2000.

Lardner, James, and David Smith, eds. *Inequality Matters: The Growing Economic Divide in America and Its Poisonous Consequences.* New York: Demos, 2005.

McChesney, Robert. *Blowing the Roof off the Twenty-First Century.* New York: Monthly Review Press, 2014.

Putnam, Robert D. *Bowling Alone: The Collapse and Revival of American Community.* New York: Simon and Schuster, 2001.

Transforming Politics from the Bottom Up

Unleashing a Community-Based Politics of Engagement to Overcome the Lobbyists and Moneyed Elites

The victory of consumers is not synonymous with the victory of citizens.
—Benjamin Barber, *Consumed*

If you're going to get serious about systemic change—not just "projects"—you're ultimately going to have to consider what government does, and how it can be used to further the vision and model you affirm. If you don't somebody else will.
—Gar Alperovitz, *What Then Must We Do?*

It appears difficult to activate citizen participation . . . without devolving powers to levels where citizens can effectively influence issues.
—Caroline Patsius, Anne Latendresse, and Lawrence Bherer, "Participatory Democracy, Decentralization and Local Governance"

When I declared my candidacy for the U.S. Congress in 2012, it was the first time I'd ever run for any kind of public office. Folks asked me why I didn't start with a local or state office and then "work my way up" to Congress, a more typical and plausible path. The answer was that I wasn't looking to embark on a career in politics but that I wanted to enter the debate about national policies, especially as they impacted our communities, economies, and environment. Perhaps in part because I was not a "typical politician," my candidacy attracted a somewhat more diverse group of supporters, including farmers, miners and retired miners, small businesspeople, even some Republicans, along with more traditional Democrats and progressives.

Let's be clear here—I lost rather resoundingly, garnering just under 39 percent of the vote. But I think it is fair to say that among the 115,000 or so people who voted for me, there was a fair number who appreciated an honest, direct approach to the issues. My foray into politics leads me to think that people will respond when we offer a clear focus on what's *wrong*—an economy that doesn't "trickle down" wealth but sucks it up from local people and communities; a politics that brazenly concentrates more and more power in a tiny elite; and when we discuss what would surely be *better*—a locally rooted, bottom-up economy that builds community resilience, and an engaged citizenry that takes power back from the elite. That's what I campaigned on, and it attracted folks of very different stripes.

There was another very basic reason I threw my hat in the political ring: I became convinced that local action, however effective and widespread, was not enough to bring about sustained positive change. Not nearly enough. Over the three decades preceding my congressional campaign, I had been involved in a good number of efforts to "build a better economy and community," and I'd come to know and sometimes work with hundreds of other folks doing similar work in almost every part of the United States. At one point I believed that this broadly based, grassroots amalgam of local food and local economy initiatives was becoming the foundation of a nationwide movement to build an economy that worked for people and their places. We were, after all, creating concrete positive benefits for ordinary people, farmers, businesses, and communities, often under very difficult circumstances. How could you argue with that?

I was wrong. So were a lot of other folks who had decided to give up on larger, often national, debates and policies. What happened instead is that our public debate and political process was overtaken, swiftly and overwhelmingly, by another amalgam of forces—the moneyed elite and the Wall Street and corporate lobbyists, supported by a media that fed anger and disenchantment among ordinary Americans. This is the "somebody else" to whom Gar Alperovitz is referring in the epigraph above. Indeed, they did get serious about changing the system, only not for the benefit of most people or their communities. I've come to call the political process they've built "WTF politics," both for the "never mind reality" policies it has spawned, and because it describes our political process pretty accurately: Wealth Trumps Fairness. WTF.

Because of the ground we've lost, the WTF political process is worse now than it has been in a very long time. An extensive 2014 analysis by Marten Gilens and Benjamin Page of nearly 1,800 different issues of public policy found that *the priorities and preferences of "average citizens" had little or no independent influence on the policies adopted.* The only times when policy adoption mirrored the will of the majority of average citizens is when it also happened to coincide with the preferences of the wealthy and/or big business associations. And more often than not, it doesn't. Recent comparisons of what the majority of Americans want versus the policy priorities of the wealthy show a sharp and consistent divergence on many issues, from increasing the minimum wage and the government's role in job creation to trade and tax policies. The interests of the rich often coincide closely to those of organized corporate, trade, and big business associations, but only infrequently with ordinary Americans. Yet as Gilens and Page show, there is a very strong correlation between the priorities of the rich and the adoption of public policy.[1]

The lack of influence in policy making has helped dampen the results of extensive "get out the vote" campaigns as more and more folks come to believe that neither their votes nor their needs and priorities have much impact on politics. This has led to a disengagement among working- and low-income people in particular. A 2013 study by Demos showed that even though there was a slight increase in voter turnout among lower-income voters for the 2008 presidential election, fewer than half of eligible voters from this group did vote, compared with more than three-fourths of wealthy voters.[2]

There are also serious questions now being raised about the very nature of our representative democracy by advocates of what is generally referred to as "participatory democracy." While still uncommon in the United States, efforts at participatory democracy have arisen in part to enliven the normal mechanisms of political participation but also to go beyond them. Is it enough, advocates would ask, to simply get more people to vote every two years, or do we need a more consistent, meaningful engagement between everyday citizens and the process of making laws and determining public priorities? And if so, how do we go about building the mechanisms and institutions that might help bring that about, and the culture to keep it going?

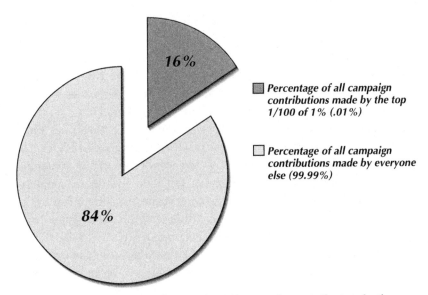

1980 political campaign contributions. In 1980, campaign contributions by the richest Americans—the top 1 out of 10,000—made up 16 percent of the total. (From CrowdPAC, "How Much Do the 1% of the 1% Control Politics? The Elite Takeover of American Politics," April 21, 2015, www.crowdpac.com.)

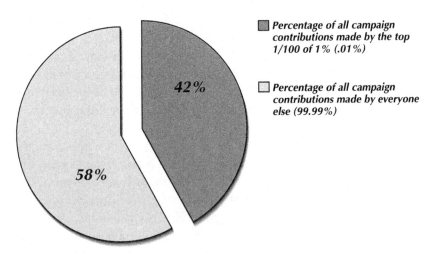

2012 political campaign contributions. By 2012, the richest 1/100th of 1 percent provided 42 percent of all campaign contributions, meaning that for every dollar given by average citizens, very wealthy people on average gave more than eight thousand dollars. (From CrowdPAC, "How Much Do the 1% of the 1% Control Politics? The Elite Takeover of American Politics," April 21, 2015, www.crowdpac .com.)

In this chapter I discuss some of these daunting challenges, as well as present some emerging efforts to *transform politics from the bottom up*, our sixth and final transition. Compared to the first five transitions, the foundation of experience I will draw from is far more limited. There are some promising initiatives and some interesting ideas—including some of my own!—but in truth we just don't have much experience with building a bottom-up political process. That's the problem, of course, and it is our starting point.

It's important to recognize that the strategies described in this chapter are meant to broaden and strengthen efforts at sweeping social change, and to ground them in the experiences emerging around the country. These experiments in civic participation can potentially enhance other, more established strategies for social change and for movement building, not supplant them. As you read this final section, be thinking about how these "synergies" might come about, how, for instance, emerging economies with a triple-bottom-line focus might link to the Black Lives Matter movement to create real opportunities in struggling communities; how efforts to build community capital and promote worker ownership can connect with the fight for a higher minimum wage, or for real financial and corporate reforms; how strategies to make democracy more participatory at the local level can ally with the national movement to overturn Citizens United and other efforts to get money out of politics.

Emerging Examples of Transforming Politics from the Bottom Up

A Northern California Town Experiments with Citizen Participation

Situated 30 miles north of San Francisco, Vallejo, California, has a diverse population of just over 180,000 people. The town made national news in 2011 when they were forced to declare bankruptcy as they struggled to come out the other side of the recession. Much less well known is a very positive step they took about that same time, initiating a citizen-led process of "participatory budgeting" (PB). One of eight U.S. cities to have begun using some form of participatory budgeting since 2010, Vallejo was the first to use it citywide.[3] Vallejo has now used PB in its annual budgeting process for three consecutive years, and the results have been encouraging.[4]

Begun in Porte Allegre, Brazil, in 1989, participatory budgeting is now used in 1,500 cities around the world, primarily in South America and Europe. In the United States, the first city to utilize PB was Chicago, beginning in 2009 and led by Alderman Joe Moore. The alderman realized that he needed to reconnect with his constituents and offer them much more meaningful ways to participate. Designed to reengage citizens in the governance of their town, community, or region, PB uses a community-focused process to gather input from residents about budget decisions, develop a set of priorities, vote on them, and then fund them. The community is involved at every step of the process, with concerted efforts made to involve young folks, people of color, and others who have been shut out from the normal world of politics. Typically, the municipality allocates a small part of their total budget to the projects selected through PB, ranging from less than 1 percent to as much as 20 percent in the case of Porte Allegre in Brazil. For Vallejo, out of a total annual budget of approximately $80 million, roughly $2 million is set aside for PB, representing about 2.5 percent of the total. About four to five thousand people participate in the public meetings and deliberations that are part of the PB process each year, or a little less than 3 percent of the total population.[5] That may not sound like a high proportion, but these folks are doing much more than just voting, as they help research ideas, develop proposals, debate with one another about the merits of different ideas, and ultimately create and select a list of priority projects.

Participatory budgeting takes different forms, but at its heart is the idea that citizens themselves can make informed decisions about the use of public funds, that is, the money that originally came from them (either as property, income, or sales taxes). In Vallejo, they begin with a series of community meetings around the city, facilitated to maximize and diversify the input. This first stage focuses on brainstorming potential projects or programs that might receive funding with the $2 million allocated.[6] In some places, the projects are limited to capital improvements, but Vallejo allows consideration of programs and services as well as capital expenditures. Turning folks out for this first stage is of course critically important, and Vallejo utilizes the full spectrum of media to announce the meetings, along with partnerships with civic and grassroots groups already working in different neighborhoods. Once the brainstorming has been completed, a smaller group of citizens is elected as delegates to work with city staff to flesh out the ideas in more detail and to attach a budget to each one. This process takes a few months.

The next step is prioritizing the projects, again done through town and community meetings, augmented by online responses. Once the projects have been narrowed in this way, a slate of potential projects, with budget estimates, is presented to the community as a whole, and a vote then determines the top-priority projects for funding. In Vallejo, this has led to support for eight to ten projects each year. These have included everything from fixing sidewalks, streets, and lighting to funding community gardens, small business assistance, youth and senior programs, and improvements to town parks and recreational areas. The city commits to funding the projects selected by the community, not just taking their views "under advisement."

In three years of using participatory budgeting, the City of Vallejo has allocated better than $6 million in funding for projects developed and chosen by a few thousand residents working together over a period of several months.[7] This process has done more than give citizens control over a small part of the city's budget. It has also helped to begin to rebuild trust and hope in a city whose financial crisis had precipitated a number of cuts in core services. According to surveys conducted by the Participatory Budgeting Project, which helped launch PB in North America, the majority of participants in the process in Vallejo said that the experience had improved their view of the government; what's more, those whose top projects were not chosen nevertheless expressed confidence and satisfaction with the process, along with a commitment to continued participation in the future.

It has also begun to build the next generation of civic leaders, like Jenny Aguilar, a teenager who now is a member of the PB Youth Committee. While she says she initially checked it out because of the free pizza being offered, she quickly became deeply involved and was impressed by how it helped build community. According to Jenny, working together and accomplishing concrete improvements for Vallejo has shown her that "the youth don't realize the power they possess to make change by participating in the process."[8] Because people as young as sixteen can fully participate, including voting on the choice of projects, young adults like Jenny can play a critical role in participatory budgeting.

In New York City, PB was launched with $1 million in each of four city council districts in 2011.[9] Three years later it had expanded to ten districts, with $14 million in funds allocated for citizen control. In the most recent year, fifty-five projects were selected at an average cost of just over $250,000. These have included a wide range of infrastructure projects along with improvements to parks and recreational facilities, and to upgrades of facilities for both seniors and schools. Eighteen thousand people participated in the process across the ten districts in 2014. One of the first council members to use PB, Melissa Mark-Viverito, has championed the process, leading to a commitment to employ participatory budgeting in twenty-three of the city's fifty-one districts in 2015, with a total of $25 million allocated.[10]

New York City has an annual budget of more than $75 billion, so the $25 million set aside for citizens' decisions in 2015 is a small fraction of 1 percent. For participatory budgeting to grow in its impact, it will need to move from the margins to a far more significant part of the city's overall budget. Nevertheless, certain patterns from New York, Vallejo, and other places are encouraging: much higher levels of participation by young people, immigrants, people of color, and low- to moderate-income people in PB, compared to traditional politics and voting; steady increases over time in those participation rates, seeming to show that people are investing themselves for the long haul and encouraging friends and family to get involved; and increases in other forms of civic participation, including joining other groups and voluntary associations.

While PB may as yet represent small potatoes in the larger budgeting decisions of major cities like New York and Chicago, the process does show potential as an effective means to rekindle democracy from the bottom up, particularly among those usually most removed from the process. One could reasonably argue that the funds allotted are little more than tokenism; that many of the projects citizens select—fixing infrastructure, supporting youth and senior centers, etc.—are things cities should be doing anyway. Both of these criticisms are true. Yet if PB becomes much more widespread, and as a result helps activate and engage millions of citizens previously estranged from politics, the bottom-up impact on our public discourse and politics could be profound.

Minipublics and Other Experiments in Citizen Engagement

"It is not enough for small groups to talk respectfully with each other, even when considerable publicity is given to the event. What is needed is a deliberative method that helps the public take strong and well-informed actions that can have significant political impact." This quote from the Minneapolis-based Jefferson Center encapsulates their commitment not only to getting different people talking to each other in civil ways but to substantially improve their understanding of the issues being debated.[11] Based on

Thomas Jefferson's views about the centrality of an informed citizenry, the Center focuses on increasing the knowledge base of citizens in an era when so many important issues have grown in complexity, even as the bulk of the information provided through the media has become increasingly simplistic.

One of the most important tools developed by the Jefferson Center to accomplish this goal is the "citizens' jury." First conceived and developed by Ned Crosby, the citizens' jury has been utilized for four decades now, in several different states and around many different issues. Like participatory budgeting, it is intended to greatly improve the depth and quality of citizen understanding of key issues and then to improve the ensuing public debate about what to do and how to do it. Unlike PB, if focuses on a very small but representative group of people from the community to undertake the process rather than engaging anyone and everyone it can. And it usually selects a single issue, or a set of closely related issues, for each jury.[12]

Most of us will think of the court system when we hear the word "jury." Citizens' juries share at least one thing with their judicial counterparts—they are intended to involve everyday people in deliberating about an important issue. But that's where the similarity ends. In a citizens' jury, from fifteen to twenty-four people come together for five, sometimes six days of intensive learning, discussion, and debate. At the end of the process, they build a consensus around a set of recommendations related to the issue they're debating, and these recommendations are then provided to elected officials and others involved in the policy process. During the jury process, they hear from people with extensive background and expertise on the issue; they engage them with questions and challenges; they learn to debate among themselves, candidly but with an open mind; and out of all of this, they build the recommendations for action. Far beyond a "town hall meeting" or a public opinion poll, these juries help diverse, ordinary citizens deeply understand an issue from all sides and then learn to bridge their differences in a spirit of open-minded, honest debate.[13]

One recent example comes from Minnesota. Following a razor-close election for the U.S. Senate in 2008, a vote recount got under way that was fraught with problems. Soon after, a citizens' jury was convened to review the existing process, understand the issues surrounding election recounts, and make recommendations for changes. Rather than meeting for one intensive five-day period, the participants met for two days at a time in a period that spanned more than a month. At the end of the process, they provided recommendations to the Minnesota secretary of state and the state legislature. By 2009, the state had changed the recount law, adopting most of the recommendations of the citizens' jury. Their work also garnered widespread positive support from other states' attorneys general and from the media. In neighboring North Dakota, the *Grand Forks Tribune* opined, "Just when we thought that Minnesota's politics was about to reach a new low, along comes the Citizens Jury for Election Recounts to offer a reminder of the state at its best."[14]

Some of the issues tackled by citizens' juries are directly tied to the legislative process. In addition to the Minnesota recount law, juries have been used to make recommendations on referendums in Oregon. They've also been used in connection to very different issues, like state regulations on animal feedlots, and national health care policy. In all cases, the selection of participants is done to ensure that the community is proportionally represented in terms of age, race, gender, geography, and political affiliations. The jury is comprised of ordinary citizens chosen randomly but proportionally. And participants are paid a stipend of approximately $150 per day to increase the likelihood that those on a tight budget, or people having to give up a few days of work, are not excluded.

Citizens' juries have picked up a bit of momentum in recent years as more politicians and government officials recognize the extent of the alienation most people feel from the current political process. It is well beyond the experimental stage, as the process has been fully tested and used with great results, both in terms of the quality of the recommendations and the sense of satisfaction and engagement among participants. But it is still relatively rarely used, considering the vast number of local, state, and national issues where it might come into play. The challenge that the Jefferson Center and other advocates of citizens' juries face is how to steadily expand the use of this tool, both to improve the recommendations provided to elected officials and to engage many more people deeply and meaningfully in our political life.

Other efforts to reengage citizens and revitalize the public debate are under way in many parts of the country, as documented in a 2013 study from the National League of Cities.[15] In Akron, Ohio, forty volunteers shared their time, first to be trained as facilitators and subsequently to help guide a series of community meetings designed to involve the public in revitalizing schools and neighborhoods. In Decatur, Georgia, fully 10 percent of the population got involved with community meetings in a long-term process of creating a strategic plan. In Austin, Texas, a similar effort engaged twenty-five thousand citizens, a smaller proportion of the public than in Decatur, but a very large number of participants nevertheless. In Detroit, community engagement efforts happened primarily outside the government, involving everything from microfinancing of new entrepreneurs working to revitalize the city's economy, to neighborhood-level efforts to engage citizens in community affairs. And in Philadelphia, a very broad, diverse group of folks have become engaged with city officials, helping to build a downtown riverfront development plan, in the process making the city's municipal planning system both more effective and more responsive to citizens' priorities.[16]

In an era of unresponsive politics and rage-filled media and Internet "discussion," these experiences present a radically different approach to public discourse and citizen involvement. Along with participatory budgeting and citizens' juries, they are part of the still-nascent field of bottom-up participatory democracy strategies. As yet, these efforts are small and far from commonplace. But they demonstrate that our democracy, to quote *Monty Python*, is "not dead yet," and that everyday people in communities and cities across this country are hungry for meaningful opportunities to make a positive difference.

Analysis of Transition Six

Few would argue—at least not publicly—with the goal of increasing public participation in the political process. (It's worth noting that in private, that's exactly what some people do, including Paul Weyrich, who famously said: "I don't want everybody to vote. . . . As a matter of fact, our leverage in the elections goes up as the voting populace goes down." Reinforcing that view, the tidal wave of state voter ID laws, even as claims of voter fraud are repeatedly debunked, is difficult to view as anything other than a deliberate and targeted reduction of public involvement in the political process.) Yet do the systems and tools described in this chapter actually increase participation and lead to more thoughtful debate and outcomes? With a small base of experience thus far, it is hard to know. However, a few trends are emerging that appear to show the potential for the range of bottom-up political tools. First, the high level of satisfaction with the process and the feeling of increased understanding and competence among participants seem widespread. This sense of empowerment has been found in the participatory budgeting under way in several U.S. cities, as well as among the much smaller groups of people who've been part of citizens' juries. It is further corroborated by other actions they take following these experiences: in Hartford, Connecticut, for instance, people who participated in the Parent Leadership Training Institute reported being twice as likely to get involved in solving community problems and twice as likely to contact their elected representatives as those who had not been through the process.[17] In New York City, one-third of all participatory budgeting participants reported increases in their involvement in community organizations following the experience, and for those in Chicago, more than half said they had never or rarely been involved in community or civic organizations prior to their participatory budgeting work.[18] All of this supports the idea that participatory democracy strategies are successfully engaging those previously disengaged, not just the activists and rabble-rousers.

Participation and deliberation, as you might expect, seem to lead to better discussions of issues, with more depth, listening to diverse viewpoints, and more subtle and practical recommendations. Two studies from across the globe bear this out. Public Agenda, a nonpartisan group formed in 1975, has worked to provide resources to both citizens and elected officials to improve the quality of public discourse. In one study, using Social Security as the issue, they compared the discussions that unfolded between four groups who were given standard political debate–type information with those given more "deliberative"—balanced, in-depth—material. In every case, they found that the deliberative materials engendered more openness to new information, more inquisitiveness, a more sustained focus on the core issues, and a more realistic search for solutions. With this study and a broad range of other experiences, they've concluded that "given the proper conditions, citizens are both able and eager to engage issues across boundaries and come to thoughtful judgments about even the most vexing problems."[19] An analysis of two cases of participatory deliberations, similar to citizens' juries, used in Australia similarly found a "liberating effect" of the deliberation, as citizens were more able to grapple with the issues and come to thoughtful recommendations. According to Simon Niemeyer, the study's author, the deliberative approach helped overcome much more simplistic and emotionally charged political symbolism attached to the issues and develop a "shared logic . . . that reflects a more holistic view of the issue at hand."[20]

So it appears that bringing people together and providing them with a solid base of information lead to more understanding of others' viewpoints and more realistic ideas for solutions. Let's repeat that: *Bringing people together and providing them with a solid base of information lead to more understanding of others' viewpoints and more realistic ideas for solutions!* This may be very difficult to even imagine in our current climate, yet it seems to consistently be the case. And also that a sizeable portion of people welcome the opportunity to be part of such processes, commitments to jobs and families notwithstanding. Given that, what would it take to expand this substantially, to make PB, citizens' juries, and similar processes much more commonplace? The Participatory Budgeting Project, the national technical support organization for PB, believes that recent success with the process and the clamoring from people around the nation for real opportunities to be heard have set the stage for a dramatic expansion of this system. With thirty-eight PB processes currently under way (that's counting each district in a city council separately), their goal is to expand to five hundred communities or districts using PB within the next ten years.[21]

Participatory budgeting provides citizens with a specific pot of money—usually quite small compared to what is being spent in that jurisdiction—for the spending of which the residents are empowered to make decisions, not simply recommendations. For most all of the other participatory mechanisms, there is a very real question as to what impact they have on actual policy decisions. A 2009 study by Robert Goodin and John Dryzek explored this question of whether the "macro-political 'takes up' micro-deliberative input." In plain English, can the priorities and recommendations of everyday citizens really impact the decisions of those in power? While the record is far from clear, Goodin and Dryzek cited several examples where impacts were real and significant. Among these was the shift in policies of Texas utilities following deliberative polls in 1996 and 1998. These demonstrated strong citizen support for energy conservation and renewable energy. Based at least in part on those results, investment in renewables expanded far beyond anything done previously (though it was still a small part of the overall energy mix), and the utilities began encouraging greater energy conservation. Similarly, a process called Reconnecting Communities and Schools in three counties of South Carolina (1998–2000) proved to be the impetus for one of those school districts to oppose—through a lawsuit—granting of tax exemptions to a major developer. Citizens had made clear their support for new forms of development and for the central role of schools. Tax breaks for traditional development that would have cut funding for local schools was clearly not part of their vision.[22] Local leaders changed course as a result.

While PB, citizens' juries, 21st Century Town Meetings, deliberative polls, and similar tools offer much-needed and carefully developed mechanisms for broader citizen engagement, we also need to rebuild the *culture* of citizenship. As Benjamin Barber has said, the current focus on individualistic consumerism has not only precipitated a lot of shopping but has also become, for many people, a substitute for the opportunities and obligations of citizenship. "Citizens," Barber says, "cannot be understood as mere consumers because individual desire is not the same thing as common ground, and public goods are always something more than an aggregation of private wants." We can't simply shop our way to a better world, in other words. Citing the need to work toward and sustain the levers of participatory democracy, Barber goes on to say, "Public liberty demands public institutions that permit citizens to address the public consequences of private market choices." When we rely too heavily on the market to express our preferences and neglect the neighborhood, community, and public sphere, "all the choices we make one by one thereby come to determine the social outcomes we must suffer together, but which we never directly choose in common."[23]

We need to rehabilitate the idea of the "public," of our shared commonwealth that was so central to the vision of the nation's founders. In a time of extreme cynicism and alienation, combined with the increasing difficulty of just getting by for so many people, this will almost surely require:

- Participation where we can make a difference. As Caroline Patsius and her colleagues found, this is most often at relatively local levels, whether the district, county, or city, as this is where direct involvement is most likely to make a difference.
- A gradual broadening to state- and national-level issues, as the knowledge, skills, and power of citizens grow. Starting locally makes sense for many reasons, but as most people discover, local issues usually have state or national dimensions that also must be addressed. Many of the people most active in their local communities tend to avoid involvement in marches, protests, or other elements of "mass movements," and many mass movement activists lack grounding in local communities. These two segments need to be connected, systematically.
- Mechanisms, like PB and citizens' juries, that use people's minds, that

push us to work for solutions with people different from ourselves, and that increase our capacity for citizenship. Clicking the button on my computer for or against something, while sometimes valuable, simply is not satisfying, nor is it likely to increase my involvement in other critical issues.

- Concrete connections between our civic and our economic behavior, between the efforts to build local living economies and the work of bottom-up participatory democracy. More than at any time since the end of World War II, we have a broadly based emergence of local food systems and vibrant local economies. Along with the tens of thousands of farmers, entrepreneurs, and small businesses, we have *millions* of people who are buying from them, their neighbors, and customers. The potential for a sizeable proportion of these "conscious consumers" to become engaged citizens has for too long been overlooked.

One approach to building a far more responsive and constructive political process would be to build on the success of the local food and local economy initiatives around the country. This idea of building "food citizens" would require a different approach than the traditional advocacy practiced by organizations supporting family farmers, sustainable agriculture, and healthy local food systems. There are a number of critically important national advocacy groups that already do this with relatively good effect, given their severe disadvantage in funding and access to politicians. These efforts should continue and deserve support from local foods advocates. Nevertheless, I am suggesting an effort to mobilize a sizeable portion of the 5 to 10 million people whom USDA estimates shop at farmers markets every week, potentially joined by others belonging to a CSA, shopping at a food cooperative, or otherwise involved with local and sustainably produced foods.

As the local food movement has grown, in places as diverse as Abingdon and New York City, it has become increasingly clear to me that many dedicated local food shoppers have come to value not only the tasty, fresh food they buy but also the farmers who grow it and the land from which it comes. Along with other farmers, I've seen a steady increase in the number of people who want to understand how their food is produced and wish to support "their" farmers in meaningful ways. Twenty-one years ago, when I started one of our region's first CSAs, I can remember one of the customer's frustration when, in the first week of June, she had not yet received sweet corn in her

With nearly 10 million people shopping at farmers markets in the United States every week, is there potential to develop millions of "food citizens" to engage with public policy issues? Courtesy of the Norton, Virginia, Farmers Market.

basket (barely three weeks after the planting date for corn in our area). Today, customers are more likely to ask, "Did you survive that frost alright?" or "How bad did the hail hurt your crops?"

Beyond expressions of concern, many farmers market shoppers are also looking for ways to help, both at the market or on the farm. There has been, I believe, a growth in real concern for the land and the people who work it. Yet very rarely has this translated into *civic or political involvement* on behalf of farmers.

My experience suggests that this may be a good time to get serious about helping people move from being "conscious consumers" to becoming "food citizens," that is, people sufficiently well informed on the issues surrounding food production, and adequately prepared to engage in the policy process. To be honest, I don't know exactly how to do this. However, drawing upon what has worked in terms of both the local food/local economy movements and the efforts to build a more participatory democracy, I'd suggest a basic outline for this process that looks something like this:

First, we should test the idea out in a few areas, a "pilot" of sorts, from which we can learn and improve subsequent efforts. These should take place in a half dozen or more communities, each with a strong farmers market, representing both urban settings and small towns in more rural areas. For the initial trial, the different communities should be clustered in one or two states to increase the chance of impact and to build common ground. Finding a handful of farmers markets willing to participate should not be difficult once we have more clearly defined both the goals and the process.

In each participating community, the goal would be to identify a representative sampling of eighteen to twenty-four market shoppers willing to participate in a process similar to the citizens' jury. They would come together to learn about the issues surrounding food and farming in their region (or state), discuss and develop ideas about how to strengthen their food systems, and then develop a set of recommendations regarding the two or three most important issues they've considered. Resource people—content "experts"—and a trained facilitator would be needed for each citizens' jury (if the timing could be worked out, some of the same people could work with two or more groups).

Although federal policy is particularly critical when it comes to food and farming, initial food citizen efforts should probably focus on local and state policy, following the findings of Caroline Patsius that it is easier to mobilize citizens when their participation is likely to make a concrete difference. This would mean identifying different issues in different communities, depending upon the particular problems or opportunities that each place represents. These might include land use ordinances related to urban farming, policies around vacant lots in town, development pressures on prime farmland near town, purchase of food by local schools or hospitals, investment in the farmers market facility itself, and similar issues.

A potentially bigger challenge would be finding communities where local leaders, whether they are city councilors or economic development and planning staff, would also be willing to sign on to the process. At a minimum, these leaders would need to make a commitment to attend a public event where the recommendations of the citizens' jury are presented, and then to give these recommendations serious consideration. While still not binding, such a commitment in advance would make it far more likely that the recommendations of the citizen panels would be adopted to at least some degree. For this reason, the scope of the recommendations and budget implications should be negotiated in advance, if possible.

With two states involved in the initial effort, each should involve at least four to six communities, from both rural and urban areas. Once each community has identified and begun work on their local issues, they could also select a subset of four to six delegates to participate in a statewide citizens' jury, a process that would focus on state-level policies. These might include food safety and food processing, land use and tax policies, economic development incentives, support for food and farming entrepreneurs, agriculture's role in climate change, and many more. The citizens' jury for the state would follow a similarly deliberative process, though likely confined to a single multiday session, given travel costs and constraints. It would probably happen the year following the local juries, in order to make it realistic for the participants. Securing the commitment of state legislators or agriculture department staff to seriously consider the recommendations of the citizen jury would almost surely be a greater challenge than getting local officials on board. But it would be essential.

As the state-level process gets under way in year two, a second set of local convenings should begin, including a mix of new and second-year communities. Assuming that some of the recommendations of various citizens' juries are put into practice and improvements in local food systems become tangible, more and more people would likely become interested in this process, and in civic engagement and public policy more broadly. We could think of it as a community-by-community, house-by-house strategy. Like Mary Kay, for democracy.

Given the urgency of so many of these issues, the hope would be that the pilot efforts focused on two states would spread steadily, even rapidly to other states and other communities, each beginning with their local farmers market community of shoppers. As this grew across multiple states, the potential to tackle national-level issues in a similarly deliberative and bottom-up fashion would emerge. So, too, would the possibility of broadening the issue base from food and farming to economic resilience, social justice, and shared prosperity. Potentially, at least.

To achieve significant impact, all of these bottom-up democracy initiatives will need to align with mass movements for change, as the force of millions of people marching, calling, writing, protesting, and using every tool of nonviolent civic engagement is utterly essential to effectively confront the problems we face. But bottom-up and participatory democracy can offer this broader movement a number of important things: active, skilled, and knowledgeable advocates, from among the ranks of everyday people; strategies to spread change to other local communities and in the process to broaden the foundation underneath state or national efforts; and a chance to break out of the boundaries of "liberal" and "conservative," based on shared experience in local communities, experience of solutions as much as problems.

Clearly this idea would need a great deal more work to flesh out the details, not to mention to build sufficient financial support to undertake this even in a few communities. My hope here is not to be prescriptive, but to suggest a new way of thinking about advocacy, an approach that is not based on professional advocates more or less permanently situated in state capitals or Washington, D.C. Instead of a handful of advocates, I'm trying to imagine hundreds, then thousands, and eventually a million or more very well-informed citizens, people already hopeful and energized about their buying habits now becoming hopeful and energized citizens.

Public Policy

Alderman Joe Moore had just squeaked by in his election when he took the leap and launched the first citizen-controlled participatory budgeting process in the United States. That was 2009. Two years later, he won reelection in a landslide. I'm not suggesting that embracing participatory democracy and increasing the influence of citizens in public policy will always get you elected. Nevertheless, being a true advocate of the power of the people will surely be a distinguishing feature for candidates for public office, not to mention being the right thing to do. Of course, we'd be kidding ourselves to think that people in power, and the corporations and moneyed interests keeping them there, are going to give that power up without a fight. In fact, it will be a very big and prolonged fight to wrest the power from the elite few and return it to ordinary citizens. But the fact is that our traditional approaches to advocacy, our special-interest politics, and our efforts at simply reforming the two major parties have borne less and less fruit. It's time to try some new approaches.

What sort of policies might make these new, participatory democracy approaches more effective, more replicable? And what might begin to level the playing field between bottom-up democracy and elite money-driven politics? For starters, the array of public policies suggested in earlier chapters would be critical. By strengthening local living economies, by building community resilience and self-reliance, and by reducing the power of hyperconcentrated media and corporations of all types, we will begin to unleash the potential of citizens, communities, local businesses, and triple-bottom-line entrepreneurs. In many local communities where this is happening, the power of the argument for wealth concentration, for giveaways to outside corporations, is declining. Living economies and healthy communities are a potent force. We've just got to start making that case at state and national levels in a much more sustained and conspicuous way.

But there are also specific policies we must change regarding our political process. Nearly all of them fall under the banner of "getting money out of politics," or, more accurately, reversing the dominant trend of the past thirty years, that money is THE driving force in all phases of our politics. It is important to understand that it is not just about campaign contributions, though that is obviously critical. Of equal importance is the undue influence of moneyed interests after the elections, through the role that lobbyists play on the development of legislation right through to funding and implementation of laws that are passed. These issues are complex, far beyond the scope of this discussion. A variety of remedies have been suggested to first constrain and then reverse the power of elites over politics (and, in most cases, the courts who have consistently sided with the elites over citizens). I would suggest exploring *Winner-Take-All Politics,* by Jacob Hacker and Paul Pierson,[24] *Blowing the Roof off the Twenty-First Century,* by Robert McChesney,[25] and *Republic, Lost,* by Lawrence Lessig,[26] to start. These are very readable books that together do an outstanding job of explaining the problem, in depth, and offering concrete and substantial steps for reform.

The current Supreme Court is almost certain to sustain and even increase the freedom to spend in order to influence elections, and almost no one in Congress is speaking about the need to restrict the "revolving door" where corporate executives become government "regulators" and government officials leave public office for lucrative private offers. But we can't lose sight of the fact that this Supreme Court is not permanent. Their decidedly perverse view that unlimited expenditures of money by an incredibly tiny fraction of the population are simply expressions of free speech is a view that need not endure forever. Changing the courts, and changing the logic of their rulings, will happen only when enough citizens demand it, consistently, coherently, and over a very long time. The rule of law, after all, is ultimately an expression of the wisdom and will of the populace, not simply an interpretation of the constitution and past rulings. *Bringing fairness and balance back to elections and politics is going to take a very long time, but no well-meaning citizen should miss a chance to talk about it, write about it, and contact their legislators about it.*

On the other side of the policy coin from these corrections is a much more readily achievable goal: for towns, cities, and states to open the door to deliberative and participatory citizen-led democratic assemblies, juries, and budgeting initiatives. To maintain their integrity and independence, these must derive from local communities. And they must recognize and give priority to the people and communities who have been neglected or deliberately marginalized in the past. But elected officials and government staff can help themselves and dramatically improve our discourse and policies by working with communities and by pledging to follow or at least pay serious attention to the results of these citizen deliberations. The Participatory Budgeting Project's goal of five hundred jurisdictions using PB within a decade is achievable, if those in power are persuaded to make room for this productive and enlivening tool of democracy.

Transition Six: Recap and Looking Forward

It's possible to build local living economies that engender much more widely shared prosperity while building community and sustaining the environment. In fact, it is happening in many places across the country. Nevertheless, the extent and the pace of this critically needed economic transition is often directly undermined by very bad, elite-driven public policy, especially at state and federal levels. This "winner-take-all politics" as Jacob Hacker and Paul Pierson have called it, is the culmination of more than thirty years of self-reinforcing policies and court decisions that have concentrated and consolidated unprecedented political power in the hands of a tiny, superwealthy elite. This is not hyperbole but rather the demonstrable truth of our current situation.

Overcoming the power of the moneyed elites and unleashing a community-based politics of engagement is the final essential transition we must make to build more just, democratic, and sustainable economies that create real prosperity. As many people experiment with both new and tested approaches to building broad political power, a few key learnings stand out:

1. Alienation from politics and from the two major political parties is at an all-time high, and this in turn has fed a destructive combination of "us versus them" rage for some people and cynicism and withdrawal for many more. As people realize how little their concerns and priorities actually impact public policy, and as their economic opportunities have declined, these two responses have become widespread.

2. The broad privatization and commercialization of our lives is steadily eroding the sense of citizenship and of shared public fortunes, that is,

of "being in this together." This viewpoint has lost ground to a private, individualistic consumer ethic.

3. The local food and local economy movements have yielded great results in hundreds of communities, but until very recently have largely neglected the broader issues of public discourse and public policy, focusing too narrowly on "what we can do right here." This is beginning to change, but that change must be accelerated and expanded.

4. The people and companies who control much of the political process, from campaigns through to the enactment and implementation of legislation, are fighting like hell to keep and increase their inordinate power. At this point in our history, the courts, particularly the Supreme Court, consistently support this concentration of wealth and power, and their freedom to use their wealth to maintain outsized influence. So, too, do most elected officials. Reducing the power and influence of elites is and will continue to be a gargantuan—and utterly essential—challenge.

5. A range of national advocacy groups has been fighting for some time to stop and reverse this extreme concentration of economic and political power. While they have occasional successes, they are badly outgunned in terms of money and lobbyists, and access to legislators, and thus can mostly just hold the line at best. These groups also offer relatively few ways for people to engage in the political process that are fulfilling, empowering, and likely to lead to ongoing civic and political engagement.

6. On the other hand, a small number of "participatory democracy" initiatives and strategies are emerging that do engage people in ways that are more gratifying, and that help build the knowledge and skills needed for full citizenship. They are, however, small and few in number at this point.

7. There is an urgent need to use these participatory democracy tools and other more traditional political advocacy strategies to systematically connect the broad base of local living economies with civic engagement and public policy. A bottom-up politics of this sort, in alignment with more traditional approaches to advocacy and movement building, could begin to undo and eventually overwhelm the concentration of political and economic power we now face.

Up next: Real and fundamental change is urgently needed in our economy and politics. It is time, as the Democracy Collaborative has put it, for "the next system" to emerge, a system where the economy puts people and their places at the center, where political power is in the hands of everyday people, and where, as Cornel West has said, justice is understood to be the public manifestation of love. In the book's conclusion, we'll look at how the emerging "new story," based upon on-the-ground experience from across the county, can help guide us toward this new system.

Further Reading

Alperovitz, Gar. *What Then Must We Do? Straight Talk about the Next American Revolution*. White River Junction, VT: Chelsea Green, 2013.

Hacker, Jacob, and Paul Pierson. *Winner-Take-All Politics: How Washington Made the Rich Richer—And Turned Its Back on the Middle Class*. New York: Simon and Schuster, 2010.

Hoene, Christopher, Christopher Kingsley, and Matthew Leighninger. "Bright Spots in Community Engagement: Case Studies of US Communities Creating Greater Civic Participation from the Bottom Up," National League of Cities. April 2013. www.nlc.org.

Lessig, Lawrence. *Republic, Lost: How Money Corrupts Congress*. New York: Hachette, 2011.

Nichols, John, and Robert McChesney. *Dollarocracy: How the Money and Media Election Complex Is Destroying America*. New York: Nation Books, 2013.

Rushkoff, Douglas. *Life Inc: How Corporatism Conquered the World, and How We Can Take It Back*. New York: Random House, 2011.

"Stacked Deck: How the Dominance of Politics by the Affluent and Business Undermines Economic Mobility in America." Demos. 2013. www.demos .org.

Conclusion

Creating a New Story, from the Bottom Up

To accept your country without betraying it, you must love it for what it might become. America—this monument to the genius of ordinary men and women, this place where hope becomes capacity, this long, halting turn of "no" into the "yes"—needs citizens who love it enough to re-imagine and re-make it.
—Cornel West

So here's the punch line: the movement toward more local economies is the same direction we will have to travel to cope with the effects of these predicaments, not just to fend them off. The logic is fairly clear: in a world threatened by ever-higher energy prices and ever-scarcer fossil fuel, you're better off in a relatively self-sufficient county or state or region. In a world increasingly rocked by wild and threatening weather, durable economies will be more useful than dynamic ones. And in both cases, the increased sense of community and heightened skill at democratic decision making that a more local economy implies will not simply increase our levels of satisfaction with our lives, but will also increase our chance of survival in a more dangerous world. Hyper-individualism is not just lonely; it's also, in the world we are starting to see emerge around us, insecure and foolhardy.
—Bill McKibben, *Deep Economy*

So the real trick, the only hope, really, is to allow the terror of an unlivable future to be balanced and soothed by the prospect of building something much better than many of us have previously dared hope.
—Naomi Klein, *This Changes Everything*

It is the day after Christmas 2014 as I complete the writing of this book. From a small café in Marina di Ragusa in southern Sicily, I've begun this conclusion with the hope that I can both distill the most important lessons from the emerging alternatives we've considered and provide the reader with a bit of guidance about how you might support and participate in the bottom-up economy and a renewed civic and political life.

There are plenty of reasons to be downright disheartened now. A budget deal that just became law in the United States dramatically increased the amount of money the wealthy can use to influence the political process, dropped a modest protection against Wall Street financial speculation, eliminated rules intended to protect small famers against agribusiness giants, and allowed public pension funds to substantially reduce the retirement payments they promised to retirees. This year's elections saw the lowest voter turnout in decades, as polls show an increasing number of people giving up on both major parties. While unemployment has been gradually falling, the number of part-time and low-wage workers continues to rise, as does the pay of corporate CEOs. The wealth gap between the few and the many continues to grow, breaking records every year. That's just some of the bad news.

Southeastern Sicily, the birthplace of my father's mom and dad, is sunny and rather warm, even this time of year. The Mediterranean Sea is clear and beautiful. Even in the off-season from tourists, the small town squares fill with people most afternoons and evenings. And mostly, they're talking to *each other*—not their phones—in that animated, gesture-filled Italian way. My wife, Laurie, and I have been in Sicily for several weeks, a sabbatical of sorts from my farm and consulting business that has allowed me to focus on this book.

Italy as a nation has plenty of problems, including a government for which many Italians have little more than contempt, and an economy struggling to overcome stagnation and bureaucratic inefficiency. But when I take a look at the *places* themselves—the vibrant "piazzas," the shops and restaurants filled with extraordinary locally produced food, the mix of ancient buildings and modern, state-of-the-art agricultural systems, the deep pride in art, music, and culture, and the lively communities of people—I'm reminded of what some environmentalists have said about climate change: it's too late to stop it altogether, so we need a strategy of both mitigation and adaptation. That is, we must find ways to both reduce the worst impacts while also preparing to live a different way, under different conditions. Still fighting for change but making the most of what we've got. I think the Italians are doing this.

Is this also our starting point for building local living economies and revitalized communities? Should we think of these efforts as strategies of mitigation and adaptation, of blunting the worst elements of an elite-controlled economy and politics, while adapting our local, daily lives to the new realities of scarcity and warming, of minimal influence on the bigger decisions that govern our lives? It would certainly be understandable to take this route. After all, we have only so much time and energy. If tackling the bigger world of corporate-controlled trade deals or money in politics seems so utterly hopeless, why not focus on just making our particular places a little better? That's certainly preferable to just giving up and going shopping at Walmart.

As I bring this book to a close, I'm going to argue for something else: *We really can't choose between better local realities and dramatic changes in the larger economic and political system.* Remember that politics is about setting the rules of the game, and increasingly, those rules are antithetical to healthy communities and vibrant local economies, to the well-being of people and their places. Hundreds of communities can embrace farmers markets and sustainable farming, but if federal policy continues to subsidize a tiny segment of agribusiness, and FDA rules make selling produce onerous for small farmers, we'll see the local food movement unravel. If communities embrace open space and rules protecting their land and water, but trade agreements allow international corporations to sue them for lost profits, those local communities will quite literally lose a lot of ground.

Of course each of us, individually, must pick our battles. We can't get involved in every important issue. But we can—we must—stop making the false choice between local and national issues, instead recognizing that *almost every positive change we make in our own communities is ultimately either undermined or supported by broader economic and political choices.* And just as important, these emerging local alternatives can change the national debate, and the policies that flow from that debate *if we* develop the strategy to make that happen.

It can take quite a long time for those local-national connections to materialize. In 1974, Bill Gable and Ed Morgan began working on an idea to start an economic development project in the rural, mountainous area known as Whitetop, Virginia. They saw it as a potential way both to help preserve important traditions and to build some skills that might improve employment opportunities for folks down the road. They convinced the Eli Lilly Foundation to support the idea of a maple syrup– and molasses-making operation, knowing that this would fit well with the land and topography of that area, and believing that it could become an important engine for tourism and jobs. Soon thereafter, local musicians and educators launched a training and mentoring program linking skilled old-time musicians to teens and other young folks. At around the same time, Bill also began working with other local people to build a community center in Konnarock (part of the Whitetop area) as a gathering place, a site for music training and much more. By 1980, the center was in place, built in part from proceeds from the community's annual Fall Festival, itself an outgrowth of the maple-syrup initiative in Whitetop.

The center continues as a vibrant part of the Konnarock community more than three decades later. In 2000, Ed Morgan was elected to the Abingdon Town Council and in 2002 and 2003, he became a critical part of the fight for the big-box ordinance that kept Walmart out of the town. Since that time, Ed has continued to work for the bottom-up economy, including the farmers market, art, music, and cultural events, and more. And he has gone on to become the town's mayor. Bill, who is a blacksmith, helped revive the Cave House Crafts cooperative and managed it for many years. More recently, he became involved with 'Round the Mountain, part of the arts, music, and culture economy discussed in chapter 3. Those initiatives, along with the emergence of a strong local food economy and the rejuvenation of numerous downtown centers around the region provided the foundation for a range of policy changes in Virginia that have begun to give local living economies a fighting chance. And beyond changes in state policy, the reorientation of a key federal agency, the Appalachian Regional Commission, toward bottom-up, "asset-based" development has been substantial, particularly in comparison to the agency's historic focus on a trickle-down, top-heavy approach to economic development.

For me, there are three lessons in this story. First, concrete local enterprises and initiatives *can* provide a foundation for broader changes in public policy. These changes can occur at local, state, and even national levels, if we are persistent enough, and explicit about the links between action and policy, between local and national. Second, it simply does not happen nearly often enough; for the most part the links have not been made explicitly enough and persistently enough. And third, we can no longer afford for it to take thirty years for these changes to trickle up. We need more bold and concerted action, networked across communities, persisting relentlessly until healthy living economies and vibrant, engaged communities become the norm. If we don't do this, it's clear what we'll get—even more concentration of wealth, sucked up from local communities and everyday folks; a political system run entirely by and for the elites; and more than likely, out-of-control climate change that will shatter communities, economies, and livelihoods. We're well on our way already.

This book has briefly described the experiences of a few dozen communities who've quit waiting for trickle-down prosperity, instead working to build their own bottom-up economies. At the center of these dynamic emerging economies are local businesses—organic farmers, ranchers and sustainable fishermen, restaurants, independent retailers, energy-efficiency and renewable-energy firms, innovative manufacturers, artists and craftspeople, community banks and credit unions, and a range of both for-profit and non-profit triple-bottom-line entrepreneurs. And the people who support them, as shoppers, as small investors, as neighbors. I've called these folks "hopeful citizens" because they believe that how they spend their money matters *and* because they still hold out some hope for the "public" in our republic, for the "we," not just the "me." I'm guessing that many of the people reading this book are hopeful citizens. I'm banking on it, actually.

Stories: Old and New

The Old, and Still-Dominant Story

In chapter 1, I presented six myths of economic prosperity that, woven together, told this basic story about the U.S. economy and the American Dream:

Money is the key to prosperity because it enables us to buy stuff, and the more stuff we have the happier and more successful we are. To achieve that success, we should all look out for Number One. Businesses and the market will respond by making everyone (who works hard) better off.

When individuals strive to make themselves better off, the market generates a rising tide of prosperity, a bigger pie, so that more and more people can have more stuff. Economic growth is what makes that rising tide possible, so it must continue indefinitely.

The only way to way to sustain that growth is through ever-bigger businesses, farms, and financial institutions, providing the lowest-cost goods and services through global free trade. This is capitalism, which rewards not only innovators but those who accumulate capital and use it to create further wealth.

Left alone, free from all but the bare minimum of government regula-tion, the market will make this happen, because the free market is always much more efficient and productive than government programs.

Because the market rewards hard work and success, there will be some inequality, but overall, everyone who makes an effort will be better off. Prob-lems that arise from economic growth—resource depletion, pollution, health problems, etc.—are short-term. Solutions to these problems will come through market demand and the technological innovation it fosters. Pros-perity will trickle down.

The market, because it rewards individual effort and ingenuity, is the greatest mechanism for prosperity and the most important tool for liberty the world has ever known. We must therefore build our political system to ensure that the market is free and that capitalism is not hindered by govern-ment; because the only alternative to deregulated capitalism is oppressive, debilitating communism.

This story has been at the center of our worldview as Americans for several generations now, either very explicitly or behind the scenes in our discussions about economics, the environment, workers and labor, and democracy. In fact, many Americans equate democracy with the free mar-ket, believing that you cannot have political freedom without "free mar-ket" capitalism, and that any limits on the market, whether they are limits on consumers or on businesses and corporations, are an infringement on political liberty and democracy.

An Emerging New Story

Yet from Arizona to Vermont, we've seen a very different reality emerging, where the health of local communities and the prosperity of everyday peo-ple are the starting point. These emerging, bottom-up economies recog-nize the power of the market but also its limits and problems. And so they are building a rich *new story* that is unfolding something like this:

"The economy" is made up of scores of smaller, regional economies, which in turn are built on the economic activities of households, neighbor-hoods, and communities. New economies are emerging to make people's lives better, fuller, happier, and more secure because the economy, after all, is for people, not the other way around. This is the transition from consumptive dependency to productive resilience.

These local and regional economies are built around a diverse array of businesses, from the most traditional to the newest and most experimental, but all with strong links to their local communities. There is a growing recognition among these businesses that they must not only serve their customers and workers but also respect the places where they reside, finding ways to conduct business utilizing the gifts and respecting the limits of the ecosystem of which they're a part. This is the transition from trickle-down problems to bottom-up, living economy solutions.

These emerging economies are building upon the strengths and assets of their particular places, including the culture, the unique skills of the people, the built environment, and the natural world. In this way, businesses and the economy develop distinctly rather than generically, and cannot easily be replaced or outsourced. The ownership of these businesses is primarily in private hands, though increasingly they are also owned by the workers, the producers, the customers, or the community. This is the transition from concentrated wealth to worker ownership and community capital.

In seeking to solve problems and build community wealth through the economy, they are also building regional and national networks of learning and exchange, of public discourse and policy, to strengthen and magnify their work. This is the transition from a thousand flickers of light to networks linked together for learning, doing, and change.

While respecting their histories and traditions, these increasingly vibrant communities are also cultivating social entrepreneurship and supporting economic innovation, new forms of media and the arts, community design and civic engagement. They are reinvigorating the public sphere as well as the private. This is the transition from concentrated corporate media to energizing civic conversations.

Most fundamentally of all, these emerging economies and energized communities are beginning to ask not, "How are we going to find jobs?" but, "What is the work that needs to be done?" In this way, fundamental economic choices are becoming fundamentally public choices, based on the health and well-being of people, on the prosperity of communities. This is the transition from a politics of lobbyists and money to a community-based politics of engagement.

None of the communities we have discussed in this book has fully made the transition from the first story to the second, from a trickle-down global economy to bottom-up local economies. However, they do provide compelling examples of *strategies that are working* in all kinds of places; and collectively, they give us a sense of what is possible when we decide that *stronger economies and a better world are two sides of the same coin, not competing interests.*

We'll bring this discussion to a close with two final segments: first, we'll look at the most important lessons we can take from the six transitions toward resilient communities and living economies, considering their successes as well as their challenges and failures. Based on this, I'll outline a strategy going forward—in broad strokes—that I hope will provide some direction for practitioners, for those involved primarily with public policy, and for the many hopeful citizens, of all political stripes, who want to help build a better world.

Key Lessons

Each chapter concluded with a short summary that included key learnings coming out of the transition discussed in that section. We'll now consider a set of overarching lessons that cut across the transitions and begin to suggest some of what we must consider to move forward productively.

1. **If you don't build it, they won't come.** A sharp focus on developing strong local economies has been necessary and fruitful up to this point. However, if we don't begin serious, sustained, and long-term work now to build the language, the communication skills and networks, and the political strategy and constituency for a bottom-up economy and politics, people won't engage. Because there isn't really much for them to engage with. We must begin to build this.

2. **To overcome the widespread alienation with and anger toward "politics," we will have to rebuild a "public life," together.** This is different from the vast majority of advocacy groups currently fighting for a range of important issues, even though some have goals that overlap local living economies. The key difference is that building a "public life" requires that we cultivate vibrant local economies and communities where very different sorts of folks both interact with each other and guide the decisions that impact their lives. Revitalized downtowns, community gardens, farmers markets, and public plazas and spaces all offer a place to begin to build this public life, together. So, too, do community theater, the arts, and independent media, connected to place. We can build on these, but must go much further.

3. **When financial resources become highly concentrated as they have, they are used almost exclusively to make more money for the people and entities that already have it, rather than to develop and sustain community capital and prosperity.** The experience of the past thirty years makes it unequivocally clear that this wealth does not "trickle down" but intensifies among a tiny elite, along with extraordinary political power. There is nothing inevitable about this, no "invisible hand" of the market that concentrates this wealth. It is public policy that has led to this concentration. It will take major policy changes to reverse it.

4. **There are viable, preferable alternatives to trickle-down economics, hyperconcentrated wealth, and global corporate capitalism, and they are emerging all over this nation.** These alternative economic strategies and structures are coming to life in rural areas, small towns, and big cities, in virtually every region of the country, and they are building stronger economies and better places to live. Unfortunately, for the most part they are swimming upstream against public policy and Wall Street. They need to be lifted up, supported, and invested in.

5. **To build broad public support for bottom-up, living economies, we need to stop beating around the bush and begin to name both the problems and the solutions in direct, straightforward language.** We cannot allow ourselves, for instance to kowtow to the utterly absurd claim that speaking out against extreme wealth concentration is a form of "class warfare" or a "war on success." And we need to support the emergence of community-based and alternative media that will help tell the stories of these emerging economies and vibrant communities, and honestly critique the dominant economic and political system.

6. **Time is of the essence.** The array of ecological problems we face—especially climate change but also the increasing scarcity of water, imminent shortages in key minerals, and degrading of productive land—makes the work of building an ecologically sustainable economy utterly critical. The social and human consequences of our current system, its inability to address poverty, and the extraordinarily expensive problems of declining health, degraded infrastructure, and dependent communities all cry out for systematic, bold solutions, not piecemeal "reform."

7. **We have reality on our side.** The amazing array of local economies that have emerged, the communities and towns they've revitalized, and the concrete improvements they've made in the lives of everyday people are undeniable. So, too, are many of the disastrous consequences of trickle-down economics and elite control of our politics. Not to mention the far greater cost-effectiveness of creating economies that build self-reliance, enterprises that preclude rather than create ecological, health, and social problems. We don't need to make things up to speculate about what might be. We need to tell real stories, support them with the facts, and relentlessly challenge the current narrative.

Moving Forward with a Bottom-Up Strategy for Transitioning to Living Economies across the Nation

Thousands of people have been building local economies and food systems for the past three decades—farmers, small businesspeople, activists, organizers, and innovative local leaders. Millions of their neighbors have become supporters of these emerging local living economies as consumers. *It is time for these two groups to move to the next level and help usher in both a vast expansion of the local economy movement and a bottom-up civic and political movement.* I believe that this is what it will take to change public policy so that it supports rather than impedes vibrant communities and healthy economies. I know of no master plan for how to do this, but drawing on the work of both practitioners in the field and strategic thinkers, I am suggesting a way forward based on five interrelated *levels of engagement,* which I'll outline below. Each of these has plenty of room for participation by people of all backgrounds, including those who've never before been much involved.

Building local living economies and the political system to support them will require concerted action over many years, at many levels. The changes we need to make will certainly be economic and political, but they will also be cultural and individual. One of the key elements of a strategy going forward is to stop sorting ourselves into "thinkers" and "doers," into "policy wonks" and "localists," but instead to realize that we all live in all of these realms, consciously or not, and have both the responsibility and opportunity to have positive impacts at each of those levels. In keeping with the fundamental theme of this book, I'm going to propose a bottom-up strategy, beginning with what we can do individually, moving through to the national level. Much like the VFW or other once-prominent voluntary associations, I believe that the work we do at each level will improve our understanding and skills for subsequent levels while also building relationships that link us to people and organizations well beyond our own communities.

That said, the urgency of our time means that this process of building from the bottom up cannot be leisurely, must not be incremental. We need to move much more quickly than that, at all of the levels discussed below. Fortunately, with the diversity of backgrounds and inclinations represented among local economy practitioners and their supporters, we should be able to work at every level from the outset.

The Five Levels of Engagement

If you've stayed with me this far, you probably want to know what you can do to help bring about the transitions to resilient communities, living economies, and a vibrant democracy. In truth, there's so much you can do, so many different ways to get involved and make a difference. But that's not very helpful. As Barry Schwartz points out in *The Paradox of Choice*,[1] having an extraordinary array of things from which to choose in fact tends to confound and immobilize most of us, often leading to either "safe" selections or even complete inaction. There's an enormous amount of critically important work to be done, big changes that need to be made, soon, now, urgently. Where do you begin? Where do *we* begin?

> First Level: What you can do *individually* or as a household
> Second Level: What you can do in *small groups,* at the neighborhood level
> Third Level: What you can do in *your community,* county, town, or city
> Fourth Level: What you can do *across communities* or cities, stretching to the state level
> Fifth Level: What you can do—yes, you—at the *national level*

In presenting a framework for moving forward in this way, my hope is to offer different starting places, recognizing that we come at this from a wide range of experiences, with our own strengths and weaknesses, things we enjoy doing and others we try to avoid, perhaps even dread. Whatever you might decide to do, I want to be clear about two things. First, *there really is no such thing as inaction.* As a consumer, your choices have impacts, shaping what type of agriculture, energy, transportation, banking, and other systems that predominate. The impacts are small and gradual, but they're real nonetheless. As a citizen, "inaction" at your town council or school board meetings, at public forums and community meetings, and in the voting booth all translates into someone else's views, somebody else's priorities determining the rules of the game. Always. And at this point in our history, that "somebody else" is much more likely to be a Wall Street investment banker or a corporate CEO than your neighbor.

I get that you're only one person, that you're justifiably busy trying to care for yourself or your family. I completely acknowledge that by yourself, you can't "change the world." I understand that your market choices alone, your votes and letters alone, are a drop in the bucket; that you can have substantial impact only as part of much, much larger collective action. Honestly, I get all that. What I'm saying is that it is precisely the larger collective *inaction* of which most of us have been a part that has enabled us to get to the critical, dysfunctional place where we are today. So again, there is no such thing as inaction, only acquiescence, only letting things happen that we don't like.

Second, whatever you choose to do, remember Wendell Berry's admonition that we must try to *"solve for pattern,"* that is, to recognize that every individual choice, every single action we take is part of a larger system, a broader "pattern." That pattern is fundamentally ecological because everything we humans do happens within ecosystems. When my friend Antoinette Goodrich integrates sheep and chickens with her cattle, she doesn't just have more products to sell to her neighbors at market, she has fewer weeds in her pasture (because the sheep eat things the cattle won't), fewer flies and pests (because the chickens eat the larvae and grubs), healthier grass and legumes (because all the animal manures and eating habits fertilize and aerate the soil), and soil that can better withstand drought and help sequester carbon from the atmosphere (because of the deep-rooted grasses and vibrant microbial life).

These patterns also exist among people and the organizations and institutions of which we're a part. When you shift your savings and checking accounts from a megabank to a community bank or credit union, you take a tiny bit of power away from Wall Street, you insulate yourself a bit from risky financial games, and you provide some more resources for investment in local homes, businesses, and civic organizations, which in turn makes your community a little stronger. When you and a few dozen of your neighbors call or write your elected officials urging them to oppose corporate trade deals, sometimes, you might just be the straw that breaks the camel's back, the ones to convince him or her to side with people over Wall Street.

Four Broad Principles for Action

First, consistently put your money to work for a better economy and community by ramping up your support for local, independent, and triple-bottom-line farms and businesses. This will also help reduce your dependence on faraway banks and corporations. We can all do this as individual consumers, and some of us can do this as business owners (buying from other local businesses), institutional leaders (procuring from local sources), and investors (investing in the local economy rather than Wall Street).

Second, find ways to link the local living economy with the broader public debate and public policy. This can be challenging at first, but to begin, stop treating them as two different worlds, one you generally like to be part of, the other that you loathe, that you've given up on. In reality, they're inextricably linked. This book should have helped you begin to see how. Go deeper now; make the links. Talk about them to neighbors, community leaders, and politicians.

Third, reconnect with your community and forsake some individual autonomy. The advertising industry wants us to believe that we can buy our way to the life we want, that our values need only be expressed as our "brand." That is total crap. We can only be fully human and happy, and we can only build a better world, as neighbors and citizens.

Last, always remember and act on these core truths:

- The economy is a subset of the ecosystem, as Herman Daly has said. Put another way, the ecosystem would get along just fine without us and all our activities, but we'd be in quite a pickle without the ecosystem.
- The economy is, or should be, for people, not the other way around. Corporations were created by people, theoretically at least for the benefit of people. We don't exist for them. Honest.
- Highly concentrated wealth always begets highly concentrated political power, and this combination always degrades and destroys democracy. I know of no example in human history that contradicts this.

The Five Levels of Engagement: Ideas for Actions

The First Level: Ourselves and Our Households

With so many things to consider, one way to look at this is what can we do with our hands, our heads, and our hearts.

The Work of Our Hands

We could all use more skills, of homemaking, of growing, cooking and preserving food, of repairing the equipment and gadgets in our lives, of building and maintaining our structures, of communicating, telling stories, making music and art. Most of these skills save us money, allow us to stay put more, make us less dependent on faraway experts or purchased solutions. They also tend to enrich our own lives and make our homes more vital. Don't try to do all of this, but instead pursue some areas of interest, some things you'd really like to be able to do for yourself.

Begin to think of your household as the first layer of your economy. Where do things come from that we use? Where do they go when we're "finished" with them? How long do they last? Are they necessary and do they enrich our lives? Where are the "leaks" that seem to always drain resources and keep us at the edge? Remember that increasing your self-reliance usually involves both addition and subtraction. What might you get rid of that you really don't need or wouldn't miss, and what can you add that makes your life fuller, your family happier, more self-reliant, and more secure?

Help your kids prepare for a different world, one likely to have more limits and constraints, by helping them learn to make the most of what they have, to care more for themselves and others, to entertain themselves and find joy in real things, close at hand. Fight consumerism in yourself and discourage it in your kids. It's difficult, but doable.

Walk places where you've usually taken the car. Don't just walk or bike for exercise, but also to get places, to do things you need to do.

Spend less and save more and teach your kids to do this. As you learn to buy less stuff, also consider paying the real, full cost for the things you do buy, whether it's sustainably produced foods, Fair Trade gifts, or American-made clothes, tools, and appliances.

The Work of Our Head

Study and learn new things, locally and beyond local. Talk to farmers, small business owners, and non-profit leaders to learn more about their challenges, how you might help or strengthen what they do. Attend a farm tour to learn more about their approach, their challenges.

Find a community radio station and start tuning in. Offer to do a program for the station, whether it's spinning your favorite disks or discussing community affairs. Find alternative media, locally and nationally, that talk about real things in thoughtful ways.

Take stock of your household's energy and water use, and the waste you generate. Look at how you can substantially reduce all of these, both through changes in habits and improved technologies.

Increase your knowledge of both the problems we face and the emerging alternatives that are beginning to provide solutions. For starters, look through the short reading lists at the end of each chapter of this book. Read Wendell Berry, Marjorie Kelly, Michael Shuman, Naomi Klein, Gar Alperovitz, Benjamin Barber. My son, Josh, once told a friend that "Dad never reads anything that doesn't add to his sense of moral outrage." That might happen to you as well when you read some of these books. Surely the information will be sobering, but it will be even more enlightening, even empowering.

The Work of Our Heart

Start breaking down the barriers of class, race, and occupation by starting or getting involved in community groups and voluntary associations. Help a neighbor or volunteer for Habitat or a local non-profit. Walk away from the TV and computer screen, shut off your phone, and start connecting to people and places you can see with your own eyes. Disengage from virtual, anonymous, unaccountable "talk" and use some of that time to have real conversations, near and far.

Remind yourself and others that we are, truly, all in this together, that we need one another, and that, ultimately, we're not as different as we now appear to be. Imagine a lively "piazza" in southern Italy and start creating your own version of it, wherever you are. Use the "Lighter, Quicker, Cheaper" approach to help bring this about.

Find the local businesses, local food, triple-bottom-line enterprises and local banks and credit unions, and shift your shopping and investing from the big chains to these folks, your neighbors. If they don't have what you want, let them know, but also consider whether or not you really need it.

Begin building community in your own home by having more meals together, even preparing them together. Sure soccer and dance class are important, but being together and learning how to do basic things together is just as important. Maybe you're exhausted after work. Cooking can be both functional (saving money, eating healthier) and energizing. Don't stop there. Think twice before buying the next hand-held device that enables you and other members of your household to live in your own world. Try living in the world together.

The Second Level: Neighborhoods and Small Communities

There are some things we can do just fine on our own, and if you're like me, you may not have the energy or desire for constant social interaction. There's nothing wrong with that. In many parts of our lives, however, it makes sense to not go it alone but to connect with small groups of people with similar goals or concerns. Like Tom and Deni and their group of six families, who bought an apple cider press. Or Ron and Cassa and their neighbors, who share a log splitter and help circulate materials and appliances to neighbors who need it. If you're not in the habit of sharing things or making joint purchases with your neighbors, consider it the next time you think you need a new yard, garden, or house tool.

If you are already part of some sharing networks, explore the potential for a tool library in your community, or look for folks who may want to save and exchange seeds. If you're feeling a bit more ambitious, look into bike and ride sharing, something you can do among friends and neighbors at least on a small scale. Uber didn't invent this.

If you don't have a farmers market close by, ask around to see if there are farmers looking for customers and if there are customers looking for local foods. Take the plunge with friends, neighbors, and coworkers to secure the space and harness the demand that farmers need.

If you already have a farmers market, talk to the farmers and the market manager to see how it's going, to see if you can help. Consider forming a "market auxiliary" that will help promote the market, build a larger, stronger customer base, maybe find and secure a better location. Many good farmers markets are now struggling with insufficient demand, even though they may appear to you to be quite busy. Find out what you can do to help, and give the vendors honest feedback on improvements they could make.

Go the next step and start a *food citizen group* to both educate yourselves and take action for better public policies. I shared some ideas in chapter 7 about "food citizens." You can start there, along with reading Wendell Berry, Barbara Kingsolver, Joel Salatin, and many others. In addition, see if there is a local food or sustainable farming group in your area and see how you can work together on this idea.

Find out if there is a BALLE network in your area, or a similar association focused on local triple-bottom-line businesses, and see how you can support them and get involved. Talk with them about forming an auxiliary or citizen group similar to, but broader in scope than, a food citizen group. Help them distribute their local business directories and talk about it with friends and coworkers.

Form *a bottom-up economy book group* with some friends and neighbors. You could start with this book and then follow suggestions for further reading listed at the end of each chapter. Structure the group to include learning and doing, reading, reflection, and action. Contact me, if you'd like me to help lead a community discussion of the issues.

If you have money to invest, even modest amounts, consider forming some sort of local investment club. Michael Shuman's *Local Dollars, Local Sense* is a great place to start to learn about both the legal issues and creative strategies emerging in this arena. Use Craigslist or other means to find others who might form a Slow Money chapter or a Local Investment Opportunity Network.

Get to know the loan officers at your community bank or credit union to see if they'd backstop you on a local currency initiative. Contact the Schumacher Center to learn about local currencies and to see what's possible in your community. Find out if there's a non-profit in your community working on building local capital, such as a microenterprise loan fund or a Community Development Finance Institution.

Take stock of what your town or community is doing in terms of forums, public debates, or other civic initiatives. Contact the Jefferson Center about their civic juries process and begin talking to the League of Women Voters and other local organizations about how to create opportunities for in-depth, ongoing education and civic dialogue. Begin talking with local or state elected officials or key institutional leaders to determine one or more issues they'd be willing to put to public dialogue in this way.

The Third Level: Community, County, or City

Working for changes at the community level can be a natural outgrowth of joining forces with friends and neighbors in some of the ways we've just described. There is no reason you can't meet with a city council member or small town mayor on your own. However, you're much more likely to have an impact if you've taken the time to become knowledgeable about the issue, made connections to others with a stake in the matter, or joined voluntary associations trying to make positive changes.

Let's take, for example, the question of support for local independent businesses versus subsidies for placeless corporations. Local leaders often feel that they must pursue all options and are likely to resist calls to end subsidies for chains and big boxes, especially if they feel that you "just don't understand" how economic development works. On the other hand, if you are part of a diverse group of citizens that has thoroughly studied the issue, that can identify both examples of better alternatives and why they are preferable, and have joined forces with local businesses or a BALLE network to shift your spending and actively support and promote them, you will be much more compelling, much more difficult to dismiss. So, build on your work with neighbors and parlay it into stronger, more effective advocacy for changes in official policies and practice. A good rule of thumb is that for everything you oppose, be sure to stand for a tangible alternative.

Identify and fight for public spaces, either preserving and enlivening those you have or creating new places from vacant lots, abandoned buildings, or neglected open space. The first step is to find out what you have, a manageable task in small towns, one you'd need help with in larger cities. Contact the Project for Public Spaces to see what tools they have and how they might help you. Start with your own neighborhood. If you venture out more broadly, be sure to first connect with local people and leaders in other parts of your community to find out what interest they have in rebuilding public spaces. Community gardens are often a good way to begin to build a sense of the importance of shared public space, and they can help you make the case for public squares, parks, or plazas as well.

Your town's policies can also provide incentives to clean up vacant lots or encourage adaptive reuse of buildings in decline. Look at the "carrot and stick" approach they've used in places like Richmond, California, where property owners must bring the structures back to code or face higher fees and penalties; or Phoenix, where productive reuse of old buildings can earn tax breaks. Where public spaces face the prospect of privatization, look into the "Lighter, Quicker, Cheaper" methodology developed by the Project for Public Spaces as a way to quickly reclaim and reenergize public squares and other spaces, and to begin to demonstrate their potential for community revitalization. If there is not already a community or neighborhood association working on community gardens or public space, consider forming one with other natural allies (advocates for walking, for downtown revitalization, for music, arts, and theater, for tourism, and for independent small businesses).

Research where your community's energy comes from, the potential for major improvements in energy efficiency and conservation, and the possibilities for major expansions of solar, wind, or other renewable sources. The laws of some states currently make it possible for groups of individuals, whether in a cooperative or an informal association, to own, lease, or share power generated by a community solar or wind project. Others make this difficult to impossible. Get to know your utility and its plans; research the successes and policies of other places through the Institute for Local Self-Reliance's community energy project; when you're ready, reach out to the Clean Energy Cooperative for guidance, expertise, and support.

Pursue participatory budgeting in your district, town, or county, working with your mayor or other elected officials who must be on board. After you've researched the successful stories from Vallejo, California, Chicago, and other communities, set up a meeting with your local representatives to consider how this might build community spirit, civic participation, and more responsive government in your area. The Participatory Budgeting Project is eager to work with communities, to dramatically increase the number and size of PB projects around the country, in communities of all sizes.

Run for local office, be it your town council, board of supervisors, school board, or other elected positions. Whether or not you win the first time, you can reach many people you're not otherwise able to through debates and forums as well as increased media attention. Use this platform to build support for the bottom-up economy and more participatory democracy, to educate and excite your fellow citizens about the emerging living economies. Help build a base of support for these ideas, and in the process, get people talking about serious issues in thoughtful ways.

In or out of the office, work for policies that encourage household savings and greater self-reliance, that promote resilient households and walkable, vibrant communities, that level the playing field for small businesses and ordinary citizens and that preserve and build on your community's unique assets, rather than those that ignore or degrade the place where you live.

The Fourth Level: Across Communities—Regionally, Statewide

Your district, town, or county is a good place to start when trying to impact public policies, and to help shape the direction your community takes in terms of economic development, transportation, building, and other important issues. But in many instances, the challenges we face go well beyond these boundaries, calling for larger efforts and for coordinated planning and action among several or many localities. This is likely to be a bit more complex and challenging, but if you've already begun to learn the ropes at the neighborhood or city level, you'll surely be able to take that experience into a bigger arena. Remember that you don't always have to initiate or lead things; just find folks already engaged and find a productive way to plug in.

One place to start is to put your community and region into its ecological context, its larger "pattern." In many places, local conservation groups, state environmental agencies, or college or academic organizations will have information about the land base, the watershed, and the ecosystem of which you're a part. You don't need to become an expert on the flora and fauna (though that can be fun) of your region to develop a much clearer, more realistic understanding of the strengths and limits of your place. If you live in an area that is increasingly dry or drought-prone, or one where storms and flooding are becoming more frequent or intense, that should be a critical part of economic and community planning. If rich agricultural soils are a part of your area but are being rapidly lost to "development," this should be a central part of both local and statewide debate, planning, and policy.

Another critical arena where a "bigger than local" perspective makes sense is in economic development and fighting poverty. You may recall from chapter 3 how PUSH Buffalo was revitalizing one of the poorest communities in the city through creation of a "Green Development Zone." Within that area, they emphasized business and job creation focused on housing rehab, green housing, and transformation of degraded properties into community gardens and parks. The Green Development Zone itself includes just twenty-seven square blocks, about as local as you can get. But that's only part of the picture. In building their strategy, leaders of PUSH discovered that many of the vacant lots and dilapidated structures in their community were controlled by the state's housing authority, part of one of those derivative deals through which these sites were earning a small return on Wall Street. Putting aside the bizarre logic of Wall Street that makes such things "profitable," the point here is that PUSH went after the state on this, eventually winning the right for the community to reclaim these properties, accompanied by a funding stream to help match and expand private resources. PUSH and its members would undoubtedly still be doing good work had they not tackled this larger issue, but in doing so they dramatically accelerated work in their own community while also enabling other towns in New York State to reclaim their own resources.

If you get more deeply involved in building your local economy and community, you'll likely discover that "extralocal" work is essential to sustaining your own efforts. This is true for at least two reasons. First, there are other folks out there, perhaps just a few counties over, maybe clear across the state, who are grappling with similar challenges. Almost surely, you can learn from one another, share what has worked and what has not, uncover new ideas without having to learn every single thing the hard way (as I did for a long time). Usually this kind of learning happens informally, and that's great. However, you may find that there are networks you can plug into that make the sharing, learning, and capacity building more systematic and easier to access. Regional networks, like the Appalachian Farmers Market Association or Slow Money Northern California formed to accelerate learning and strengthen work at the local level, and they've succeeded in doing that.

Those networks help describe the second reason for extralocal collaborations—garnering more resources and impacting public policy. Regional and statewide BALLE networks have increased awareness of and support for local living economies, from coastal South Carolina to Washington State. If you own or work for an independent local business or a community-based organization, see if there is a BALLE network in your area and, if so, consider becoming a member. If not, you can gather other local businesses to watch one of BALLE's many webinars as a first step toward potentially forming a network affiliate.

If you're not part of a small business or community organization, you can still work on regional and state issues that impact your community. One way to do this is through a focus on increasing knowledge and understanding about the critical but complex issues we face. A good and timely example of this is in the realm of campaign finance and "money in politics." Since the Supreme Court ruling in *Citizens United,* there has been a grassroots movement to pass a constitutional amendment to overturn the decision and, further, to limit the rights and influence of money in our political process. While the vast majority of Americans believe that the political process is rigged in favor of the very wealthy, most of us have limited knowledge about many of the key issues involved, from "corporate personhood" to the view that the unlimited expenditure of money is "protected free speech."

Understanding these ideas and how to effectively challenge them will be critical to the passage of a constitutional amendment or other substantial changes in policy. For your own study of these issues, read Lawrence Lessig's *Republic, Lost*[2] or Jacob Hacker and Paul Pierson's *Winner-Take-All Politics*.[3]

But to do more than just educate yourself, join the "Move to Amend" movement, focused on overturning *Citizens United* as a first step.

Another means to get engaged and to connect your community's challenges to others is to join a grassroots advocacy group. In Virginia we're lucky to have Virginia Organizing, a statewide group that supports and links nearly a dozen local chapters. Each grassroots local chapter determines its own agenda, issues, and priorities. The chapters often include a diverse mix of folks, sometimes uniting libertarians and progressives in common cause for positive change and greater citizen control. Virginia Organizing supports their efforts with training, education, and a methodology that gets people of different stripes talking to each other and learning how to address local and state officials. The local chapters then help build a statewide agenda that reflects similar priorities and values, and these are then taken to the state legislature. Kentucky has a couple of similar organizations—Community Farm Alliance and Kentuckians for the Commonwealth—as do many other states. You can find and connect to these groups on the Web.

And, of course, you could consider becoming part of a third party if, like many other folks, you're fed up with both the Republicans and Democrats. One such party that seems to represent at least some of the bottom-up economy priorities is the Working Families Party (WFP), begun in New York State and now building its base in Oregon, Wisconsin, Pennsylvania, New Jersey, Connecticut, Maryland, and the District of Columbia. Before I go any further, let me just say that I understand the risks and downside of voting for third-party candidates, how this can "dilute" the vote for a more "viable" candidate and help elect someone you really don't support. Those concerns are real. However, so too is the pervasive alienation from politics as neither major party responds to or represents the concerns of everyday people, what I call WTF politics. In its very brief history—they only formed in 2011—the Working Families Party has demonstrated that they can seriously impact the views and positions of major-party politicians while also fielding their own candidates. Some of this is due to the laws in New York and a few other states that allow an individual to run for office as the candidate of two different parties. But even without that law, the WFP is beginning to build the foundation for an alternative political voice. Check them out.

The Fifth Level: National

For most of us, this is the most daunting and difficult level with which to engage. Many people have given up entirely, while perhaps a slightly greater number of us engage every couple of years to vote in congressional elections. A bit over half of eligible voters still turn out for presidential elections every four years. It's important to keep doing this, but it has become for many of us a purely defensive action. We vote more to oppose a person and his or her positions than we vote for someone who gets us excited, who we believe speaks for us. That is the dreadful but common reality, and it is part of why more and more people are withdrawing from the process. This widespread alienation also has helped enable the near-complete takeover of our economy and politics by an elite few.

Voting is still important, still an expression of what it means to be a citizen. Laws and policies that make voting more difficult, expensive, and restrictive are some of the worst, most un-American nonsense we've seen in generations. These should and will be fought, and sooner or later the fallacy of "voter fraud" will become so obvious that I believe such laws will be overturned. Do your part to make that happen.

But that, again, is a defensive move. To be proactive at the federal level, to help bring about resilient communities, living economies, and a vibrant democracy, we need to figure out how to act *for* these things, not just against the unjust and wholly depressing status quo. One place to start is to recognize and learn about the proactive efforts already under way, the significant and potentially transformative work taking hold in so many places. If nothing else, I hope this book has provided you with a sampling of these emerging alternatives and some understanding of how the people involved have made them work.

Focusing our attention on the emerging and substantive alternatives, rather than just the problems and defeats we've faced, is part of what Gar Alperovitz has called a *checkerboard strategy* for social and economic change.[4] Alperovitz, an economist who helped found the Democracy Collaborative, believes that we must build a strategy that goes far beyond the voting booth alone, one that is more systematic and grounded than are the traditional issue advocacy strategies for political change. Imagining a checkerboard, Alperovitz invites us to focus on certain "pieces," to look at where they are in relation to both the "open squares" and those that are "blocked." Recognizing that we must continue to fight defensive battles in order to keep things from getting even worse, he argues that we must simultaneously look at where we can build on positive developments already under way and where the openings on the checkerboard give us space to move, to progress, to grow stronger. Alperovitz points out that historically, major shifts in *national* policy were often preceded by innovative local experiments and *state-level* policy changes, as happened during the years leading up to women gaining the right to vote.

More recently, experiments in crowd funding and local investment clubs helped build the case for the Jumpstart Our Business Startups (JOBS) Act, signed into law in 2012. The JOBS law was designed to ease some securities laws that make it nearly impossible for ordinary people to directly invest in businesses, while recognizing the importance of emerging new sources of local and community capital. It came about only after several states passed their own laws, and after dozens of local communities pioneered a range of local investing strategies. A similar process is under way regarding minimum-wage increases at municipal and state levels.

Similar "openings" on the public policy checkerboard are beginning to emerge around distributed energy and community-owned solar power; in the realm of laws allowing greater investment by cooperatives and fewer hurdles to cooperative startup and expansion; in farm-to-consumer food laws that allow for some processed foods without excessive fees and regulations; in student-debt relief, a movement spawned in part by Occupy Wall Street; and in procurement policies that encourage local sourcing of food, supplies, or services. Each of these areas and many others face more hurdles than opportunities before they might become common practice or policy at the national level. The checkerboard strategy refocuses our attention on where the next "openings" might exist rather than immediately pushing for national policy prescriptions. It's more organic, more bottom-up, yet far beyond an incremental, purely local approach.

Another critical step you can take is to become better informed about national issues and the public policies surrounding them. Stacy Mitchell of the Institute for Local Self-Reliance has developed a working paper that provides a succinct outline of policies that would help level the playing field for local communities and independent businesses.[5] These policy ideas are based on what works, on the experience of BALLE networks and others working to bring about stronger local economies and resilient communities. Once you've familiarized yourself with them, begin presenting the ideas to your legislators, to candidates for office, to economic development and other agency staff, and to the public through letters to the editor, presentations to civic clubs, and even classes you might teach at your local adult learning center. You may not be an "expert," but armed with this book and some of the other resources I've suggested, *you really do know plenty to actively help shape the public debate about our economy and our democracy.*

Some Final Thoughts

I've written this book for largely the same reasons that I ran for Congress: to make the case for emerging economic alternatives so that people would no longer believe that we have "to choose between rapacious capitalism and debilitating communism"; to make clear that local alone is not nearly enough to build and sustain these better alternatives; to help explain and clarify what can sometimes be some pretty complex issues; and to offer a framework and some specific ideas for what you can do to help bring about a better world. I hope that I've been at least partially successful.

And there's one last reason. I've come to see my role in this work much like I felt, and still feel, as a parent. When Josh was born thirty-two years ago, I hadn't a clue how to be a dad. When Maria came along seven years later, I had some experience under my belt but nevertheless faced challenges about which I knew very little. Several years later, when Laurie and I married and Alex entered my life as my stepson, altogether different issues arose, again with me decidedly a "layman" when it came to knowledge or experience. Of course, I read a bit along the way, I talked with other young parents, and I tried to learn from what other folks did, good and bad.

My experience as a parent has included a difficult divorce, a period as a single dad, and a new era as a "blended" family with Laurie and Al. My life was then and continues to be almost unimaginably more comfortable, safe, and secure than the circumstances into which millions upon millions of people are born. But that doesn't mean it was easy, or without some big uncertainties and disappointments. It doesn't mean that it wasn't humbling to realize that I was but one of many factors shaping who my children would become, and that half the time I didn't know what the hell I was doing.

What got me through, what helped me play a small role in nurturing three amazing young people, was, ultimately, love. I'm not talking about abstract, lofty, or principled love. I mean the love that comes from experience, from getting your hands dirty (we washed cloth diapers, so I mean this quite literally), from making mistakes and doing it a little better the next time; from seeing that all your ignorance, inexperience, and personal flaws notwithstanding, you can be part of something wondrous, a flourishing beyond your wildest dreams.

Not all parents do love their kids, of course, and some kids and many kinds of circumstances can make it much more difficult than what I faced. But at some point early on as a parent, *you decide whether or not you're all in, for the long haul, through pain and sorrow every bit as much as joy and cele-bration.* When you turn that corner and accept that these are *your* kids, it doesn't get easy. But your hands, your head, and your heart start working together to help you be a more willing learner, a more persistent and skillful doer, a resilient though imperfect lover.

Our kids live in our homes for but a small part of their lives, spending many more years in the larger world. That's the very same world that many of us have given up on, a world we sometimes hope just doesn't get any worse. We can do better than that. We can go all-in as willing learners, skillful doers, and resilient lovers. But first, we've got to turn that corner and recognize that this is *our* world, *our* democracy, *our* communities, *our* economy. That's not an easy path to take, and the outcome is far from certain. For me at least, it sure beats the alternative.

I'll leave you with the words of a young woman, Kayla Jean Mueller, who in February 2015 was killed while being held hostage by extremists in Syria. This remarkable young woman was there because she had been working to help refugees in one of the most dangerous and degraded places in the world. A year before her death, at the age of twenty-five, she said this in an interview with her hometown paper in Prescott, Arizona: "For as long as I live, I will not let this suffering be normal. It's important to realize what we have, why we have it and how privileged we are. And from that place, start caring and get a lot done."[6]

I don't have the courage and fortitude that Kayla had; my commitment pales in comparison. But I know that I am among the very privileged. I know that a world of extreme injustice should never be normal. And I know that when enough of us start caring, it's possible to get a lot done.

Further Reading

Brand, E. Cabell. *If Not Me, Then Who? How You Can Help with Poverty, Economic Opportunity, Education, Healthcare, Environment, Racial Justice, and Peace Issues in America.* New York: iUniverse, 2010.

Fisher, Stephen L., and Barbara Ellen Smith, eds. *Transforming Places: Lessons from Appalachia.* Urbana: University of Illinois Press, 2012.

Flanders, Laura. *Blue Grit: Making Impossible, Improbable and Inspirational Political Change in America.* New York: Penguin, 2008.

Klein, Naomi. *This Changes Everything: Capitalism vs. the Climate* New York: Simon and Schuster, 2014.

McKibben, Bill. *Deep Economy: The Wealth of Communities and the Durable Future.* New York: Henry Holt, 2007.

West, Cornel. *Race Matters.* Boston: Beacon, 2001.

Acknowledgments

This book has come out of the experiences I've been fortunate to have over the past three decades, and from the nagging sense that the serious problems of our times demand broader, more holistic, and more urgent responses. With this in mind, there are two distinct groups of people whom I wish to acknowledge here: first, the hundreds of practitioners I've come to know who have persisted through thick and thin, often swimming against the tide, to make their towns, communities, and regions better, healthier, more just. While they are all, indeed, "practitioners," this diverse group of women and men are also among the most insightful "thinkers" in the country. These folks have inspired me, rejuvenated me when I've been down, and built the foundation upon which this book rests. More important by far, they're building the foundation for a dramatically more just, pleasant, and sustainable world. It's an amazing bunch! The pages that follow briefly highlight a handful of these exceptional innovators; many, many more are left out. My gratitude to all of you.

I also owe a profound debt to the great writers and thought leaders who have relentlessly challenged the status quo of an often-destructive economy and politics, who have brought to me the deepest insights about both what is wrong and what promises to be much better. There are quite a few folks in this group, but I'll mention a few to whom I always return: David Korten, Marjorie Kelly, Benjamin Barber, Thomas Frank, Barbara Ehrenreich, Bill Moyers, Naomi Klein, Cornel West, Gar Alperovitz, Robert McChesney, Paul Krugman, Leonard Pitts, Justin Maxson, Tom Philpott, Laura Flanders, all of the BALLE Fellows, and, most of all, Wendell Berry. My understanding has been enriched and my assumptions challenged by all of these marvelous people, and they have helped put the work that I and my many colleagues do into the larger context in which we all live.

More than three dozen people whose work and communities are described in this book took time out of their very busy lives to respond to my questions, send me additional information, talk to me on the phone or in person. I sometimes felt bad about this additional work I was giving you, but I absolutely could not have written the book without you.

I'm extraordinarily grateful to my collection of "readers" who took the time to review the manuscript as it was unfolding, and who provided both encouragement and excellent, thoughtful critiques, all of which dramatically improved the book: Nancy Blaney, Rana Duncan-Daston, Steve Fisher, Josh Flaccavento, Maria Flaccavento, Bill Gable, David Korten, Kimber Lanning, Sara Saavedra, and Rees Shearer. Thank you all very, very much.

Thanks also to Megan Jamison and Josh Flaccavento for help in information gathering, running down leads, and creating some of the graphs used in the text, and to Laurel Flaccavento for help with formatting the citations and bibliography.

I appreciate the wonderful support and encouragement I've received throughout this process from the team at the University Press of Kentucky: Norman Wirzba, Steve Wrinn, and Allison Webster. You've made the experience simple and pleasant throughout, taking this rookie under your wings. And Norman, thanks for coming up to me in North Carolina that day and forcefully telling me that I needed to write a book. My wife had been telling me that for years, but I never thought much about it until that day. Doggone it, she was right again.

And finally, I wish to thank my two "hosts" in Sicily, the place where the majority of the research and writing for this book took place. Particularly, I am grateful to the staff at the two cafés where I did most of the work: Caffe Pascucci in Siracusa, and the Marina Café in Marina di Ragusa. Day after day, I plopped myself down, plugged in my computer, had an espresso doppio or two (and somedays, a cornetta), and worked for hours and hours. In both places, they never pressured me to buy more or leave but instead were welcoming, helpful, and interested in my progress on the book. And they greatly improved my Italian! Per Antonella, Ugo, Valentina, Giusseppe, e Denise a Caffe Pascucci, e per Francesca e Biaggio a Marina Café: Grazie mille, grazie per tutto: La vostra pazienza, gentilezza e ospitalita. E anche per il buono espresso, dolce e cibo. Non vi dimenticheró, amici miei!

Notes

Introduction

First epigraph: Robert McChesney, *Blowing the Roof off the Twenty-First Century: Media, Politics, and the Struggle for Post-Capitalist Democracy* (New York: Monthly Review Press, 2014), 27.

Second epigraph: Janisse Ray, *Ecology of a Cracker Childhood* (Minneapolis: Milkweed, 1999), 69.

Third epigraph: Gar Alperovitz, *What Then Must We Do? Straight Talk about the Next American Revolution* (White River Junction, VT: Chelsea Green, 2013), 139.

1. Marjorie Kelly, *Owning Our Future: The Emerging Ownership Revolution* (San Francisco: Berrett-Koehler, 2012), 210.

2. Van Jones, *The Green Collar Economy: How One Solution Can Fix Our Two Biggest Problems* (New York: Harper Collins, 2008).

3. Bill McKibben, *Deep Economy: The Wealth of Communities and the Durable Future* (New York: Henry Holt, 2007), 3, 97.

4. Naomi Klein, *This Changes Everything: Capitalism vs. the Climate* (New York: Simon and Schuster, 2014), 9.

5. Wendell Berry, "The Whole Horse," in *Citizenship Papers,* by Berry (Washington, DC: Shoemaker and Hoard, 2003), 122.

1. What's Wrong with What We've Got?

First epigraph: Mitt Romney qtd. in *USA Today,* September 18, 2012, www.usatoday.com/news/politics.

Second epigraph: Adam Smith, *The Wealth of Nations: An Inquiry into the Nature and Causes of the Wealth of Nations* (London: Methuen, 1776), 1.8.35.

1. Joseph E. Stiglitz, *The Price of Inequality: How Today's Divided Society Endangers Our Future* (New York: Norton, 2012), 24–25.

2. Daniel Wesley, "The State of the 40-Hour Work Week," CreditLoan, http://visualeconomics.creditloan.com/the-state-of-the-40-hour-workweek.

3. Maggie Winslow, "Increasing Labor Productivity: A Mixed Blessing?" *TriplePundit,* January 24, 2012, www.triplepundit.com.

4. Stiglitz, *The Price of Inequality,* 18–19.

5. Richard Wilkinson and Kate Pickett, *The Spirit Level: Why Greater Equality Makes Societies Stronger* (New York: Bloomsbury, 2010), 159–61.

6. A more recent result of this myth has been the growing tendency to view and, in some cases, approach decisions about seemingly "noneconomic" issues through the prism of the market. As Michael J. Sandel has pointed out in *What Money Can't Buy: The Moral Limits of Markets* (New York: Farrar, Straus and Giroux, 2012), this thinking has spawned some rather perverse new forms of "investment." One has been the creation of a commodity futures exchange trading in the probability of terrorist attacks, where people essentially bet on the probability of terrorist attacks (150–53). Another is the massive buyout of life insurance policies on seniors and the terminally ill by big banks and hedge funds, where those who are financially strapped receive a cash payout that is well below the value of their life insurance policies. The buyers gamble that the person won't live too long, in which case, the actual payout of the life insurance policy represents a "return on investment." This has come to be called "the longevity and mortality-related marketplace" (156–61).

7. Benjamin R. Barber, *Consumed: How Markets Corrupt Children, Infantilize Adults, and Swallow Citizens Whole* (New York: Norton, 2007), 16.

8. David C. Korten, *Agenda for a New Economy: From Phantom Wealth to Real Wealth* (San Francisco: Berrett-Koehler, 2009), 7, 13–16.

9. Ibid., 67. Korten cites a 2008 report for the Bank of International Settlements stating that the notional value of all over-the-counter derivatives was $648 trillion. That same year, the world GDP was estimated at just under $61 trillion, a tenfold difference.

10. Marjorie Kelly, *The Divine Right of Capital: Dethroning the Corporate Aristocracy* (San Francisco: Berrett-Koehler, 2001), 33.

11. Paul Hawken, Amory B. Lovins, and Hunter Lovins, *Natural Capitalism: The Next Industrial Revolution* (New York: Little, Brown, 1999), 51.

12. Craig Cox, Brett Lorenzen, and Soren Rundquist, "Washout: Spring Storms Batter Poorly Protected Soil and Streams," Environmental Working Group, July 3, 2013, www.ewg.org.

13. Charles T. Driscoll et al., "Nitrogen Pollution in the Northeastern United States: Sources, Effects and Management Options," *BioScience* 53, no. 4 (April 2003): 62–64.

14. "2013 Report Card for American Infrastructure," American Society of Civil Engineers, www.infrastructurereportcard.org.

15. Melanie Greenberg, "Is Money the Secret to Happiness?" posted in *Psychology Today*, September 10, 2012, www.psychologytoday.com/blog/the-mindful-self-express.

16. Daniel Kahneman and Angus Deaton, "High Income Improves Evaluation of Life but Not Emotional Well-Being," *Proceedings of the National Academy of Sciences* 107, no. 38 (August 4, 2010): 16489–93.

17. Annual surveys from the National Opinion Research Council, qtd. in Bill McKibben, *Deep Economy: The Wealth of Communities and the Durable Future* (New York: Henry Holt, 2007), 35–36.

18. Hara Estroff Marano, "Teens: Suburban Blues," *Psychology Today*, March 22, 2005, www.psychologytoday.com.

19. Barber, *Consumed*, 9–10.

20. Review of U.S. Census of Agriculture reports for selected years.

21. Michael Shuman, *The Small-Mart Revolution: How Local Businesses Are Beating the Global Competition* (San Francisco: Berrett Koehler, 2006), 64.

22. Adam S. Davis et al., "Increasing Cropping System Diversity Balances Productivity, Profitability and Environmental Health," *PLOS One*, October 10, 2012, www.journals.plos.org.

23. "Frequently Asked Questions," Small Business Administration, September 2012, www.sba.gov/sites/default/files/FAQ.

24. Marc-Andre Gagnon and Joel Lexchin, "The Cost of Pushing Pills: A New Estimate of Pharmaceutical Promotion Expenditures in the United States," *PLOS Medicine*, Public Library of Science, January 3, 2008, www.journals.plos.org.

25. Stacy Mitchell, *Big-Box Swindle: The True Cost of Mega-Retailers and the Fight for America's Independent Businesses* (Boston: Beacon, 2006), 42–45.

26. Ibid.

27. Cited in Shuman, *Local Dollars, Local Sense*. 74.

28. Jeffrey K. O'Hara, "Market Forces: Creating Jobs through Public Investment in Local and Regional Food Systems," Union of Concerned Scientists, August 2011, www.ucsusa.org.

29. Thomas Lyson study, as cited in Mitchell, *Big-Box Swindle*, 76.

30. Shuman, *Local Dollars, Local Sense*, 22.

31. Robert E. Scott, "U.S. Trade Deficit Declined in 2012, but Goods Trade Deficits with China, and in Non-Petroleum Products, Rose Sharply," Economic Policy Institute, February 11, 2012, www.epi.org.

32. Robert E. Scott, "Growing U.S. Trade Deficit with China Cost More Than 2.7 Million Jobs between 2001 and 2011, with Job Losses in Every State," Economic Policy Institute, August 23, 2012, www.epi.org.

33. Ibid.

34. John Aravosis, "Petco to Stop Selling Treats from China, after 1000 Dog Deaths," *Americablog*, May 22, 2014, www.americablog.com.

35. Brad Racino, "Flood of Food Imported to U.S., but Only 2 Percent Inspected," NBCNews.com, October 3, 2011 http://www.nbcnews.com/id/44701433/ns/health-food_safety/t/flood-food-imported-us-only-percent-inspected/#.VuOj8_krLIU.

36. Deborah Zabarenko, "With Imported Seafood Flooding US, Are Inspections Enough?" Food and Environment Reporting Network, July 8, 2014, http://thefern.org/2014/07/imported-seafood-flooding-us-inspections-enough.

37. Lydia Zuraw, "WTO Rejects US Appeal of COOL Ruling," *Food Safety News*, May 18, 2015, www.foodsafetynews.com/2015.

38. William Safire, "Ode to Greed," *New York Times,* January 5, 1986, www.nytimes.com.

39. Stacy Mitchell, "One in Four Local Banks Has Vanished since 2008: Here's What's Causing the Decline and Why We Should Treat It as a National Crisis," Institute for Local Self-Reliance, May 15, 2015, https://lsr.org.

40. Stacy Mitchell, "Working Paper: A Local Business Policy Roadmap," September 2014, 1, available at www.ruralscale.com.

41. Katie Halbesleben and Charles M. Tolbert, "Small, Local and Loyal: How Firm Attributes Affect Workers' Organizational Commitment," *Local Economy: The Journal of the Local Economy Policy Unit* 29 (December 2014), www.baylor.edu.

42. Michael Cooper, Huseyin Gulen, and P. Raghavendra Rau, "Performance for Pay? The Relation between CEO Compensation and Future Stock Price Performance," Social Science Research Network, October 1, 2014, http://papers.ssm.com.

43. This is discussed in detail in chapter 4, with corroborating references.

44. Laura Flanders, "How America's Largest Worker Owned Co-op Lifts People out of Poverty," *Yes Magazine,* August 2014, www.yesmagazine.org.

45. Steffie Woolhandler, Dan Ariely, and David Himmelstein, "Will Pay for Performance Backfire? Insights from Behavioral Economics," *Health Affairs Blog,* October 11, 2012, http://healthaffairs.org.

46. "Fast Food Business Overview and Trends, 2012," www.SBDCnet.org.

47. Samara Joy Nielson and Barry M. Popkin, "Patterns and Trends in Food Portion Sizes, 1977–1998," *Journal of the American Medical Association* 289, no. 4 (January 22, 2003): 450–53.

48. Lisa Young and Marion Nestle, "Reducing Portion Sizes to Prevent Obesity: A Call to Action," *American Journal of Preventive Medicine* 43, no. 5 (November 2012): 585.

49. "Talent Report: What Workers Want in 2012," Net Impact, May 2012, netimpact.org.

50. Wilkinson and Pickett, *The Spirit Level,* 160.

51. Chrystia Freeland, "A U.S. Recovery, but Only for the 1 Percent," Reuters, March 8, 2012. www/nytimes.com/2012.

52. Jacob Hacker and Paul Pierson, *Winner-Take-All Politics: How Washington Made the Rich Richer—And Turned Its Back on the Middle Class* (New York: Simon and Schuster, 2010), 24.

53. G. William Domhoff, "Wealth, Income and Power," quoting economist Edward N. Wolff of New York University, WhoRulesAmerica.net.

54. Wilkinson and Pickett, *The Spirit Level.*

55. Stiglitz, *The Price of Inequality,* 19.

56. Ibid.

57. Wilkinson and Pickett, *The Spirit Level.*

58. Herman E. Daly, "From Empty-World Economics to Full-World Eco-

nomics: Recognizing an Historical Turning Point in Economic Development," 1–2, www.science.duq.edu/esm.

59. Herman E. Daly and John Cobb Jr., *For the Common Good: Redirecting the Economy toward Community, the Environment and a Sustainable Future* (Boston: Beacon, 1994), 143–44.

60. Lew Daly and Steven Posner, "Beyond GDP: New Measures for a New Economy," Demos Institute, 2011, www.demos.org.

61. James Gruber, "Why Shale Oil Boosters Are Charlatans in Disguise," *Forbes,* January 26, 2014. www.forbes.com.

62. "US Coal Reserves," Energy Information Agency, January 21, 2015, www.eia.gov/coal/reserves.

63. "Frequently Asked Questions," Energy Information Agency, December 3, 2014, www.eia.gov/tools/faqs.

64. Korten, *Agenda for a New Economy,* 25.

2. Renewing Households and Communities

First epigraph: Rhoda H. Halperin, *The Livelihood of Kin: Making Ends Meet "The Kentucky Way"* (Austin: University of Texas Press, 1990), 11.

Second epigraph: David C. Korten, *Agenda for a New Economy: From Phantom Wealth to Real Wealth* (San Francisco: Berrett-Koehler, 2009), 110.

1. Jeanine Stein, "Tending to a Community Garden May Foster Higher Fruit and Vegetable Consumption," *Los Angeles Times,* August 5, 2011, articles.latimes.com/2011/aug/05/news.

2. Katherine Alaimo et al., "Fruit and Vegetable Intake among Urban Community Gardeners," 2008, *Journal of Nutrition Education and Behavior,* March–April 2008, www.jneb.org.

3. J. N. Davis et al., "LA Sprouts: A Gardening, Nutrition and Cooking Intervention for Latino Youth," August 2011, www.ncbi.nim.nih.gov.

4. Quotation from presentation by Adrienne Maree Brown at the BALLE Annual Conference, June 9, 2015, Phoenix, Arizona.

5. Lester R. Brown, "Learning from China: Why the Existing Economic Model Will Fail," Earth Policy Institute, September 8, 2011, www.earth-policy.org.

6. P. Ryan, "U.S., World's Growing Household Debt: The New Face of Economic Downturns and Upturns," Marubeni Research Institute, June 2004, 2–3, www.marubeni.com/dbps.

7. Rebecca Sato, "The Consumer Paradox: Scientists Find That Low Self-Esteem and Materialism Goes Hand in Hand," *Daily Galaxy,* November 13, 2007, citing study by Lan Nguyen Chaplin and Deborah Roedder John, www.dailygalaxy.com.

8. Patrick Dunn, "How to Start a Tool Library," Shareable website, May 9, 2012, www.shareable.net.

9. From Clean Energy Collective website, www.easycleanenergy.com.

10. "Midwest Energy, Clean Energy Collective Commission 1 MW Array," *Hays Daily News*, January 29, 2015, www.hdnews.net.

11. Peter Kelly-Detwiler, "Clean Energy Collective's Goal: Bring Mass Financing to Solar, One Panel at a Time," *Forbes Magazine*, May 15, 2014, www.forbes.com.

12. Nick Safay, e-mail exchange with the author, October 2014.

13. From Energy Co-op website, November 2014, www.theenergy.coop.

14. Dan Barber, phone conversation with the author, October 21, 2014.

15. Ibid.

16. Justin Maxson, e-mail exchange with the author, October 2014, and review of website, www.maced.org.

17. Lauren Severe, e-mail exchange with the author, February 2015.

18. Two sources were used to construct this graph: USDA Economic Research Service, "Americans' Budget Shares Devoted to Food Have Flattened in Recent Years" stated that "between 1960 and 2007, the share of disposable personal income spent on total food by Americans fell from 17.5% to 9.6%" and has remained relatively flat since that time. Regarding health care expenditures, Henry J. Kaiser Family Foundation, "Health Care Costs: A Primer," May 1, 2012, http://kff.org/health-costs, contained a graph showing that between 1960 and 2010, per-capita health care expenditures in the United States rose from an average of 5.2 percent to 17.9 percent.

19. Ellen-Marie Whelan, "The Importance of Community Health Centers," Center for American Progress, August 9, 2010, www.americanprogress .org.

20. Jack Wall, e-mail exchange with the author, October 2014.

21. National Gardening Research Association, "The Impact of Home and Community Gardening in America," 2009 Annual Report, 4–5.

22. Grace Lee Boggs, conversation with the author, September 17, 2001.

23. Ashley Atkinson, e-mail exchange with the author, November 2014.

24. Surveys done by Keep Growing Detroit, 2013. For more information on these surveys, contact Ashley Atkinson, Executive Director, Keep Growing Detroit, aatkinso@umich.edu.

25. Denise Peterson, e-mail exchange with the author, January 2015.

26. Qtd. in Benjamin R. Barber, *Consumed: How Markets Corrupt Children, Infantilize Adults, and Swallow Citizens Whole* (New York: Norton, 2007), 16.

27. Rhoda H. Halperin, *The Livelihood of Kin: Making Ends Meet "The Kentucky Way"* (Austin: University of Texas Press, 1990), 1–15.

28. Ann Tickamyer and Teresa Wood, "Identifying Participation in the Informal Economy Using Survey Research Methods," *Rural Sociology* 63, no. 2 (May 1998): 323–39.

29. C. Menchen and S. Maggard, "Informal Economic Activity in West Virginia," in *Inside West Virginia Public Policy Perspectives for the 21st Cen-*

tury, ed. B. Keith and R. Althouse (Morgantown: West Virginia University Press, 1999), as cited in Eric D. Cohen and Andrea Stephens, "Informal Economic Activity in a Deindustrialized Rural Pennsylvania Community: A Preliminary Profile," *Journal of Rural Community Psychology* E8, no. 2 (Fall 2005), available at www.marshall.edu/jrcp.

30. Jan L. Losby, Marcia E. Kingslow, and John F. Else, "The Informal Economy: Experiences of African Americans," Institute for Social and Economic Development Solutions; the Aspen Institute, Washington, DC, December 2002, www.ised.org.

31. Eric D. Cohen and Andrea Stephens, "Informal Economic Activity in a Deindustrialized Rural Pennsylvania Community: A Preliminary Profile," *Journal of Rural Community Psychology* E8, no. 2 (Fall 2005), www.marshall .edu/jrcp.

32. Taylor Barnes, "America's Shadow Economy Is Bigger Than You Think—and Growing," *Christian Science Monitor,* November 12, 2009, www .csmonitor.com.

33. Colin C. Williams and Sara Nadin, "Entrepreneurship and the Informal Economy: An Overview," *Journal of Developmental Entrepreneurship* 15, no. 4 (December 2010): 364, 370–72, www.academia.edu/640233.

34. Lynn Karoly and Constantiju Panis, "The Future at Work—Trends and Implications," RAND Research Brief, Rand Corporation, 2004, www .rand.org.

35. "The Onrushing Wave," *Economist,* January 18, 2014, www.economist .com.

36. Barber, *Consumed,* 15.

37. Ibid., 13.

38. Atif Mian and Amir Sufi, "Consumers and the Economy, Part II: Household Debt and the Weak U.S. Recovery," *FRBSF Economic Letter,* June 2011, www.frbsf.org.

39. "June 2013 Financial Security Index Charts," Bankrate, bankrate.com.

40. Reid Cramer and Elliot Schreur, "Personal Savings and Tax Reform: Principle and Policy Proposals for Reforming the Tax Code," New America Foundation, July 2013, community-wealth.org.

41. Ibid.

42. John P. Millhone, "The 'Longest Running and Perhaps Most Successful' U.S. Energy Efficiency Program," Federation of American Scientists, 2008, https://.fas.org.

43. Ann O'M. Bowman and Michael A. Pagano, "Urban Vacant Land in the United States," Lincoln Institute of Land Policy, January 2001, www .brookings.edu/research/reports.

44. Ibid.

45. Ibid.

46. Diane Cardwell, "Solar and Wind Energy Start to Win on Price vs.

Conventional Fuels," *New York Times*, November 23, 2014, www.nytimes
.com.

47. Christopher Helman, "Solar Power Is Booming, But Will Never
Replace Coal: Here's Why," *Forbes Magazine*, April 24, 2014, www.forbes.com.

48. General Electric International, Inc., "PJM Renewable Integration
Study: Executive Summary Report, Revision 05," March 31, 2014, www.pjm
.com.

49. Richie Bernardo, "2014's Most and Least Energy Efficient States," WalletHub, October 2014, https://wallethub.com.

50. Sustainable Economies Law Center and Shareable, *Policies for Shareable Cities: A Sharing Economy Policy Primer for Urban Leaders*, Sustainable
Economies Law Center and Shareable, September 9, 2013, www.shareable
.net.

3. Unleashing Local Living Economies

First epigraph: David C. Korten, *Agenda for a New Economy: From Phantom
Wealth to Real Wealth* (San Francisco: Berrett-Koehler, 2009), 25.

Second epigraph: Van Jones, *The Green Collar Economy: How One Solution Can Fix Our Two Biggest Problems* (New York: Harper Collins, 2008), 14.

1. Derek Thompson, "Who Got the Biggest Tax Break in the Last 30
Years? (The Rich, of Course)," *Atlantic*, December 1, 2012, www.theatlantic
.com/business/archive/2012.

2. Rich Smith, "Why Are U.S. Corporations Still Hoarding $1.5 Trillion
in Cash?" *Daily Finance*, January 16, 2014, www.dailyfinance.com.

3. Thomas Lyson, qtd. in Stacy Mitchell, *Big-Box Swindle: The True Cost
of Mega-Retailers and the Fight for America's Independent Businesses* (Boston:
Beacon, 2006), 76.

4. See, for example, Garrett Martin and Amar Patel, "Going Local:
Quantifying the Economic Impacts of Buying from Locally Owned Busi-
nesses in Portland, Maine," Maine Center for Economic Policy, December 5,
2011, www.mecep.org; Troy C. Blanchard, Charles Tolbert, and Carson
Mencken, "The Health and Wealth of U.S. Counties: How the Small Business
Environment Impacts Alternative Measures of Development," *Cambridge
Journal of Regions, Economy and Society* 5, no. 1 (2011): 149–62; Stephan J.
Goetz and Anil Rupasingha, "Wal-Mart and Social Capital," *American Journal of Agricultural Economics* 88, no. 5 (December 2006): 1304–10; Anil
Rupasingha, "Locally Owned: Do Local Business Ownership and Size Matter
for Local Economic Well-Being?" discussion paper, Federal Reserve Bank of
Atlanta, August 2013, www.frba.org. Several other studies are also summarized on the website of the Institute for Local Self-Reliance (https://ilsr.org)
under the title "Key Studies: Why Local Matters."

5. Korten, *Agenda for a New Economy*, 126.

6. Leslie Schaller, e-mail exchange and conversation with the author, ACEnet, February and March 2015.

7. Tom Redfern, Rural Action, e-mail exchange with the author, December 2014.

8. Elissa Hillary, Executive Director, Local First, Grand Rapids, conversation with the author, September 2014.

9. "Art Prize 2013: Economic Impact and Attendee Profile," Anderson Economic Group, January 9, 2014, www.andersoneconomicgroup.com.

10. Elissa Hillary, conversation with the author, September 2014.

11. Tim Kelly, planning manager, Downtown Grand Rapids, Inc., e-mail exchange with the author, May 2015.

12. Ibid.

13 *Case Study: Electric Buses Energize Downtown Chattanooga*, U.S. Department of Energy, August 1997, www.afdc.energy.gov.

14. Kelly McCartney, "The Top 11 Shareable Innovations in Chattanooga, Tennessee," Shareable, August 2014, www.shareable.net.

15. Ibid.

16. Ibid.

17. W. Arthur Mehrhoff, "Case Study: Chattanooga Shapes a Sustainable Future," Minnesota Sustainable Communities Network, available at www .ruralscale.com.

18. McCartney, "The Top 11 Shareable Innovations in Chattanooga, Tennessee."

19. Ibid.

20. Ibid.

21. Mehrhoff, "Case Study: Chattanooga Shapes a Sustainable Future."

22. Ibid.

23. "Massachusetts Avenue Park: Whose Park? Our Park!" PUSH Buffalo, 2012, greendevelopmentzone.org.

24. Aaron Bartley, e-mail exchange with the author, November 2014.

25. "Toward Zero Waste Case Studies," Sustainable Connections, 2014, sustainableconnections.org.

26. Derek Long, e-mail exchanges and phone interview with the author, September 5–12, 2014.

27. "Wind Power," Puget Sound Energy, 2015, www.pse.com.

28. Nora Weaver and Karl Unterscheutz, e-mail exchange with the author, May 2015.

29. Sara Southerland, e-mail exchange with the author, February 2015.

30. Benjamin J. Newman and John V. Kane, "Backlash against the 'Big Box': Local Small Business and Public Opinion toward Business Corporations," *Public Opinion Quarterly* 78, no. 4 (November 19, 2014), poq .oxfordjournals.org.

31. From John Molinaro, e-mail to the author, June 2015; and 2011 presen-

tation and report on the WCI strategy and results. The information on job creation and wages can be found at www.wcif.org. The information on youth migration patterns can be found in the John Molinaro presentation and report, available at www.ruralscale.com.

32. Jeffrey K. O'Hara, "Market Forces: Creating Jobs through Public Investment in Local and Regional Food Systems," Union of Concerned Scientists, August 2011, www.ucsusa.org.

33. "Measuring the Impact of Public Markets and Farmers Markets on Local Economies," Project for Public Spaces, 2002 study, www.pps.org.

34. "Farmers Markets and Local Food Marketing," USDA Agriculture Marketing Service, September 29, 2014, ams.usda.gov.

35. Ibid.

36. Duncan Hilchey, Thomas Lyson, and Gilbert W. Gillespie, *Farmers Markets and Rural Economic Development: Entrepreneurship, Business Incubation and Job Creation in the Northeast*, Community Agriculture Development Series, Ithaca, NY, Cornell University Farming Alternatives Program, Department of Rural Sociology, 1995.

37. Dr. Phil Howard, "Who Owns Organic?" qtd. in *Cornucopia Newsletter*, May 22, 2013, www.cornucopia.org/who-owns-organic.

38. Lynn Stout, *The Shareholder Value Myth: How Putting Shareholders First Harms Investors, Corporations, and the Public* (San Francisco: Berrett Koehler, 2012), 24–25.

39. Jim Kleinschmit, "Agriculture and Climate—The Critical Connection," Institute for Agriculture and Trade Policy, November 30, 2009, www .iatp.org.

40. "Healthcare Statistics: Small Businesses and the Healthcare Crisis," Small Business Majority, 2015, www.smallbusinessmajority.org.

41. Ibid.

42. Leslie Schaller, e-mail exchange with the author, February 2015.

43. National Farmers Market Directory website search, January 2015, www.nfmd.org.

44. Anthony Flaccavento, "Is Local Food Affordable for Ordinary Folks? A Comparison of Farmers Markets and Supermarkets in Nineteen Communities in the Southeast," SCALE, November 1, 2011, www.ruralscale.com.

45. "Voice GR Survey Results: Local First Data Brief," January 2014, Johnson Center at Grand Valley University, www.johnsoncenter.org/resources/community-data/2014.

46. "EWG Farm Subsidies Database: The United States Summary Information," Environmental Working Group, 2012, www.ewg.org.

47. Stacy Mitchell, "Working Paper: A Local Business Policy Roadmap," September 2014, 1.

48. "Policies and Tools: Community Benefits Agreements and Policies," Partnership for Working Families, 2014, www.forworkingfamilies.org.

49. Alexis Stephens, "Detroit Is Taking the Lead in the Community Benefits Movement," Next City, March 10, 2015, https://nextcity.org.

50. Stacy Mitchell, "One in Four Local Banks Have Vanished since 2008: Here's What's Causing the Decline and Why We Should Treat It as a National Crisis," May 15, 2015, https://ilsr.org.

51. "A New Farm Economy Rises from Tobacco's Ashes," Farm Aid, July 6, 2014, citing Census of Agriculture statistics, www.farmaid.org.

4. Building Broadly Based and Durable Prosperity

First epigraph: Marjorie Kelly, Owning Our Future: The Emerging Ownership Revolution (San Francisco: Berrett-Koehler, 2012), 210.

Second epigraph: Woody Tasch, Inquiries into the Nature of Slow Money: Investing as if Food, Farms, and Fertility Mattered (White River Junction, VT: Chelsea Green, 2008), 93–94.

1. Website research, www.sustainablebusinesscenter.com; Cindy Teel, e-mail exchange with the author, October 2014.

2. Andrea Chen, e-mail exchange with the author; review of Propeller website, press releases.

3. "Quick Facts" Wild Ramp, wildramp.org.

4. Clark Davis, "Wild Ramp Continues to Succeed in Huntington," West Virginia Public Broadcasting, January 31, 2014.

5. Tom Rossmassler, telephone conversation with the author, February 6, 2015.

6. Co-op Power, www.cooppower.coop.

7. Ibid.

8. Ibid.

9. Sandi Kronick, conversation with the author, March 2014.

10. Ibid.

11. Robin Seydel, "Rooting the Local Food System in Cooperation," Cooperative Grocer Network, September/October 2013, www.grocer.coop.

12. Robin Seydel, e-mail exchange with the author, November 2014.

13. Michael Shuman, Local Dollars, Local Sense: How to Shift Your Money from Wall Street to Main Street and Achieve Real Prosperity (White River Junction, VT: Chelsea Green, 2012), 18–21.

14. Alice Maggio, e-mail exchange with the author, November 2014.

15. Jane O'Brien, "BerkShares Boost the Berkshires in Massachusetts," BBC News, Washington, September 6, 2011.

16. Ibid.

17. Review of participating businesses on Schumacher website.

18. Alice Maggio, e-mail exchange with the author, November 2014.

19. "Our Early History," Southern Exposure Seed Exchange, www.southernexposure.com.

20. Irena Hollowell and Paul Blundell, e-mail exchanges, December 2014.

21. Ibid.

22. Ibid.

23. Kelly, *Owning Our Future*, 107–8.

24. For an introduction to the history of discriminatory federal housing policy, see, for instance, Alexis C. Madrigal, "The Racist Housing Policy That Made Your Neighborhood," *Atlantic*, May 22, 2014, www.theatlantic.com.

25. Steven Deller et al., "Research on the Economic Impact of Cooperatives," University of Wisconsin Center for Cooperatives, 2006, www.reic.uwcc.wisc.edu.

26. Georgeanne Artz and Younjun Kim, "Business Ownership by Workers: Are Worker Cooperatives a Viable Option?" Iowa State University Deparment of Economics, 2011, http://coop.econ.iastate.edu/presentations_publications/businessownership.pdf.

27. Patrizia Battilani and Harm G. Schroter, eds., *The Cooperative Business Movement, 1950–Present* (London: Cambridge University Press, 2012), 202.

28. Ben Craig and John Pencavel, "Participation and Productivity: A Comparison of Worker Cooperatives and Conventional Firms in the Plywood Industry," Brookings Papers: Microeconomics, Brookings Institution, 1995, www.brookings.edu.

29. "What Works: Using a Cooperative Model to Increase Latina Wages," Initiative for a Competitive Inner City, October 21, 2014, www.icic.org.

30. Loren Rodgers and J. Michael Keeling, "ESOPs as Retirement Benefits: An Analysis of Data from the U.S. Department of Labor," National Center for Employee Ownership, September 20, 2010, www.nceo.org.

31. John Pencavel, Luigi Pistaferri, and Fabiano Schivardi, "Wages, Employment and Capital in Capitalist and Worker-Owned Firms," *Industrial and Labor Relations* 60, no. 1 (2006): 41–42.

32. "Findings of the 2013 National Food Hub Survey," Wallace Center, National Good Foods Network, September 2013, http://ngfn.org/resources/food-hubs/food-hubs.

33. Ibid.

34. Ibid.

35. This includes food hubs at various stages of development in Virginia, North Carolina, New York City, Kentucky, New Mexico, and other places.

36. Larry Fisher, "Rebuilding the Local Food System," *IEDC Economic Development Journal* 12, no. 4 (Fall 2013), www.iedconline.org.

37. See Charlie Jackson and Allison Perrett, "At What Cost? Food Hubs, Walmart, and Local Food," ASAP, March 26, 2014, asapconnections.org; and Brendan Smith, "Don't Let Your Children Grow Up to Be Farmers," *New York Times*, August 9, 2014, www.nytimes.com.

38. Qtd. in Ben Block, "Local Currencies Grow during Economic Reces-

sion," working paper, World Watch Institute Papers, November 2014, www .worldwatch.org.

39. Mina Kimes, "Caterpillar's Douglas Oberhelman: Manufacturing's Mouthpiece," *Bloomsburg Business,* May 16, 2013, www.bloomberg.com.

40. Gar Alperovitz, *What Then Must We Do? Straight Talk about the Next American Revolution* (White River Junction, VT: Chelsea Green, 2013), 77.

41. Ibid., 81.

42. Quote from live webinar titled "Next System Project Launch," May 20, 2015, www.democracycollaborative.org/content/next-system-project.

43. Hilary Abell, "Worker Cooperatives: Pathways to Scale," Democracy Collaborative, Takoma Park, MD, June 2014, community-wealth.org.

44. "Job Creation Strategies for Shareable Cities," P2P Foundation, December 28, 2013, p2pfoundation.net.

45. Ibid

46. Michael Shuman, *Local Dollars, Local Sense: How to Shift Your Money from Wall Street to Main Street and Achieve Real Prosperity* (White River Junction, VT: Chelsea Green, 2012), 96.

5. Taking Sustainability to Scale

First epigraph: Jacob S. Hacker and Paul Pierson, *Winner-Take-All Politics: How Washington Made the Rich Richer—And Turned Its Back on the Middle Class* (New York: Simon and Schuster, 2010), 6–7.

Second epigraph: Catherine H. Clark et al., "Scaling Social Impact: A Literature Toolkit for Funders," Social Impact Exchange, Growth Philanthropy Network, and Duke University, www.socialimpactexchange.org.

1. USDA Agriculture Marketing Service, www.ams.usda.gov.

2. Based on comparison of Walmart's annual U.S. grocery sales of $140 billion in 2010, as cited in Bruce Blythe, "Wal-Mart's U.S. Grocery Sales Rise 2.1%," *Packer,* March 31, 2011, versus USDA's estimate of all "local and regional food sales" of $6.1 billion in 2012, cited in Sarah A. Low et al., "Trends in U.S. Local and Regional Food Systems: Report to Congress," Administrative Publication No. 068, USDA Economic Research Service, January 2015, www.ers .usda.gov.

3. Jim Baldwin and Todd Christenson, e-mail exchanges with the author, November and December 2014.

4. Robert R. Jones, "Economic Impact Assessment of the Crooked Road: Virginia's Heritage Music Trail," Sustainable Development Consulting International, December 5, 2008, www.myswva.org.

5. Diana Blackburn, e-mail exchange with the author, December 4–5, 2014, plus review of website, www.myswva.org/rtm.

6. Leif Pettersen, "10 Best: City Art Districts around the U.S.," *USA Today Travel,* May 7, 2014, www.usatoday.com.

7. From Local First Arizona website and reports.

8. Heather Rodriguez and Dan Houston, "Procurement Matters: The Economic Impact of Local Suppliers," Civic Economics, November 2007, www.community-wealth.org.

9. Kimber Lanning, e-mail exchange with the author, February 2015.

10. Ibid.

11. Chris Hubbuch and Allison Geyer, "Organic Valley: Big Business in Tiny Towns," *Wisconsin State Journal,* May 20, 2013, www.madison.com.

12. Marjorie Kelly, *Owning Our Future* (San Francisco: Berrett-Koehler, 2012), 201–9.

13. Ibid.

14. S. W. Stevenson, "Values-Based Food Supply Chains: Organic Valley," University of Wisconsin Madison Center for Integrated Agriculture Systems, April 2013, www.cias.wisc.edu.

15. Ibid.

16. John Farrell, "Anya Schoolman: Episode 1 of Local Energy Rules Podcast," Institute for Local Self-Reliance, January 16, 2013, https://ilsr.org.

17. Ibid.

18. Ibid.

19. Emily Stiever, e-mail exchange with the author, December 2014.

20. Anya Schoolman, e-mail exchange with the author, December 2014.

21. Judy Wicks, conversation with the author, October 2014.

22. From BALLE website, https://bealocalist.org.

23. Michelle Long, conversation with the author, February 2015.

24. B Corporation website, www.bcorporation.net.

25. Natalie Woodroofe and Leslie Schaller, "Cultivating a Garden of Eatin: Reinventing Appalachia Ohio's Local Food System," ACEnet, October 2013, www.acenetworks.org.

26. Larry Fischer, "Rebuilding the Local Food System," *IEDC Economic Development Journal* 12, no. 4 (Fall 2013): 40.

27. Woodroofe and Schaller, "Cultivating a Garden of Eatin."

28. Ibid.

29. Ibid.

30. Ibid.

31. Kimber Lanning, e-mail exchange with the author, November 22, 2014.

32. "Measuring the Impacts of Public Markets and Farmers Markets on Local Economies," Project for Public Spaces, 2002, www.pps.org.

33. Excerpted from interview with Bill Moyers on *Moyers and Company,* December 12, 2014.

34. Stacy Mitchell, "Working Paper: A Local Business Policy Roadmap," September 2014, 2, available at www.ruralscale.com.

35. "Internet Sales Tax Fairness," Institute for Local Self-Reliance, December 22, 2014, https://ilsr.org.

36. Richard Marosi, "Product of Mexico: Hardship on Mexico's Farms, a Bounty for US Tables," *LA Times,* December 7, 2014, www.latimes.com.

6. Rebuilding a Meaningful Public Debate

First epigraph: Joel Bakan, "Corporations Unbound," in *Inequality Matters: The Growing Economic Divide in America and Its Poisonous Consequences,* ed. James Lardner and David A. Smith, 188–202 (New York: New Press in collaboration with Demos, 2005), 202.

Second epigraph: Mimi Pickering, e-mail exchange with the author, December 2014.

Third epigraph: Cornel West, from "Cornel West Quotes," www.goodreads.com.

1. Andy Morikawa, e-mail exchange with the author, January 2014.

2. Ibid.

3. Robert D. Putnam, *Bowling Alone: The Collapse and Revival of American Community* (New York: Simon and Schuster, 2001). Putman's focus is wider than consumerism, encompassing the decline of civic organizations and networks as central to the diminishment of a public life together, a phenomenon that complements and augments what might be called autonomous consumerism.

4. Benjamin R. Barber, *Consumed: How Markets Corrupt Children, Infantilize Adults, and Swallow Citizens Whole* (New York: Norton, 2007). The role of pervasive commercialization, relentless marketing, and an individualistic consumerist identity in undermining civic virtues and public life is woven throughout Barber's book.

5. Kevin Coe, Kate Kenski, and Stephen A. Rains, "Online and Uncivil? Patterns and Determinants of Incivility in Newspaper Website Comments," *Journal of Communication* 64, no. 4 (June 16, 2014): 658–79.

6. Mimi Pickering, e-mail exchanges with the author, December 2014 and February 2015.

7. Ibid.

8. "Who Killed All the Coal Jobs?" *National Journal,* November 4, 2013, www.nationaljournal.com.

9. Michael Shuman, "Making the Case for Localism: Case Studies of Successful Localist Businesses," Business Alliance for Local Living Economies, 2012, https://bealocalist.org.

10. Ibid.

11. Ibid.

12. Ibid.

13. Ibid.

14. Devyn Creech, conversation with the author, May 27, 2015, as well as website information.

15. Jennifer Lunden, "How to Save a Park," *Portland Phoenix,* October 23, 2014, www.portland.thephoenix.com.

16. "The Story of Congress Square Park: How a Derelict Plaza Got a New Identity Downtown," Project for Public Spaces, October 1, 2014, www.pps.org.

17. Ibid.

18. For information on Policy Link, its research, tools, and analyses related to urban development, gentrification, and related issues, go to www.policylink .org.

19. Putnam, *Bowling Alone.*

20. From *The Moral Foundations of Trust,* excerpted from Richard Wilkinson and Kate Pickett, *The Spirit Level: Why Greater Equality Makes Societies Stronger* (New York: Bloomsbury, 2010).

21. Theda Skocpol, "America Disconnected," in *Inequality Matters,* ed. James Lardner and David A. Smith, 178–87 (New York: New Press in collaboration with Demos, 2005), 178–80.

22. Ibid., 179, 187.

23. Ibid., 180.

24. Jonathan Rowe, "The Vanishing Commons," in *Inequality Matters,* ed. James Lardner and David A. Smith, 150–64 (New York: New Press in collaboration with Demos, 2005), 154–55.

25. Ibid., 156.

26. Ashley Lutz, "These 6 Corporations Control 90% of the Media," *Business Insider,* June 14, 2012, www.businessinsider.com.

27. "Who Owns the Media?" Free Press, June 12, 2012, www.freepress.net.

28. Steven Waldman, "FCC Report: The Information Needs of Communities," June 2011, 5–13, www.fcc.gov/infoneedsreport.

29. Philip Napoli and Michael Yan, "Media Ownership Regulations and Local News Programming on Broadcast Television: An Empirical Analysis," *Journal of Broadcasting and Electronic Media* 51, no. 1 (March 2007), www.questia.com.

30. Thomas A. Lyson, "Big Business and Community Welfare," *American Journal of Economics and Sociology* 65, no. 5 (November 2006): 1001–23.

31. Troy Blanchard, Charles Tolbert, and Carson Mencken, "The Health and Wealth of U.S. Counties: How the Small Business Environment Impacts Alternative Measures of Development," *Cambridge Journal of Regions, Economy and Society* 5, no. 1 (October 19, 2011): 149–62.

32. Troy Blanchard and Todd L. Matthews, "The Configuration of Local Economic Power and Civic Participation in the Global Economy," *Social Forces* 84, no. 4 (June 2006): 2241–57.

33. Richard Campanella, "Street Surveys of Business Reopenings in Post-Katrina New Orleans," Tulane University, January 2007, www.richcampanella .com.

34. Sarah Sobieraj and Jeffrey M. Berry, "From Incivility to Outrage: Political

Discourse in Blogs, Talk Radio and Cable News," *Political Communication* 28, no. 1 (February 2011): 19–41.

35. Donn Esmonde, "Canalside Light Show Reflects a Change in Thinking," *Buffalo News,* May 11, 2013, www.buffalonews.com.

36. Angela Glover-Blackwell et al., "Equitable Development Toolkit," Policy Link, 2015, www.policylink.org/equitable. The Toolkit is very easy to navigate, organized into twelve topical areas, such as "Access to Healthy Food," "Affordable Housing Development 101," "Commercial Stabilization," etc., each of which contains a set of practical tools, along with an analysis of the problems and challenges in that arena.

37. Robert McChesney, *Blowing the Roof off the Twenty-First Century: Media, Politics, and the Struggle for Post-Capitalist Democracy* (New York: Monthly Review Press, 2014), 220.

38. Report on Prometheus Radio Project website, www.prometheusradio .org.

39. Ibid.

7. Transforming Politics from the Bottom Up

First epigraph: Benjamin R. Barber, *Consumed: How Markets Corrupt Children, Infantilize Adults, and Swallow Citizens Whole* (New York: Norton, 2007), 4.

Second epigraph: Gar Alperovitz, *What Then Must We Do? Straight Talk about the Next American Revolution* (White River Junction, VT: Chelsea Green, 2013), 55.

Third epigraph: Caroline Patsius, Anne Latendresse, and Lawrence Bherer, "Participatory Democracy, Decentralization and Local Governance: The Montreal Participatory Budget in the Light of 'Empowered Participatory Governance,'" *International Journal of Urban and Regional Research* 37, no. 6 (November 2013): 2214.

1. Martin Gilens and Benjamin L. Page, "Testing Theories of American Politics: Elites, Interest Groups and Average Citizens," *Perspectives on Politics* 12, no. 3 (September 2014): 574–76.

2. "Stacked Deck: How the Dominance of Politics by the Affluent and Business Undermines Economic Mobility in America," Demos, 2013, www.demos .org.

3. Carolyn Jones, "Vallejo Is Participatory Budgeting Pioneer," SF Gate, June 10, 2013, www.sfgate.com.

4. From Participatory Budgeting Project, www.participatorybudgeting.org.

5. Ibid.

6. Ibid.

7. City of Vallejo, California, website, www.pbvallejo.org.

8. From "PB Stories," Participatory Budgeting Project, www .participatorybudgeting.org.

9. Sonia Sangha, "Putting in Their 2 Cents," *New York Times*, March 30, 2012, www.nytimes.com.

10. "Participatory Budgeting" on website of New York City Councilwoman, Melissa Mark-Viverito, www.nyc.gov/d8 (follow the "Participatory Budgeting" link on the homepage).

11. Audrey Wall, "The Citizens Jury Process," Council of State Governments Knowledge Center, July 1, 2011, knowledgecenter.csg.org.

12. Ibid.

13. Ibid.

14. Qtd. in ibid.

15. Christopher Hoene, Christopher Kingsley, and Matthew Leighninger, "Bright Spots in Community Engagement: Case Studies of U.S. Communities Creating Greater Civic Participation from the Bottom Up," National League of Cities, April 2013, www.nlc.org.

16. Ibid. Discussion of the Decatur case can be found on pp. 12 and 21–22; of Austin, on pp. 15 and 43–46; of Detroit, on pp. 29–31; and of Philadelphia, on pp. 14 and 33–37.

17. Ibid., 19–20.

18. Participatory Budgeting Project, "Participatory Budgeting in North America, 2014–2015: A Year of Growth," June 25, 2015, 4, www .participatorybudgeting.org.

19. Alison Kadlec and Will Friedman, "Beyond Debate: Impacts of Deliberative Issue Framing on Group Dialogue and Problem Solving," Occasional Paper No. 4, Public Agenda, 2009, www.publicagenda.org.

20. Simon Niemeyer, "The Emancipatory Effect of Deliberation: Empirical Lessons from Mini-Publics," *Politics and Society* 30, no. 1 (2011): 107.

21. Participatory Budgeting Project website, www.participatorybudgeting .org.

22. Robert E. Goodin and John S. Dryzek, "Deliberative Impacts: The Macro-Political Uptake of Mini-Publics," *Politics and Society* 34, no. 2 (June 2006): 219–44.

23. Benjamin R. Barber, *Consumed: How Markets Corrupt Children, Infantilize Adults, and Swallow Citizens Whole* (New York: Norton, 2007), 126.

24. Jacob S. Hacker and Paul Pierson, *Winner-Take-All Politics: How Washington Made the Rich Richer—And Turned Its Back on the Middle Class* (New York: Simon and Schuster, 2010).

25. Robert W. McChesney, *Blowing the Roof off the Twenty-First Century: Media, Politics, and the Struggle for Post-Capitalist Democracy* (New York: Monthly Review Press, 2014).

26. Lawrence Lessig, *Republic, Lost: How Money Corrupts Congress* (New York: Hachette, 2011).

Conclusion

First epigraph: Cornel West, "Cornel West Quotes," www.goodreads.com.

Second epigraph: Bill McKibben, *Deep Economy: The Wealth of Communities and the Durable Future* (New York: Henry Holt, 2007), 231.

Third epigraph: Naomi Klein, *This Changes Everything: Capitalism vs. the Climate* (New York: Simon and Schuster, 2014), 28.

1. Barry Schwartz, *The Paradox of Choice* (New York: Harper Perennial, 2004), 1–5.

2. Lawrence Lessig, *Republic, Lost: How Money Corrupts Congress* (New York: Hachette, 2011).

3. Jacob S. Hacker and Paul Pierson, *Winner-Take-All Politics: How Washington Made the Rich Richer—And Turned Its Back on the Middle Class* (New York: Simon and Schuster, 2010).

4. Gar Alperovitz, *What Then Must We Do? Straight Talk about the Next American Revolution* (White River Junction, VT: Chelsea Green, 2013), 65–71.

5. Stacy Mitchell, "Working Paper: A Local Business Policy Roadmap," September 2014, available at www.ruralscale.com.

6. Lisa Irish, "Prescott Woman Gives Aid to Syrian Refugees," *Daily Courier*, May 31, 2013, www.dcourier.com.

BALLE — Business Alliance for Local Living Economy

Index

Oakland, CA., 75, 119, 126, 154
Obama, Barack, 190–91, 203
Oberhelman, Douglas, 158
obesity, 32, 48, 62, 77
Occupy Wall Street, 270
Ohio University, 187, 188
oil, 36, 39, 58; BP Deep Water Horizon oil-spill disaster, 30, 38, 51
Oregon, 56, 67, 162, 210, 232
organic farming, 53–54, 120, 136, 193; Eastern Carolina Organics (ECO) and, 143–44, 160; growth in and, 112, 114–15, 187; La Montañita Cooperative and, 146; Organic Valley and, 178–80; production systems and, 23–24, 72; vs. tobacco and, 1–2, 3, 130–31; World Wide Workers On Organic Farms (WWOOF) and, 156
Organic Food Production Act of 1990, 72
Organic Valley, 177–79
outsourcing, 27, 53, 122

Page, Benjamin, 225
Paradox of Choice, The (Schwartz), 257
Parent Leadership Training Institute (Hartford, CT), 234
parks, 99, 101, 207–10
participatory budgeting (PB), 6, 227–30, 231, 234, 235, 241, 243, 265
Participatory Budgeting Project, 229, 235, 243, 265
Patagonia, 33
patents, 24
Patsius, Caroline, 223, 236, 239
Patton, Gail, 139
Pennycress Energy Company, 136
People United for Sustainable Housing (PUSH Buffalo). See PUSH Buffalo
permaculture, 55
pesticides, 23, 193

Peterson, Deni, 53–54, 262
Peterson, Tom, 53–54, 262
pharmaceutical industry, 24
Philadelphia, 58, 66, 126, 181, 182, 184, 233
Phoenix, AZ, 5, 174–77, 264
photosynthesis, 36
Pickering, Mimi, 197
Pickett, Kate, 34, 35
Pierson, Paul, 167, 242, 243, 267
Policies for Sharable Cities (Sustainable Economies Law Center), 80
Policy Link, 210, 217, 290n18
population growth, 36, 40, 50–51
Porte Allegre, Brazil, 228
Portland Phoenix, 207
poverty, 17, 22, 25, 34, 35, 40, 63, 266
procurement, city and state, 175–76
productive land, 21, 40, 41, 51, 76, 112, 124
Project for Public Spaces, 113, 208, 209, 264
Prometheus Radio Project, 218
Propeller Social Innovation Center (New Orleans), 137–38, 144, 160
property ownership, 30
Prospera, 154
prosperity, 13, 18, 22, 27; "greed is good" and, 32–33; sustainability and, 42, 243; trickle-down economy and, 86, 88, 123, 126, 251, 252. See also economic myths; economic transitions; wealth
Psychology Today, 22
Public Agenda, 234
public life, 211, 254, 289nn3–4
public policy: bottom-up economy and, 120–25, 256–57; community gardens and, 76–77, 80, 85, 264; from concentrated wealth to community capital and, 158–63, 164; from consumerism to

CPSIA information can be obtained at www.ICGtesting.com
Printed in the USA
BVOW08s0857050416

442961BV00002B/3/P